INCLUSIVE EDUCATION

A Casebook and Readings for Prospective and Practicing Teachers

INCLUSIVE EDUCATION

A Casebook and Readings for Prospective and Practicing Teachers

Edited by
Suzanne E. Wade
University of Utah

LAWRENCE ERLBAUM ASSOCIATES, PUBLISHERS
2000   Mahwah, New Jersey   London

Lawrence Erlbaum Associates, Inc., Publishers
10 Industrial Avenue
Mahwah, NJ 07430

Cover design by Kathryn Houghtaling Lacey

Library of Congress Cataloging-in-Publication Data

Inclusive education : a casebook and readings for prospective and practicing teachers / edited by Suzanne E. Wade.
    p.   cm.
"A companion volume—Preparing teachers for inclusive education : case pedagogies and curricula for teacher educators—is available to accompany this book"—Pref.
Includes bibliographical references and index.
ISBN 0-8058-2508-8 (pbk. : alk. paper)
1. Inclusive education—United States Case studies. 2. Handicapped children—Education—United States Case studies. 3. Teachers of handicapped children—United States Case studies. I Wade, Suzanne E.
LC1201.I527   1999
371.9'046—dc21   99-37804
                                                                              CIP

Books published by Lawrence Erlbaum Associates are printed on acid-free paper, and their bindings are chosen for strength and durability.

Printed in the Untied States of America
10   9   8   7   6   5   4   3   2   1

CONTENTS

*These names are pseudonyms.

FOREWORD

On behalf of the Joseph P. Kennedy, Jr. Foundation, I am pleased to write this foreword for *Inclusive Education: A Casebook and Readings for Prospective and Practicing Teachers*. This exciting new book introduces teachers to real-life experiences shared by students, their families, and educators that will better prepare them to work with students with mental retardation and other disabilities in inclusive classroom settings. Historically, university and college teacher education programs in this country have not provided any systematic training to future general educators on how to adapt their classrooms to meet the instructional needs of students with disabilities. Although a significant number of students with mental retardation and other disabilities have been placed in general education classrooms since passage of the Individuals with Disabilities Education Act in 1975, few elementary or secondary teachers have received the necessary training to meet the specialized instructional demands of this population. This is why the development of a casebook and readings by Suzanne Wade at the University of Utah is so important. Professor Wade and the parents and professionals who contributed to this project are to be applauded for making a significant contribution to teacher training that will ultimately facilitate more acceptance and support for students with mental retardation and other disabilities in U.S. schools and classrooms.

Professor Wade was one of four recipients of the Kennedy Foundation Career Development Award in 1994. In response to the growing need to better prepare general educators to work with students with mental retardation and other disabilities, the Kennedy Foundation established the career development program to provide an opportunity for university professors in general education to focus their teaching and research on creating new and innovative ways to work with special education faculty to appropriately include students with mental retardation and other disabilities in the educational mainstream. This book is the culmination of four years of curriculum development, teaching, and research for Professor

Wade during her tenure as a Kennedy Foundation Career Award recipient. One other award recipient, Karen Karp from the University of Louisville, also contributed to the chapters found in this book.

This book on inclusive education is part of a changing national focus in the preparation of general and special education teachers. The growing emphasis on higher expectations for this nation's children calls for the appropriate education of all students regardless of ability, gender, language, and ethnicity. This book clearly communicates the value—one that is the responsibility of teachers—of providing a quality educational experience for not only the best and brightest, but also for those who traditionally have been left behind. It is my hope that through their work on this book, the Kennedy Foundation Career Development Award recipients will have made a significant contribution to this effort.

To those prospective and practicing teachers who have the opportunity to learn through the readings and cases presented in this book, I wish you every success in your careers as educators. I hope that you find teaching a successful and rewarding experience. Perhaps you will meet students with mental retardation or other disabilities in the future who will remind you of those you read about in the cases found in this book. I also hope that you will be a teacher whom your students—both those with disabilities and those without—remember fondly as having made a difference in their lives.

—Eunice Kennedy Shriver

PREFACE

As inclusive education becomes more widespread, significantly more students will require specialized support in the general education classroom. Consequently, there is an increasing need for both general and special education teachers who will be able to teach students with and without disabilities in inclusive classrooms. The purpose of this book is to prepare teachers for inclusive education by providing readings and teaching cases. *Inclusive Education: A Casebook and Readings for Prospective and Practicing Teachers* is organized in two parts. Part I, consisting of chapters 1 through 4, provides an overview of issues related to inclusive education and describes approaches for creating inclusive classrooms and schools. These chapters are designed to provide prospective and practicing teachers with background information on curricular, instructional, assessment, and collaborative problem-solving strategies that foster inclusive education. Thus, they can be assigned as course readings to help teachers analyze cases and construct and evaluate possible solutions or plans of action. Chapter 1, by Wade and Zone, is an introduction to issues of inclusive education. It covers topics such as special education and the inclusive education movement, general curricular and instructional approaches that facilitate inclusive education, alternative assessment, and collaborative teamwork. In chapter 2, Karp describes mathematics and science curricula and pedagogy for learners with special needs in inclusive classrooms. In chapter 3, Giangreco and Doyle describe curricular and instructional approaches designed to meet the needs of all students, including those with disabilities. Part I concludes with a chapter by Welch, who describes collaborative problem-solving strategies that are effective in helping general education teachers, special educators, administrators, and parents work collaboratively to plan and implement educational programs for students with special needs in inclusive settings.

Part II consists of an introduction to the concept and use of cases and 14 teaching cases that can be used in a variety of teacher education courses.

These cases are narratives based on actual events as experienced by the case authors. They describe in rich detail the experiences of parents, students, and teachers related to inclusive education. Most of the cases pose problems or dilemmas to be resolved, including the struggles of parents seeking inclusive education for their children; students' attempts to succeed in the general education classroom; experiences of special educators, principals, and teachers as they collaborate in moving toward inclusive programs; and teachers' concerns for the future success of their students. Many of these cases describe situations that were not in compliance with the Individuals With Disabilities Education Act (IDEA) and other federal and state program guidelines. Therefore, we urge readers to obtain copies of relevant state and federal guidelines as reference materials. For example, you could contact the education or special education office in your state for the most recent guidelines for implementing IDEA.

The cases were either written or narrated by the case authors. Those that were narrated (designated by the phrase *as told by*) were written from transcripts of interviews I held with parents and educators (the narrators). With the help of my research assistants, the interviews were then constructed as teaching cases and returned to the narrators for their approval and modifications, in case they wished to make any. The book's case authors, case narrators, chapter authors, and I, as editor, have decided to share royalties from the book equally, and some of us have donated our royalties to various support groups.

A companion volume, *Preparing Teachers for Inclusive Education: Case Pedagogies and Curricula for Teacher Educators,* is available to accompany this book. It includes a general introduction to case pedagogies; describes curricula that teacher educators have developed, using cases designed to prepare teachers for inclusive education; and provides teaching notes that correspond to the 14 cases in the present text.

ACKNOWLEDGMENTS

Many people helped make this project possible. First and foremost, I would like to thank Eunice Kennedy Shriver, the trustees, and board members of the Joseph P. Kennedy, Jr. Foundation, and the many others involved in the Foundation's work. In particular, I would like to acknowledge Michael Hardman, who played a key role in creating the Foundation's Career Development Awards to fund this and other projects on inclusive education, and Steven Eidelman, former director of the Foundation, whose help and sense of humor made him a delight to work with. Special thanks go to my colleagues at the University of Utah, who were willing to try new ideas in their courses and to contribute teaching notes and chapters to this book from their experiences with cases related to inclusive education; to colleagues at other universities who wrote several of the chapters and cases; and to Ralph Reynolds, former chair of the Department of Educational Studies, and Colleen Kennedy, former dean of the Graduate School of Education at the University of Utah, who were always supportive and encouraging. Of course, special thanks also go to the teachers, special educators, parents, and administrators who generously shared their time and experiences so that we could develop the cases and teaching notes, which are the centerpiece of this project. These could not have been completed without the talents of Larry Johnson, Braden Lindstrom, Charles Otis, and Judy Zone, who helped to develop many of the cases from interview transcripts. I would also like to thank our editor at Lawrence Erlbaum Associates, Naomi Silverman, and the reviewers she recruited, who offered many valuable suggestions. Finally, I would like to acknowledge Judith and Lee Shulman, who first introduced me to case pedagogies in teacher education and whose pioneering work in this area continues to be an inspiration to me. All of us hope that readers will find this book helpful in thinking about the issues of inclusive education and in incorporating into their practice the curricular and pedagogical ideas and materials that it offers.

—Suzanne E. Wade

CONTRIBUTORS

CHAPTER AUTHORS (PART I)

Dr. Mary Beth Doyle is an assistant professor of education at Trinity College of Vermont. She has 15 years of experience as a special education teacher, community residence counselor, technical assistance provider, and educational consultant. Dr. Doyle has coauthored a series of books and articles in the areas of inclusive education, collaboration, curriculum development and adaptations, and working with paraprofessionals. She frequently consults with school districts around the country that are working toward creating school communities where children and adults are welcomed and supported.

Dr. Michael F. Giangreco is research associate professor in the Department of Education, assigned to the Center on Disability and Community Inclusion at the University of Vermont, where he has been on the faculty since 1988. He has spent more than 20 years working with children and adults in a variety of capacities including as a special education teacher, community residence counselor, summer camp counselor, school administrator, educational consultant, university teacher, and researcher. Dr. Giangreco has conducted numerous research studies and written extensively on inclusive education, individualized and adapted curriculum and instruction, and coordination of support services in schools. He is a frequent national, and occasional international, presenter on these and other topics pertaining to educating children in inclusive school communities.

Dr. Karen Karp is an associate professor of mathematics education in the Department of Early and Middle Childhood Education at the University of Louisville. She received her bachelor's degree in elementary education and her master's degree in special education from Adelphi University in New York. She received her doctoral degree in educational administration and policy from Hofstra University. She has numerous publications centering on mathematics education and equity. In collaboration with several classroom teachers, she is involved in a project to develop mathematics lessons based on strong female characters in children's literature, which are designed to encourage all children, particularly girls, to think mathematically. She is also the recipient of the Joseph P. Kennedy, Jr. Career Development Award. With the assistance of a Dwight D. Eisenhower Grant, Dr. Karp is currently researching instructional approaches for teaching mathematics and science to students with mental retardation and other special needs.

Dr. Suzanne E. Wade is a professor in the Department of Educational Studies at the University of Utah. She received her doctorate in 1984 from the Harvard Graduate School of Education. Her areas of specialization include the teaching of reading and learning strategies in the subject areas, assessment and instruction of reading difficulties, inclusive education, and the use of cases in teacher education. Dr. Wade has published numerous book chapters and articles in journals such as *Reading Research Quarterly, Review of Educational Research, Journal of Educational Psychology, JRB: A Journal of Literacy, The Reading Teacher, Journal of Reading, Journal of Educational and Psychological Consultation*, and *Teaching and Teacher Education*. She has been supported in her work by a National Academy of Education Spencer Fellowship, awarded in 1990, and a Career Development Award from the Joseph P. Kennedy, Jr. Foundation, awarded in 1994 to design and teach an experimental course for preservice and inservice teachers on inclusive education. In 1999, she was a recipient of the University of Utah's Distinguished Teaching Award.

Dr. Marshall Welch is an associate professor and coordinator of the teacher education program in mild to moderate disabilities in the Department of Special Education at the University of Utah. Prior to receiving his doctorate at Southern Illinois University in 1987, Dr. Welch was a social studies teacher and a special education resource teacher in secondary settings. He is coauthor of a college textbook entitled *Educational Partnerships: Serving Students at Risk,* and has published numerous articles on teacher education and collaboration in journals such as *Learning Disabilities Quarterly, Journal of Learning Disabilities, Journal of Educational and Psychological Consultation, Teacher Education and Special Education, Remedial and Special Education, Teaching Exceptional Children,* and *Journal of Teacher Education.* Dr. Welch has been the principal investigator of three innovative, federally funded projects awarded by the U.S. Department of Education. In addition to his administrative responsibilities, Dr. Welch teaches graduate courses on collaboration, instructional methods, learning strategies, and curricula.

Judy Zone is a high school English teacher working in Utah. She has also taught classes in the preservice teacher education, masters cooperative, and reading programs at the University of Utah while enrolled in the graduate program there. At the secondary level, she has been involved for the past 16 years in developing programs to foster inclusion and improve student writing and reading skills across the curriculum.

CASE AUTHORS (PART II)

Karen Hahne is the mother of Reed and director of "Kids on the Move."

Dr. Janine Remillard is an assistant professor of mathematics education at the University of Pennsylvania.

Mary Anne Schmidt teaches English and ESL and is chair of the ESL Department in a junior high school.

Sione Ika teaches ESL and band in a high school.

Linda Nesi is an elementary school teacher.

Carminda Ranches is a high school teacher.

Judy Zone teaches high school English.

Dr. Elizabeth B. Moje is an assistant professor of educational studies at the University of Michigan.

Wendy Besel Hahn teaches high school English literature and writing.

Heather and Bill Bonn are the parents of Scott.

Bonnie Reynolds teaches an at-risk first grade class in an elementary school.

Lisa Foster is a special education teacher in an elementary school.

Sue McGhie is an educational administrator.

Dr. Suzanne E. Wade is a professor of literacy and teacher education at the University of Utah.

I
READINGS

1

Creating Inclusive Classrooms: An Overview

Suzanne E. Wade
Judy Zone

As teachers, you know that students in today's increasingly diverse classrooms differ in language, culture, experiences, background knowledge, talents, interests, and cognitive ability. This is especially true as the movement grows to include in general education classrooms students with special needs, who in the past have been placed in separate special education classrooms. Therefore, you will need to carefully consider how you can structure your classroom and adapt your curriculum and teaching to meet the needs of all your students. The purpose of this chapter is to describe inclusive education and its origins and to outline in broad strokes curricular, pedagogical, and collaborative approaches that have been associated with successful inclusive classrooms.

A BRIEF HISTORY OF SPECIAL EDUCATION

Throughout the 20th century, various labels have been applied to students who were considered "the hard-to-teach, the hard-to-reach, and the least privileged" (Allington, 1994, p. 97). Whether they have disabilities, are at-risk, are low achieving, have limited English proficiency, or are marginalized for some other reason, they have traditionally been placed in

Labels	Programs
irregular attendants	truant schools
unmanageables	disciplinary classes
neglected	home visitors
defectives	vocational schools/classes
incorrigibles	suspension from school
backwards	mentally handicapped schools
truants	adjustment classes
immigrants	child guidance clinics
subnormals	crippled, blind, & deaf schools
low-grade children	ungraded schools/classes
laggards	pupil personnel services
feeble-minded	home tutors
high-grade morons	Negro schools
dull normals	achievement tracking/grouping
immatures	retention in grade
maladjusted	remedial classes/courses
coloreds	fresh air classes
slow learner	social promotion
reluctant learner	summer schools
dyslexic	special education schools
educable mentally retarded	paraprofessional assistance
educationally disadvantaged	special education classes
remedial readers	extended day programs
emotionally disturbed	drug therapies
developmentally delayed	consultant teachers
learning disabled	in-school suspension rooms
attention deficit disordered	multi-age groupings
language impaired	inclusionary education
differently abled	magnet schools

FIG. 1.1.   *Labels and programs for marginalized students in American elementary schools, 1900–2000 (Allington, 1994, p. 99; reprinted with the permission of Richard Allington and the National Reading Conference.)*

specialized programs that excluded them from the regular educational system. Examples of programs developed for students with disabilities and the ways those students have been labeled throughout this century are listed in Fig. 1.1.

In response to federal legislation and court rulings, these labels and programs have changed over time and grown in number. The most important federal legislation affecting special education was the Education for All Handicapped Children Act, known as Public Law 94-142, renamed the Individuals With Disabilities Education Act (IDEA, (PL 101-476) in 1990). Originally passed by Congress in 1975, the purpose of IDEA was to provide equal educational opportunity and access to the public schools for students with disabilities. In addition to mandating that students with disabilities have access to a free, appropriate public education, IDEA also established the concept of the *least restrictive environment* (LRE). The intent of LRE is to educate students with disabilities along with their nondisabled peers to the maximum extent appropriate, and for special classes, separate schooling, or other removal of students with disabilities to occur "only when the nature of the severity of the disability is such that education in regular classes with the use of supplementary aid and services cannot be achieved satisfactorily" (IDEA, 1990, p. 169). Although LRE has often been confused with *mainstreaming*, these terms should not be used interchangeably (Osborne & DiMattia, 1994). Whereas LRE refers to a range of possible placements, with a preference for general education settings, mainstreaming refers to the practice of placing students with disabilities in the general education classroom, which is only one of the options available in LRE. However, to many educators mainstreaming has become associated with cost-cutting measures in which students with disabilities are placed in general education classes without the necessary additional supports and services (see Hardman, Drew, & Egan, 1996).

Since IDEA went into effect in 1976, special education has grown enormously. In 1994/1995, for example, more than 5.2 million children (10% of all students enrolled in school) were receiving special education services (U.S. Department of Education, 1997). Tens of thousands of additional special educators have been hired, representing 13% of all teachers in the United States in 1990 (Fuchs & Fuchs, 1994). Not surprisingly, state-reported expenditures for special education have also grown enormously. For example, $18.6 billion was spent on special education and related services in 1989/1990 (Chaikind, Danielson, & Brauen, 1993).

As the number of students in special education has grown, so have the different kinds of specialized programs in segregated settings and the special education personnel to staff them (Allington, 1994). Critics of LRE (see Lipsky & Gartner, 1996; Taylor, 1988) have argued that, although LRE states a preference for the education of students with disabilities in regular education settings, it legitimates segregated, restrictive environments. Taylor (1988) argued that defining LRE operationally in terms of a continuum of educational placements, ranging from the most restrictive environment to the least, suggests that the most restrictive setting, such as an institution or special school, would be appropriate under some circumstances. Further, according to Taylor, the continuum of placements confuses the physical setting with intensity of services; that is, it assumes that the most restrictive and segregated placements offer the most intensive services, whereas the least restrictive and integrated settings provide the least intensive services. Yet, as critics note, intensive services can be provided in integrated settings, and some of the most segregated settings have provided the least effective services. Another criticism is that LRE is based on the readiness model, which assumes that people must acquire certain skills and thus "earn" the right to move to the least restrictive setting. However, critics argue that restrictive environments do not prepare people for more integrated settings. Yet another criticism is that the criteria for assigning labels and determining placements are ambiguous, vary widely, and are influenced by issues of race, class, and gender, as well as funding considerations.

The percentage of students who are classified as needing special education varies enormously from state to state. Based on an analysis of

Department of Education data, *U.S. News & World Report* (Shapiro, Loeb, & Bowermaster, 1993) reported that 15% of students in Massachusetts were labeled as special needs students compared to only 7% in Hawaii and 8% in Georgia and Michigan. In Alabama, 28% of special education students were classified as mentally retarded, compared to 3% in Alaska. Furthermore, a disproportionate number of special education students were from minority groups. For example, African-American students were two to three times as likely as White students to be classified as mentally retarded; when White students were classified, they tended to be given the less stigmatizing label of "learning disabled" (LD). Wide discrepancies also occurred among states in their labeling of African-American students: Whereas five states (Alabama, Ohio, Arkansas, Indiana, and Georgia) labeled 36% to 47% of their African-American students in special education as mentally retarded, five other states classified less than 10% of such students as mentally retarded (Nevada, Connecticut, Maryland, New Jersey, and Alaska).

According to statistics from the Report of the American Association of University Women (AAUW, report 1992), far more boys than girls are referred to special education, although medical reports indicate that disabilities occur almost equally in boys and girls. Furthermore, girls who are identified as LD have lower IQs than boys labeled as LD, suggesting that boys are overreferred. Socioeconomic status (SES) also plays a role in referrals to special education, although it is a complicated one. Teachers who perceive themselves as ineffectual are far more likely to refer lower SES children with mild learning problems to special education than similar children from higher SES families (Podell & Soodak, 1993).

According to Allington (1994), classification has more to do with lack of early literacy experience than with innate ability: "The most direct route to being identified as at risk or handicapped in schools today is to arrive at school with few experiences with books, stories, or print and then exhibit any sort of difficulty with the standard literacy curriculum" (p. 95). Others argue that labels and segregated settings are designed to serve the needs of schools and society—not students—by attributing the problem of school failure to deficiencies in students, their parents, or their culture, rather than to inappropriate educational programs or practices (McDermott & Varenne, 1995; Skrtic, 1991). A related concern is that decisions regarding classification and placement are highly influenced by funding patterns rather than clinical evidence or objective judgments (Kliewer & Biklen, 1996).

Finally, there is growing evidence that separate education programs have not been beneficial for students with disabilities (see Allington,

1994; Lipsky & Gartner, 1996). A recent U.S. Department of Education report (1997) reveals that less than 50% of students with disabilities receive a regular diploma at graduation, and 38% drop out before graduation. Other national reports indicate that two thirds of persons with disabilities are unemployed, although the vast majority say they would like to be working; when they do obtain employment, it tends to be in part-time and low-status jobs; and more youth with disabilities are arrested than are nondisabled youth (Lipsky & Gartner, 1996).

As a result of criticisms of LRE and separate classes, there has been a renewed call to educate *all* students in the regular educational system. Referred to as *inclusive education*, this movement is currently a hotly debated topic among general and special educators and in the media. For example, some organizations, such as The Association of Persons with Severe Handicaps, have become strong advocates of inclusion, whereas other groups, such as The Council for Exceptional Children and the Learning Disabilities Association, support a continuum of educational placements (Fuchs & Fuchs, 1994). (For an overview of the debate among special and general educators, see the 1994/1995 and February 1996 issues of *Educational Leadership*.)

INCLUSIVE EDUCATION

While focusing on individuals with disabilities, advocates of inclusion seek to change the philosophy and structure of schools so that *all* students, despite differences in language, culture, ethnicity, economic status, gender, and ability, can be educated with their peers in the regular classroom in their neighborhood schools. Inclusive education calls for the merger of regular and special education (cf. Lipsky & Gartner, 1996; Stainback, Stainback, & Ayres, 1996) and represents a shift from a continuum of educational placements to a continuum of educational services. To many, inclusive education also represents a shift from changing individuals (who must become "ready" and earn the right to be in integrated settings) to changing the curriculum and pedagogy (Taylor, 1988). To these educators, inclusion would mean the end to labeling and segregated education classes but not the end of necessary supports and services, which would follow students with special needs into the regular classroom. According to Sapon-Shevin (1994/1995), "What we need is a continuum of *services*. . . . Inclusion is saying: How can we meet children's individual educational needs within the regular classroom context—the community of students—without segregating them?" (p. 8).

Inclusive education is becoming an ideal that many in regular education are striving for as well. For example, the National Committee on Science Education Standards and Assessment (NCSESA, 1993) has advocated an inclusive position in its call for *science for all*:

> We emphatically reject the current situation in science education where members defined by race, ethnicity, economic status, gender, physical disability or intellectual capacity are discouraged from pursuing science and excluded from opportunities to learn science. By adopting the goal of *science for all*, the standards prescribe the inclusion of all students in challenging science learning opportunities and define a level of understanding that all should develop. . . . Every person must be brought into and given access to the ongoing conversation of science. (p. 1)

Similar statements have been made by the Association for Supervision and Curriculum Development (1992), the Council of Chief State School Officers (1992), and the National Association of State Boards of Education (1992).

Regardless of the individual positions teachers may take regarding inclusive education, most will find themselves teaching children who vary greatly in ability, culture, language, and background. For inclusive education to be successful, fundamental changes are needed in curriculum, instructional practice, and assessment. Also needed is a redefinition of the professional relationships among general and special educators so that both children and teachers receive the necessary supports and services. The remainder of this chapter and the chapters that follow in this "Readings" section of the book are devoted to describing these fundamental changes, which will be needed to successfully include diverse populations of students in the general education classroom.

CURRICULAR AND INSTRUCTIONAL APPROACHES THAT FACILITATE INCLUSION

Curricular and instructional approaches that promote the active, social construction of knowledge; that are interactive, experiential, and inquiry based; and that provide guided instruction have been recommended in the literature as ways to include and motivate students who traditionally have been excluded from success in the mainstream. Reviews of the literature on inclusive science classes, for example, concluded that an approach that emphasizes concrete, meaningful experiences and cooperative learning is more successful for students whose learning difficulties are related to language, literacy, and lack of prior knowledge than a curriculum that emphasizes vocabulary acquisition, lecture or textbook learning, and whole- group recitations (Mastropieri & Scruggs, 1992; Scruggs & Mastropieri, 1994). Moll (1994) has argued that interactive, "participatory" approaches that emphasize authentic activities, guided instruction, and student ownership of learning are well suited to Latino and other children:

These "participatory" approaches highlight children as active learners, using and applying literacy as a tool for communication and for thinking. The role of the teacher is to enable and guide activities that involve students as thoughtful learners in socially meaningful tasks. Of central concern is how the teacher facilitates the students' "taking over" or appropriating the learning activity. (p. 80)

Participatory approaches are also congruent with the cultural values and verbal interaction styles of many American Indian and Alaskan Native communities, in which shared authority among adults and children, voluntary participation, competence prior to public performance, and cooperation are the norm (Deyhle & Swisher, 1997). According to Deyhle and Swisher, these values help to explain why some American Indian children are more likely to participate actively and verbally in cooperative group projects and similar situations in which they have control in volunteering participation. In contrast, many American Indian children are less apt to participate in teacher-dominated activities such as responding on demand to a question asked in a large group:

In these "silent" classrooms, communication is controlled by the teacher, who accepts only one correct answer and singles out individuals to respond to questions for which they have little background knowledge. Many of these educators expect passivity and fail to provide Indian students with enriched opportunities for open-ended discussions about challenging academic content. (Deyhle & Swisher, p. 153)

The participatory approach is similar to what Cummins (1986) called the "reciprocal interaction" model of pedagogy, which he advocates for students from minority groups. Reciprocal interaction, he argued, "requires a genuine dialogue between student and teacher in both oral and written modalities, guidance, and facilitation rather than control of student learning by the teacher, and the encouragement of student/student talk in a collaborative learning context" (p. 28). The result, Cummins argued, is an instructional approach that empowers students, enabling them "to assume greater control over setting their own learning goals and to collaborate actively with each other in achieving these goals" (p. 28). Thus, participatory and reciprocal approaches provide a sense of efficacy and inner direction to students whose experiences, Cummins argued, have usually been the opposite of empowering.

In the sections that follow, we look in more detail at two aspects of participatory approaches to curriculum and instruction. The first is cooperative project learning, which emphasizes socially constructed knowledge and student ownership of learning. The second is scaffolded instruction, which provides students with the cognitive and metacognitive strategies to learn independently, so that they eventually take over the learning activity, as Moll (1994) advocated.

Cooperative Group and Project Learning as Inclusion Strategies

Cooperative groups working on student-led projects or complex problems are one of the most frequently recommended ways to encourage motivated, active learning; prosocial behavior; and higher order thinking among students. In a classroom structured for cooperative learning, students work in heterogeneous, mixed-ability groups on academic tasks. Group rewards are often based on everyone's improvement of past performance, and lower achieving students are reinforced for the gains or contributions they make. This way of structuring the classroom and organizing the curriculum supports inclusion because it enables all students to participate in activities and to complete assignments that they could not do on their own. The students' peers can help to clarify assignments and instructions as well as give feedback, encouragement, and help in solving problems or completing tasks. This structure also provides opportunities for *metacognitive exchanges* among students as they discuss their goals, tasks, and strategies (Paris, Wasik, & Turner, 1991). Finally, small-group work allows for "private practice," which Deyhle and Swisher (1997) report is important for some minority children before performing publicly in a large group.

In applying Vygotsky's (1978) theory of cognitive development, Slavin (1995) has argued that children learn more when they work together in cooperative groups because they are likely to operate in one another's *zone of proximal development*, which is the distance between what students can do independently and what they can accomplish with adult guidance or in collaboration with more capable peers. Slavin argued that students can do an excellent job of explaining difficult ideas to one another by translating the teacher's language into language they can understand. As a result, students who would otherwise become frustrated can become involved in challenging tasks and activities. Peer assistance also benefits those who are providing the help because explaining a concept or the results of a research project to others is an effective way to increase one's own understanding (McNamara & Moreton, 1993).

Cooperatively structured classrooms also increase motivation because academic effort is socially reinforced by peers, especially when each individual's increase in achievement leads to the success of the group (Slavin, DeVries, & Hulten, 1975). Such classrooms also promote acceptance of differences and more liking among students despite differences in ability level, sex, ethnicity, or social class (Johnson & Johnson, 1994). According to Johnson and Johnson, students also like the teacher more, because they perceive the teacher as more supportive and accepting. In contrast, low-achieving students in traditional, competitively structured classrooms have been found to be less well accepted and even rejected by peers who are achieving at average or higher levels (Clever, Bear, & Juvonen, 1992; Larrivee & Horne, 1991; Scranton & Ryckman, 1979).

Elements of Successful Cooperative Learning

Successful cooperative group work in inclusive classrooms does not just happen; it requires certain conditions. The first involves the type of task in which students are engaged. Unfortunately, the tasks in cooperative groups too often focus on rote learning or the mastery of discrete skills, which could be completed by individuals working alone, rather than on creative thinking, problem solving, or the integration of ideas. However, when students are working on true group tasks, such as student-led projects or open-ended problem-solving tasks that are optimally challenging, they engage in higher order thinking and rely on the resources and efforts of all group members (Cohen, 1994). Student-led projects provide students with some degree of choice in selecting topics and learning activities, allow them to see a whole task through to its completion, and provide opportunities to share their work. For example, students writing a group report might choose which planet to study, generate their own research questions, construct the final product, and prepare a presentation of their findings. Or, they might conduct research on the literature and history of their communities and cultures, perhaps recording and publishing stories and oral histories for class members, which is one way to integrate minority students' cultures and languages in the curriculum (Nieto, 1996). Such activities are highly motivating and enable students to view their contributions as meaningful and valuable; they also help to develop feelings of competence and, in turn, a willingness to exert effort in learning (Deci, 1992). Further, students perceive such choice and responsibility as reflecting their teachers' beliefs and expectations that they can reach challenging goals (Roehler & Duffy, 1991).

Heterogeneous grouping is another key element in successful group work. This requires that the teacher organize groups to maximize diversity rather than allow students to form their own groups. As Sapon-Shevin, Ayres, and Duncan (1994) noted, student choice usually results in groups that are homogeneous in gender, ability, and race. Once groups are formed, group work needs to be carefully structured to create what Johnson and Johnson (1994) called positive interdependence within groups. This can be fostered by creating different, although flexible, roles for students and by individualizing student responsibilities. When students perceive that they can succeed only if everyone in the group succeeds, they are likely to see a need to coordinate their efforts.

In addition to carefully structuring group work, teachers also need to establish an ethic of cooperation. Sapon-Shevin et al. (1994) emphasize the need to create a safe, caring community in the classroom for all students at all times, whether they are working in cooperative groups or not. This can be accomplished by talking with students about how to work cooperatively in groups, what they hope to accomplish, what some of the barriers to cooperation might be, and strategies they might use to prevent or resolve problems. Sapon-Shevin et al. argued that two critical values in this process are that "1) Everyone is good at something and can help others, and 2) Everyone is entitled to and can benefit from help and support from others" (p. 50). These values challenge the stereotypes of certain children as needing help and others as providing help. They also increase the participation and thus the performance of low-status students, who might otherwise let other students take over and do all the talking (Cohen, 1994). Sapon-Shevin et al. also advocate openly talking with students about differences and problems as they arise, using a collaborative problem-solving process in which students and teachers identify issues, generate possible solutions, choose and implement a solution that seems feasible, and finally evaluate the success of the solution. The circle of friends is a formalized version of this process in which students with disabilities, an inclusion facilitator, and classmates discuss problems, needs, and ways to create an inclusive environment (Perske, 1989; Sherwood, 1990).

Learning in cooperative groups is also increased when groups are recognized or rewarded based on the individual learning of each of their members as opposed to group competitions in which students compete against other peer groups (Davidson, 1985; Mergendollar & Packer, 1989; Newman & Thompson, 1987; Slavin, 1995). Johnson and Johnson (1994) suggest that each member of a group receive the same reward when the group achieves its goals.

Finally, the advantages of cooperative learning are enhanced when it is combined with explicit instruction that teaches students to engage in cognitive and metacognitive strategies that increase active learning (Fantuzzo, King, & Heller, 1992; Meloth & Deering, 1992; Palincsar & Brown, 1984). Well-implemented strategy instruction encourages children to be active learners—to *learn how to learn*. In long-term studies, cooperative learning combined with explicit strategy instruction or individualized instruction was found to have significant and strong achievement effects (cf. Slavin, Madden, & Leavey, 1984). Because of its importance for students with disabilities, explicit strategy instruction is described in detail in the next section.

Scaffolded Strategy Instruction in the Context of Meaningful Learning Activities

An extensive body of research indicates that a source of academic difficulty for children with learning disabilities is a lack of cognitive and metacognitive strategies (deBettencourt, 1987; Wong, 1985). Cognitive strategies are defined as task-specific and are used to achieve a certain goal, such as the ability to add a column of numbers or to summarize a story. Metacognitive strategies refer to those used by an individual to monitor and evaluate cognitive strategies to assure that the goal has been reached (Flavell, 1979). Metacognitive strategies are particularly important for poor readers and students with learning disabilities, who often go through the motions of executing a strategy that they have been taught, perhaps achieving the overt goal, but not understanding what they are doing or why they are doing it (Paris, Wasik, & Turner, 1991; Swanson, 1989).

Research has shown that strategy instruction can significantly increase the performance of students with learning disabilities, often bringing their achievement on academic tasks up to par with their peers who are not disabled (deBettencourt, 1987; Deshler & Schumaker, 1993; Graham & Harris, 1993; Wong, 1985). Research has also shown that strategies can be taught successfully to children with learning disabilities in inclusive classrooms. According to Deshler and Schumaker (1993), "successful strategy instruction is not necessarily the result of *where* students are placed but rather a result of the instructional conditions that are present in the learning setting" (p. 162). The principles of instruction are the same for all students, although students with disabilities may need more explicit explanation, practice, and elaborated feedback than their nondisabled peers (Kline, Shumaker, & Deshler, 1991). Barry (1994/1995) stated this idea well when she said, "Good teaching is good teaching. Someone who works with children with special needs may have to spend much more time explaining, modeling, interacting, or practicing particular strategies, but strategies that work well with labeled children usually work just as well with nonlabeled children" (p. 6).

One of the most effective approaches to strategy instruction is known as *scaffolded instruction* (Graves, Graves, & Braaten, 1994/1995; Langer, 1984; Paris, Wasik, & Turner, 1991; Pearson, 1996; Rosenshine & Meister, 1992). A teacher who scaffolds instruction is continuously assessing the knowledge and strategies of her students and using that information to design and structure learning activities that they could not accomplish on their own but could with guidance. As the students learn the strategies that will enable them to accomplish these challenging tasks, the teacher's and students' roles change, with students becoming more proficient and independent. This change in roles and responsibilities, referred to as "the gradual release of responsibility," is depicted in Fig. 1.2 (Pearson & Gallagher, 1983, p. 337).

At first, the teacher provides a great deal of structure and help in the form of modeling, demonstrating, explaining, questioning, and directing, which Roehler and Duffy (1991) call *information giving*. Students with reading and other learning difficulties may have a greater need for information giving than do peers without disabilities (Deshler & Schumaker, 1993; Reeve & Brown, 1985; Sears, Carpenter, & Burstein, 1994). Further, Delpit (1988) argued that explicit information giving gives minority students access to the "culture of power" that exists in all classrooms. Although she was referring to the ways of talking, writing, presenting oneself, and interacting with others, we can extend this idea to include access to strategies for learning. Explicit instruction is particularly important in teaching metacognitive strategies because it lets students know why, when, and where they should use a particular strategy, and consequently how to use it independently in new contexts. Especially helpful to struggling learners are *think-alouds*, in which the teacher models and explains both the overt procedures of the strategy and the covert thinking processes that are involved (Anderson & Roit, 1993; Duffy, Roehler, & Meloth, 1984; Rosenshine & Meister, 1992).

As students become more proficient in using strategies, the teacher may then offer help in the form of *coaching*. Coaching includes feedback, questioning, reminders, and clues as well as more elaborated explana-

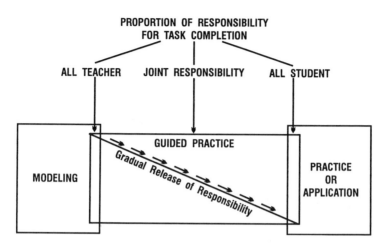

FIG. 1.2.   *A model of explicit instruction. (Pearson & Gallagher, 1983, p. 337. Reprinted the permission of P.D. Pearson and Academic Press, Inc.)*

tions, further modeling, and directives, depending on what is needed at the time (Roehler & Duffy, 1991). Although the coach's role is that of a facilitator and director, it is always the students who are responsible for using the strategy. Thus, in contrast to information giving, in which the teacher is highly directive, coaching involves shared responsibility between the teacher and students, who work together to achieve a common goal.

Although initially the teacher may need to select the strategies and skills to teach in the context of particular learning activities, students should be encouraged to independently select and flexibly adapt strategies to meet their needs (Wade, Trathen, & Schraw, 1990). One way to achieve this goal is to ask students to evaluate their own existing strategies and discuss them with peers, in a search for alternative approaches to a task. However, Graham and Harris (1993) caution that, although students should be "encouraged to *make strategies their own* by modifying and personalizing them," this should be "monitored to ensure that students do not change strategies in ways that make them less effective" (p. 172).

Some Cautions

As with any instructional approach, there are concerns associated with some aspects of instructional scaffolding. The major concern is that information giving be kept to a minimum; otherwise, students may become passive observers of demonstrations or be "talked at" too much of the time (Palincsar, 1986). To avoid this problem, it is helpful to think of instructional scaffolding as a collaborative social dialogue, in which students are encouraged to participate as soon as possible (Englert, Raphael, Anderson, Anthony, & Stevens, 1991). Regardless of the type of instructional actions the teacher engages in at any one time—whether it be information giving or coaching—his or her role is always one of collaboration rather than evaluation. As Langer (1984) described it, the teacher's role "is one of helping students toward new learning, rather than of testing the adequacy of previous learning. The teacher's responses to student work help the students rethink efforts and rework ideas as they move toward more effective solutions to the problem at hand" (p. 124).

In summary, effective strategy instruction for students of all abilities is not linear, or lock-step, but constructivist, allowing students to construct their own interpretations and applications of a strategy through active processing and interaction with other students as well as the teacher (Anderson & Roit, 1993; Deshler & Schumaker, 1993; Graham & Harris, 1993; Wade, Trathen, & Schraw, 1990). Studies of children with and without learning disabilities during strategy instruction reveal "thinking that is multidirectional rather than linear. This is in contrast to the *step-by-step* or serial thinking adhered to in some 'strategy-instruction' packages" (Swanson, 1989, p. 10). Strategy instruction that allows for open-ended discussion and individual adaptation may be more aligned with all children's thinking and more effective than prescriptive, lock-step strategy instruction.

ALTERNATIVE ASSESSMENT

To develop a curriculum that is meaningful, motivating, and supportive for students—one that involves higher thinking and problem solving, cooperative and project learning, and scaffolded strategy instruction—alternatives are needed to current educational assessment practices, particularly standardized achievement tests. Achievement tests are "high stakes" assessments because results are frequently used to compare districts, schools, and even teachers, and to determine district funding, promotions, merit pay, and placement of students in special programs. Real estate agents have even been known to use test scores to sell houses (Paris, Lawton, Turner, & Roth, 1991). The annual cost of standardized achievement testing in the United States has been estimated at half a billion dollars and 100 hours of instructional time to prepare students for the tests and administer them—a loss of 3 to 4 weeks of the school year (Paris, Lawton, et al., 1991; Smith, 1991).

Yet, according to critics, standardized achievement tests are not good indicators of learning because they measure only isolated bits of students' knowledge. Some critics also have argued that assessment practices serve to legitimize the "disabling" of minority students by locating the problem or deficiency in the student rather than in school practices that are disempowering (cf. Allington, 1994; Cummins, 1986; Deyhle & Swisher, 1997). Students may perform poorly on traditional standardized tests because of the misalignment between the tests and the students' cultural background, proficiency in English, or lack of test-taking experience (Deyhle & Swisher, 1997; Putnam, 1992; Scruggs & Mastropieri, 1988).

Furthermore, results are often inflated by unethical practices that are pervasive in American schools (Haladyna, Nolen, & Haas, 1991). These include dismissing low-achieving students on days the test is administered, giving hints or answers to students taking the tests, increasing the time students are given to complete the tests, and developing a curriculum to match the test. It is this last practice that has the greatest impact on what happens in the classroom.

In an extensive study of elementary schools, Smith (1991) found that achievement testing programs "substantially reduce the time available for instruction, narrow curricular offerings and modes of instruction, and potentially reduce the capacities of teachers to teach content and to use methods and materials that are incompatible with standardized testing formats" (p. 8). In the interview below, a teacher describes how standardized tests, in this case, the Iowa Test of Basic Skills (ITBS), affected the use of an innovative math program that was not closely matched to test items:

The first year I used Math Their Way [a program designed for conceptual understanding of math concepts through manipulation of concrete materials], I was teaching a second grade class and they scored at grade level. But other second grades in that school scored higher than grade level, and I had to do an awful lot of talking before they allowed me to use that program again. . . . I was really angry because so many of the things I had taught those children about math were not on the test—were not tested by the test. And, indeed, the following year they did extremely well in the third grade. I had no children who were [placed] in any of the low math classes and a great many of my children were in the advanced classes doing better than some of the children who had scored higher than they had on the ITBS. . . . But it's very hard to start a new program knowing that the Iowa may be used against you. (Smith, 1991, p. 8)

Unfortunately, this math teacher's persistence is unusual. Smith (1991) found that to avoid feelings of shame and anxiety, many teachers teach to the test. In one school, for example, elementary school teachers pushed to substitute a science textbook for the hands-on science program they had used in the past. Thus, the current emphasis on standardized tests, which involve isolated and decontextualized factual recall or recognition, not conceptual understanding or problem solving, tends to make teaching more testlike and to align the curriculum with what is covered on the tests (Smith, 1991). The use of standardized tests also affects students' strategies and motivation. In a survey of students, Paris, Lawton, et al. (1991) found that large numbers of students, especially low-achieving adolescents, become both cynical and anxious about tests, cheat, refuse to try, and use poor test-taking strategies such as guessing.

Performance-Based Assessment

Performance-based assessment is an umbrella term for alternative assessments that ask students to use their knowledge rather than to recall isolated bits of knowledge or to select responses in contrived testing situations. For example, in performance assessments, students might "produce, demonstrate, perform, create, construct, apply, build, solve, plan, show, illustrate, convince, persuade, or explain" what they know (Poteet, Choate, & Stewart, 1993, p. 5). Thus, performance assessment is in keeping with constructivist views of learning that emphasize problem solving and higher order thinking (Coutinho & Malouf, 1993; Doran & Sentman, 1994; Resnick & Resnick, 1992).

Reflecting the assumption that "all students are intelligent, although not in the same way" (Gage & Falvey, 1995, p. 64), performance assessments provide students with a variety of ways to demonstrate their knowledge. For example, assessments that rely on visual representations may enable some students with learning disabilities to express their knowledge more effectively (Bergerud, Lovitt, & Horton, 1988; Dalton, Morroco, Tivnan, & Rawson, 1994). Following a unit on electricity, Dalton et al. found that average and low-achieving fourth grade students, including those with learning disabilities, who were given a constructed diagram test were better able to demonstrate their knowledge than a similar group of students who were given a written questionnaire. Interestingly, test mode had no effect on high-achieving students, who performed equally well on the diagram or the questionnaire tests.

Performance assessments can help teachers make instructional decisions by providing them with meaningful and useful information about students' learning—their accomplishments and progress as well as their difficulties (Darling-Hammond, 1996). This use of assessment is consistent with our discussion of scaffolded instruction, in which assessment helps to determine where instruction should begin in order to build on what students already know and can do. In the reading literature, Lipson and Wixson (1997) see such assessment as the key to the assessment–instruction cycle, in which continuous assessment takes place as part of ongoing instruction, each informing the other. In their model, teachers evaluate a reader's strengths and needs through interviews, observations, and informal measures of literacy performance, which occur as a part of the classroom routine. Similarly, in mathematics, teachers can use observations, interviews, holistic scoring of paper-and-pencil problem solving, and journal writing as assessment tools for instruction (Cross & Hynes, 1994). The data collected serves to shape future instruction, the outcomes of which can be assessed in the same way.

Paris, Lawton, et al. (1991) list four critical ingredients for effective performance assessment. First, assessments should be *authentic*, involving students in meaningful texts and activities. For example, students might perform a science experiment, participate in a debate, write a persuasive letter to the editor, or solve a practical problem with math knowledge. Teachers can assess students' performance in such activities by analyzing the resulting products, such as research projects, journals, or portfolios of students' work. Portfolios are collections of student performances in a variety of modes, compiled to show progress toward specific instructional goals (Pierce & O'Malley, 1992). Performance assessments may also consist of teachers' observations during the course of instruction, for example, during a minilesson, class or small-group discussion, think-alouds, guided practice, and student–teacher conferences. By carefully observing and listening over time, teachers can gain valuable information for future instructional planning. Second, performance assessments should be *multidimensional*, involving different competencies, complex strategies, and higher level thinking processes for different purposes. Third, they should be *collaborative*, and therefore motivating for students, involving them in goal setting and encouraging them to assess their own progress toward those goals. Finally, such assessments should be *longitudinal*, examining student development over time.

It is naive to think that informal assessments like the ones just described will replace high-stakes testing, which serves political purposes, as we have seen. Still, performance assessment is becoming more prevalent in the United States. The U.S. Congress, Office of Technology Assessment (1992) reported that more than half the states were using some type of performance assessment on a voluntary, experimental, or mandatory basis. In addition, many educators and policy makers in states such as Illinois, Arizona, and Michigan, and at the U.S. Department of Education, which oversees the National Assessment of Educational Progress (NAEP), are developing new standardized achievement tests to measure more of what students know and can do, including their use of strategies and background knowledge and their ability to compare, synthesize, and solve problems.

In sum, the trend toward more authentic assessment is in keeping with inclusive education. It is aligned with instruction that emphasizes the active, experiential construction of knowledge; it has the potential to enable students to express their learning in a variety of modes; and it can improve instruction by revealing both students' strengths and their difficulties. However, although performance assessments are not new to vocational, special, or regular education, little empirical research has been done on them (Coutinho & Malouf, 1993; Doran & Sentman, 1994; Maeroff, 1991; Poteet, Choate, & Stewart, 1993). As a result, we do not know whether students with disabilities or students from diverse cultural and linguistic backgrounds will do better under performance assessment conditions (Linn, Baker, & Dunbar, 1991). Further, they are time consuming, costly, and require more teacher training than standardized testing, and are problematic in terms of reliability and generalizability (Linn, 1993; O'Neil, 1992). Finally, Darling-Hammond (1996) cautions that *"changes in the forms of assessment are unlikely to enhance equity unless we change the ways in which assessments are used as well"* (p. 247, italics in original). Only if they are used for diagnostic and instructional purposes, to insure that all students learn successfully, will performance-based assessments support the goals of inclusive education.

COLLABORATIVE TEAMWORK

As teachers know very well, successful inclusion requires adequate resources and support. To provide these, many educators in both regular and special education are calling for fundamental changes in schools. Sapon-Shevin (quoted in O'Neil, 1994/1995), for example, argues: "We shouldn't think of choosing between special education services and regular classrooms as they currently look, but to rethink, restructure, and recreate a different kind of classroom" (p. 10). What Sapon-Shevin has in mind is a flexible curriculum involving project learning, thematic instruction, cooperative learning, and authentic assessment—the themes of this book. But to make it happen, she contends, "we need to move away from the kind of isolation where we have one teacher who is in charge of 30 kids. Instead, we need to say: How do we arrange classrooms where there may be two or three adults who share responsibility and expertise and collaborate to meet the needs of a wide range of learners?" (p. 10).

Collaboration in the inclusive classroom is a relatively new idea, one that brings with it a different conceptualization of the roles and responsibilities of both classroom teachers and special educators, English as a second language (ESL) teachers, administrators, school psychologists, and other resource people. For example, it involves the idea of a partnership among school personnel, who work together as equals, pooling their expertise in content knowledge, teaching strategies, and child development for the benefit of all students in the classroom (Welch & Sheridan, 1995).

Collaborative teamwork within the inclusive classroom may take different forms. In one model, the special educator (or other resource personnel) plays a complementary role to the classroom teacher, who assumes responsibility for overall instructional planning and content teaching. In a history class, for example, a special educator or reading specialist might be responsible for the informal assessments and strategy minilessons we discussed earlier, which would help all students learn assigned text material and complete assignments. In another type of collaborative model, the classroom teacher and special educator share responsibility for supplementary instructional support. In this model, teachers take turns: As one works with students experiencing difficulty, the other works with the larger group. Regardless of the form collaboration takes, it is a way to provide classroom teachers with support and resources. As Welch and Sheridan (1995) note, "no one alone can achieve what the partners in collaboration can achieve together" (p. 23).

Collaboration is a reality in many schools, and most teachers are generally receptive to the idea. A questionnaire survey found that 13% of teachers and specialists surveyed indicated an interest in assuming an active leadership role in a collaborative project, and an additional 70% reported an interest in learning more about schoolwide collaborative efforts and/or receiving collaborative support within their classrooms to serve students with learning disabilities (Wade, Welch, & Jensen, 1994).

Still, collaboration is not an easy undertaking: It requires administrative support, communication skills, shared goals, and commitment.

Parents are another source of information and support for the classroom teacher, and the benefits of collaboration are mutual. The issue of collaboration between educators and parents is of special importance to students and communities who traditionally have been excluded from participation in schools. As Cummins (1986) noted, "when educators involve minority parents in their children's education, parents appear to develop a sense of efficacy that communicates itself to children, with positive academic consequences" (p. 26). To communicate effectively with parents for whom English is not their first language, teachers may need to work closely with ESL and bilingual teachers or aides. Collaboration also means valuing what parents have to offer and finding ways to involve them in their children's education.

CONCLUSION

As Deshler and Schumaker (1993) noted, "a prevailing trend in education today is toward the full inclusion of students with disabilities within regular schools and classrooms" (p. 153). A similar trend is toward providing services in the general education classroom to other types of students, such as those with limited English proficiency. In this chapter, we have looked at conditions that foster inclusive education at both the classroom level and the school level. These include curricular and instructional approaches that have been described as participatory, strategy instruction that is integrated and scaffolded, collaborative relationships among school personnel and with parents, and alternative assessment practices. Unlike pedagogies in which students compete with one another or work alone to master a standardized, lock-step curriculum, participatory approaches have the potential to achieve the goals of inclusive education, such as building community and affirming diversity. Theoretically, participatory approaches foster learning for all students, as they emphasize the social construction of knowledge, encourage diverse approaches to problem solving, and allow for adaptations to accommodate individual needs and multilevel learning. In such contexts, struggling learners can be actively involved, socially accepted, and motivated to achieve to the best of their individual and multiple abilities.

However, systemic changes are necessary. What Slavin wrote in 1990 is still true today in many schools:

If basic school and classroom organization practices remain unchanged, moving larger numbers of academically handicapped students into general classes is likely to be futile; classroom methods in widespread use today are simply inadequate to deal with the amount of student diversity that exists now, much less that which would exist if mainstreaming of academically handicapped students in major instructional areas were significantly increased. (p. 48)

To make inclusion work, Slavin (1990) called for the development of well-researched, comprehensive instructional programs that provide "systematic, carefully constructed, complete alternatives to traditional methods" (p. 48). Teachers in inclusive classrooms also must be prepared adequately for these settings and must have the support and collaboration of special educators, who can assist in individualizing instruction for students with special needs. It is the purpose of these two volumes to provide that much-needed preparation and assistance.

REFERENCES

Allington, R. L. (1994). What's special about special programs for children who find learning to read difficult? *Journal of Reading Behavior, 26,* 95–115.

American Association of University Women (1992). *How schools shortchange girls: The AAUW report.* New York: Marlowe.

Anderson, V., & Roit, M. (1993). Planning and implementing collaborative strategy instruction for delayed readers in grades 6-10. *Elementary School Journal, 94,* 121–137.

Association for Supervision and Curriculum Development (1992). *Resolutions 1992: Critical priority resolutions endorsed by resolutions committee.* Washington, DC: Author.

Barry, A. (1994/1995). Easing into inclusive classrooms. *Educational Leadership, 52,* 4–6.

Bergerud, D., Lovitt, T. C., & Horton, S. (1988). The effectiveness of textbook adaptions in life science for high school students with learning disabilities. *Journal of Learning Disabilities, 21*(2), 70–76.

Chaikind, S., Danielson, L. C., & Brauen, M. L. (1993). What do we know about the costs of special education? A selected review. *The Journal of Special Education, 26,* 344–370.

Clever, A., Bear, G., & Juvonen, J. (1992). Discrepancies between competence and importance of self-perception of children in integrated classes. *Journal of Special Education, 26,* 125–138.

Cohen, E. G. (1994). Restructuring the classroom: Conditions for productive small groups. *Review of Educational Research, 32,* 99–120.

Council of Chief State School Officers (1992, March). Special education and school restructuring. *Concerns, 35,* 1–7.

Coutinho, M., & Malouf, D. (1993). Performance assessment and children with disabilities: Issues and possibilities. *Teaching Exceptional Children, 25*(4), 62–67.

Cross, L., & Hynes, M. C. (1994). Assessing mathematics learning for students with learning differences. *Arithmetic Teacher, 41*(7), 371–377.

Cummins, J. (1986). Empowering minority students: A framework for intervention. *Harvard Educational Review, 56,* 18–35.

Dalton, B., Morroco, C. C., Tivnan, T., & Rawson, P. (1994). Effect of format on learning disabled and non-learning disabled students' performance on a hands-on science assessment. *International Journal of Educational Research, 21*(3), 299–316.

Darling-Hammond, L. (1996). Performance-based assessment and educational equity. In E. R. Hollins (Ed.), *Transforming curriculum for a culturally diverse society*. Mahwah, NJ: Lawrence Erlbaum Associates.

Davidson, N. (1985). Small-group learning and teaching in mathematics: A selective review of the research. In R. E. Slavin, S. Sharan, S. Kagan, R. Hertz-Lazarowitz, C. Webb, & R. Schmuck (Eds.), *Learning to cooperate, cooperating to learn* (pp. 211–230). New York: Plenum.

deBettencourt, L. U. (1987). Strategy training: A need for clarification. *Exceptional Children, 54,* 24–30.

Deci, E. L. (1992). The relation of interest to the motivation of behavior: A self-determination theory perspective. In K. A. Renninger, S. Hidi, & A. Krapp (Eds.), *The role of interest in learning and development*. Hillsdale, NJ: Lawrence Erlbaum Associates.

Delpit, L. (1988). The silenced dialogue: Power and pedagogy in educating other people's children. *Harvard Educational Review, 58,* 280–298.

Deshler, D. D., & Schumaker, J. B. (1993). Strategy mastery by at-risk students: Not a simple matter. *Elementary School Journal, 94,* 153–167.

Deyhle, D., & Swisher, K. (1997). Research in American Indian and Alaska Native education: From assimilation to self-determination. *Review of Research in Education, 22,* 113–194.

Doran, R. L., & Sentman, J. R. (1994). Science and special education: A science education perspective. *Remedial and Special Education, 15*(2), 128–133.

Duffy, G. G., Roehler, L. R., & Meloth, M. S. (1984). The effects and some distinguishing characteristics of explicit teacher explanation during reading strategy instruction. In J. Niles & L. Harris (Eds.), *Changing perspectives on research in reading/language: Processing and instruction* (pp. 223–229). Thirty-third yearbook of the National Reading Conference. Rochester, NY: National Reading Conference.

Englert, C. S., Raphael, T. E., Anderson, L. M., Anthony, H. M., & Stevens, D. D. (1991). Making writing strategies and self-talk visible: Cognitive strategy instruction in writing in regular and special education classrooms. *American Educational Research Journal, 28,* 337–372.

Fantuzzo, J. W., King, J. A., & Heller, L. R. (1992). Effects of reciprocal peer tutoring on mathematics and school adjustment: A component analysis. *Journal of Educational Psychology, 84* (3), 331–339.

Flavell, J. (1979). Metacognition and cognitive monitoring: A new area of cognitive-developmental inquiry. *American Psychologist, 34,* 906–911.

Fuchs, D., & Fuchs, L. S. (1994). Inclusive schools movement and the radicalization of special education reform. *Exceptional Children, 60,* 294–309.

Gage, S. T., & Falvey, M. A. (1995). Assessment strategies to develop appropriate curricula and educational programs. In M. A. Falvey (Ed.), *Inclusive and heterogeneous schooling: Assessment, curriculum, and instruction* (pp. 59–110). Baltimore: Paul H. Brookes.

Graham, S., & Harris, K. R. (1993). Self-regulated strategy development: Helping students with learning problems develop as writers. *Elementary School Journal, 94,* 169–181.

Graves, M. F., Graves, B. B., & Braaten, S. (1994/1995). Scaffolded reading experiences for inclusive classes. *Educational Leadership, 52,* 14–16.

Haladyna, T. M., Nolan, S. B., & Haas, N. S. (1991). Raising standardized achievement test scores and the origins of test score pollution. *Educational Researcher, 20,* 2–7.

Hardman, M. L., Drew, C. J., & Egan, M. W. (1996). *Human exceptionality: Society, school, and family.* Boston: Allyn & Bacon.

Individuals With Disabilities Act of 1990, Pub. L. No. 94–142, § 1412(5b).

Johnson, R. T., & Johnson, D. W. (1994). An overview of cooperative learning. In J. S. Thousand, R. A. Villa, & A. I. Nevin (Eds.), *Creativity and collaborative learning: A practical guide to empowering students and teachers* (pp. 31–44). Baltimore: Paul H. Brookes.

Kliewer, C., & Biklen, D. (1996). Labeling: Who wants to be called retarded? In W. Stainback & S. Stainback (Eds.), *Controversial issues confronting special education: Divergent perspectives* (pp. 83–95). Boston: Allyn & Bacon.

Kline, F. M., Schumaker, J. B., Deshler, D. D. (1991). The development and validation of feedback routines for instructing students with learning disabilities. *Learning Disability Quarterly, 14*(3), 191–207.

Langer, J. (1984). Literacy instruction in American schools: Problems and perspectives. *American Journal of Education, 93*, 107–132.

Larrivee, B., & Horne, M. D. (1991). Social status: A comparison of mainstreamed students with peers of different ability levels. *Journal of Special Education, 25*, 90–101.

Linn, R. L. (1993). Educational assessment: Expanded expectations and challenges. *Educational Evaluation and Policy Analysis, 15*(1), 1–16.

Linn, R. L., Baker, E. L., & Dunbar, S. B. (1991). Complex, performance-based assessment: Expectations and validation criteria. *Educational Researcher, 20*(8), 15–21.

Lipsky, D., & Gartner, A. (1996). Inclusive education and school restructuring. In W. Stainback & S. Stainback (Eds.), *Controversial issues confronting special education: Divergent perspectives* (pp. 3–15). Boston: Allyn & Bacon.

Lipson, M. Y., & Wixson, K. K. (1997). *Assessment and instruction of reading and writing disability: An interactive approach.* (2nd edition) New York: Longman.

Maeroff, G. I. (1991). Assessing alternative assessment. *Phi Delta Kappan, 73*(4), 272–281.

Mastropieri, M. A., & Scruggs, T. E. (1992). Science for students with disabilities. *Review of Educational Research, 62*, 377–411.

McDermott, R., & Varenne, H. (1995). Culture as disability. *Anthropology and Education Quarterly, 26*, 324–348.

McNamara, S., & Moreton, G. (1993). *Teaching special needs: Strategies and activities for children in the primary classroom.* London: David Fulton Publishers.

Meloth, M. S., & Deering, P. D. (1992). The effects of two cooperative conditions on peer group discussions, reading comprehension, and metacognition. *Contemporary Educational Psychology, 17*, 175–193.

Mergendollar, J., & Packer, M. H. (1989). *Cooperative learning in the classroom: A knowledge brief on effective teaching.* San Francisco: Far West Laboratory.

Moll, L. C. (1994). Literacy research in community and classrooms: A sociocultural approach. In R. B. Ruddell, M. R. Ruddell, & H. Singer (Eds.), *Theoretical models and processes of reading* (pp.179–207). Newark, DE: International Reading Association.

National Association of State Boards of Education (1992). *Winners all: A call for inclusive schools.* Washington, DC: Author.

National Committee on Science Education Standards and Assessment (1993). *National science education standards: July '93 Report.* Washington, DC: National Research Council.

Newman, F. M., & Thompson, J. (1987). *Effects on cooperative learning on achievement in secondary schools: A summary of research.* Madison: University of Wisconsin, National Center on Effective Secondary Schools.

Nieto, S. (1996). *Affirming diversity: The sociopolitical context of multicultural education.* White Plains, NY: Longman.

O'Neil, J. (1992). Putting performance assessment to the test. *Educational Leadership, 49*, 14–19.

O'Neil, J. (1994/1995). Can inclusion work? A conversation with Jim Kauffman and Mara Sapon-Shevin. *Educational Leadership, 52*, 7–11.

Osborne, A. G., Jr., & DiMattia, P. (1994). The IDEA's least restrictive environment mandate: Legal implications. *Exceptional Children, 61*, 6–14.

Palincsar, A. S. (1986). The role of dialogue in providing scaffolding instruction. *Educational Psychologist, 21*, 73–98.

Palinscar, A. S., & Brown, A. L. (1984). Reciprocal teaching of comprehension monitoring strategies. *Cognition and Instruction, 2*, 117–175.

Paris, S. G., Lawton, T. A., Turner, J. C., & Roth, J. L. (1991). A developmental perspective on standardized achievement testing. *Educational Researcher, 20,* 12–20.

Paris, S. G., Wasik, B. A., & Turner, J. C. (1991). The development of strategic readers. In R. Barr, M. L. Kamil, P. B. Mosenthal, & P. D. Pearson (Eds.), *Handbook of reading research* (Vol. II, pp. 609–640). New York: Longman.

Pearson, P. D. (1996). Reclaiming the center. In M .F. Graves, P. Van den Broek, & B. M. Taylor (Eds.), *The first R: The right of all children* (pp. 259–274). New York: Teachers College Press.

Pearson, P. D., & Gallagher, M. C. (1983). The instruction of reading comprehension. *Contemporary Educational Psychology, 8,* 317–344.

Perske, R. (1989). *Circle of Friends.* Nashville: Abingdon Press.

Pierce, L. V., & O'Malley, J. M. (1992). *Performance and portfolio assessment for language minority students.* Washington, DC: National Clearinghouse for Bilingual Education.

Podell, D. M., & Soodak, L. C. (1993). Teacher efficacy and bias in special education referrals. *Journal of Educational Research, 86,* 247–253.

Poteet, J. A., Choate, J. S., & Stewart, S. C. (1993). Performance assessment and special education: Practices and prospects. *Focus on Exceptional Children, 26*(1), 1–20.

Putnam, M. L. (1992). Characteristics of questions on tests administered by mainstream secondary classroom teachers. *Learning Disabilities Research and Practice, 3,* 129–136.

Reeve, R., & Brown, A. (1985). Metacognition reconsidered: Implications for intervention research. *Journal of Abnormal Child Psychology, 13,* 343–356.

Resnick, L. B., & Resnick, D. P. (1992). Assessing the thinking curriculum: New tools for educational reform. In B. R. Gifford & M. C. O'Connor (Eds.), *Changing assessments: Alternative views of aptitude, achievement and instruction* (pp. 38–75). Boston: Kluwer.

Roehler, L. R., & Duffy, G. G. (1991). Teachers' instructional actions. In R. Barr, M. L. Kamil, P. B. Mosenthal, & P. David Pearson (Eds.), *Handbook of reading research* (Vol. II, pp. 861–883). New York: Longman.

Rosenshine, B., & Meister, C. (1992). The use of scaffolds for teaching higher-level cognitive strategies. *Educational Leadership, 49,* 26–33.

Sapon-Shevin, M., Ayres, B. J., & Duncan, J. (1994). Cooperative learning and inclusion. In J. S. Thousand, R. A. Villa, & A. I. Nevin (Eds.), *Creativity and collaborative learning: A practical guide to empowering students and teachers* (pp. 45–58). Baltimore: Paul H. Brookes.

Scranton, T., & Ryckman, D. (1979). Sociometric status of learning disabled children in an integrative program. *Journal of Learning Disabilities, 12,* 402–407.

Scruggs, T. E., & Mastropieri, M. A. (1988). Are learning disabled students "test-wise"? A review of recent research. *Learning Disabilities Focus, 3,* 87–97.

Scruggs, T. E., & Mastropieri, M. A. (1994). Successful mainstreaming in elementary science classes: A qualitative study of three reputational cases. *American Educational Research Journal, 31,* 785–811.

Sears, S., Carpenter, C., & Burstein, N. (1994). Meaningful reading instruction for learners with special needs, *The Reading Teacher, 47,* 632–638.

Shapiro, J. P., Loeb, P., & Bowermaster, D. (1993, December 13). Separate and unequal. *U.S. News and World Report, 115,* 46–50, 54–56, 60.

Sherwood, S. K. (1990). A circle of friends in a 1st grade classroom. *Educational Leadership, 48,* 41.

Skrtic, T. M. (1991). The special education paradox: Equity as the way to excellence. *Harvard Educational Review, 61,* 148–206.

Slavin, R. E. (1990). General education under the regular education initiative: How must it change? *Remedial and Special Education, 11,* 40–50.

Slavin, R. E. (1995). *Cooperative learning* (2nd ed.). Boston: Allyn and Bacon.

Slavin, R. E., DeVries, D. L., & Hulten, B. H. (1975). *Individual vs. team competition: The interpersonal consequences of academic performance* (Report No. 188). Baltimore: Johns Hopkins University, Center for Social Organization of Schools.

Slavin, R. E., Madden, N. A., & Leavey, M. B. (1984). Effects of cooperative learning and individualized instruction on mainstreamed students. *Exceptional Children, 50,* 434–443.

Smith, M. L. (1991). Put to the test: The effects of external testing on teachers. *Educational Researcher, 20,* 20–11.

Stainback, S., Stainback, S., & Ayres, B. (1996). Schools as inclusive communities. In W. Stainback & S. Stainback (Eds.), *Controversial issues confronting special education: Divergent perspectives* (pp. 31–43). Boston: Allyn & Bacon.

Swanson, H. L. (1989). Strategy instruction: Overview of principles and procedures for effective use. *Learning Disabilities Quarterly, 12,* 3–14.

Taylor, S. (1988). Caught in the continuum: A critical analysis of the principle of the least restrictive environment. *Journal of the Association of Persons with Severe Handicaps, 13,* 41–53.

U.S. Congress, Office of Technology Assessment. (1992). *Testing in American schools: Asking the right questions (OTA-SET-519).* Washington, DC: U.S. Government Printing Office.

U. S. Department of Education (1997). *Nineteenth annual report to Congress on the implementation of the Individuals With Disabilities Education Act.* Washington, DC: Department of Education.

U.S. Department of Education. (1994). *Sixteenth annual report to Congress on the implementation of the Individuals With Disabilities Education Act.* Washington, DC: Department of Education.

Vygotsky, L. S. (1978). *Mind in society: The development of higher psychological processes.* (M. Cole, V. John-Steiner, S. Scribner, & E. Souberman, Eds.). Cambridge, MA: Harvard University Press.

Wade, S. E., Trathen, W., & Schraw, G. (1990). An analysis of spontaneous study strategies. *Reading Research Quarterly, 25,* 147–166.

Wade, S. E., Welch, M., & Jensen, J. B. (1994). Teacher receptivity to collaboration: Levels of interest, types of concerns, and school characteristics as variables contributing to successful implementation. *Journal of Educational and Psychological Consultation, 5,* 177–209.

Wang, M. C., Reynolds, M. C., & Walberg, H. J. (1994/1995). Serving students at the margins. *Educational Leadership, 52,* 12–17.

Welch, M., & Sheridan, S. M. (1995). *Educational partnerships: Serving students at risk.* Orlando, FL: Harcourt Brace.

Wong, B. Y. L. (1985). Metacognition and learning disabilities. In D. L. Forrest-Pressley, G. E. MacKinnon, & T. G. Waller (Eds.), *Metacognition, cognition, and human performance* (Vol. 2, pp. 137–180). Orlando, FL: Academic Press.

2

Weaving Lessons: Strategies for Teaching Mathematics and Science in Inclusive Settings

Karen Karp

A visit to two very different classrooms in a local elementary school illustrates the current issues in school reform for students with special needs. As we enter Mr. D's classroom, we see a group of students seated at desks, reading from a chapter in a textbook about dinosaurs. Children are taking turns reading one paragraph at a time out loud while the teacher frequently interjects questions as important points arise. Each illustration is examined in detail, and the teacher directly highlights critical components, such as how adaptations of the dinosaur's body show whether they were meat or plant eaters. Important vocabulary is written on the chalkboard, and as the words emerge in the narrative, the definitions are noted. After completing several pages, the students are given worksheets with short-answer questions, fill-in-the-blank items, and vocabulary words and asked to respond with one- or two-word answers.

In Ms. T's classroom, the students are circulating around learning stations that are based on topics relating to the life of dinosaurs. One group is engaged in creating a fossil from a cast, another is using hand-held microscopes to examine the fossilized remains of sea creatures that once lived in the area, and a third is trying to tear paper using pointed pieces of cardboard and flat, squared-off ones in an effort to mimic the effect of different kinds of dinosaur teeth. Ms. T moves among the groups asking students to describe and justify their thinking while posing alternative problems. The children are asked to write lab reports of their findings using both narrative and drawings.

As a result of national concerns about student achievement in mathematics and science and in an effort to make these disciplines more accessible to all students, educators are moving from the instruction described in the first classroom to that in the second setting. In the first classroom, the children are working in a relatively passive learning situation, absorbing scientific knowledge from oral, written, and visual clues. The teacher provides information that the students are expected to remember and recite back on demand. The following questions arise: Are these students engaged in meaningful activities? Will instruction that is so dependent on the teacher prepare students to respond independently to scientific inquiries that might arise in the future? How will students with special needs respond to this method of instruction?

In the second classroom children are constructing their own knowledge, confirming predictions, and developing conclusions. Students are learning how to learn through the process of becoming active thinkers and explorers. This hands-on and minds-on approach accommodates diverse learning styles while discouraging teacher-dependent behaviors. In this setting there is the potential for the student with special needs to succeed.

In several research studies of students with learning disabilities and mild mental handicaps, teachers coached the students on developing explanations of scientific events. This proved to be a successful method for developing student reasoning skills and increased recall of the explanations (Sullivan, Mastropieri, & Scruggs, 1995). In one study, students in separate groups were either given facts about animals and asked to repeat them, given the same facts and the explanations for each fact, or given facts and coached through explanations (developing the knowledge themselves through artful teacher questioning). The third group, which engaged in the more autonomous development of information, showed significant gains over the other students in both immediate and delayed assessments of information. Teachers reported that the use of highly structured and guided questioning to support student thinking was essential. Thus, active knowledge construction by students and structured teaching are not at odds with each other.

Scruggs, Mastropieri, Bakken, and Brigham (1993) compared two science instructional programs in classrooms of students with learning disabilities. Although the content was exactly the same, one lesson was based on a textbook approach, where there was group reading, teacher-directed discussion, examination of illustrations, and worksheet tasks for reinforcement. The other lesson used an inquiry-oriented, activity-based approach, where students were encouraged to think and solve problems on their own in an effort to promote student-constructed knowledge. The findings indicated that the students with special needs learned and remembered more—both immediately and after a period of time—from the teaching methods that encouraged an inquiry-oriented model. In addition, almost all of the student participants indicated that they preferred the investigatory style to the textbook and worksheet design.

School mathematics and science curriculum are currently being restructured in terms of what is taught, how it is taught, and how results are evaluated. This shift to more engaging learning experiences is reflected in documents such as the Standards (1989, 1991) of The National Council of Teachers of Mathematics (NCTM), *The National Science Education Standards* (National Committee on Science Education Standards and Assessment, 1996), and the Department of Education's *Goals 2000* (1994), all of which clearly articulate a reform agenda for improving instruction in mathematics and science. All groups call for "environments in which [teachers] and their students work together as active learners" (National Committee on Science, 1996, p. 4), "settings where students work on a variety of interesting, real world problems requiring the application and integration of knowledge" (National Education Goals Panel, 1994, p. 40), and a focus on "reasoning—away from merely memorizing procedures" (NCTM, 1991, p. 3). NCTM expands the reform to embrace equity when they suggest, "Today's society expects schools to insure that all students have an opportunity to become mathematically (and scientifically) literate, are capable of extending their learning, have an equal opportunity to learn, and become informed citizens capable of understanding issues in a technological society. As society changes, so must its schools" (NCTM, 1989, p. 5). The constructivist, inquiry-based approaches recommended by these educational organizations facilitate learning in inclusive settings, which is the context for successfully including students with special needs.

However, there is a significant gap between what is proposed and what is practiced. Despite overwhelming evidence from theorists, researchers, and practitioners favoring change in mathematics and science education, teachers still present a curriculum highly characterized by paper-and-pencil tasks and rote learning. Even in cases where students are discovering concepts in engaging and meaningful tasks, some children are obviously left out of the equation. This is particularly evident in instructional situations dealing with students with special needs, who make up fully 10% of all school-aged children (Cawley, 1994). These students often are not considered in the proposed reforms and thereby are not effectively included in the instructional activities. Many leaders in The Council of Exceptional Children reiterate the critical need for educational reform, but make a plea to other educational leaders not to overlook the learner with special needs in the process (Anderson, 1992).

In research supported by a Career Development Award from the Joseph P. Kennedy, Jr. Foundation, I have examined best practice in teaching science and mathematics to students with special needs in inclusive settings. From my work with collaborative teams of elementary and special education teachers in classrooms, details about successful instructional approaches are emerging. This chapter describes the curricular and pedagogical approaches of our research and our findings, organized around two of the most critical questions in education today: What constitutes appropriate mathematics and science curriculum for learners with special needs? and What pedagogies match curricular reforms and best serve students with special needs? Although many teachers have made incidental changes to curriculum and instruction, most of these changes result in merely cosmetic alterations. For example, you will see more concrete materials on students' desks, but the actual instruction still prescribes how the materials are used. Instead of the students exploring concepts through hands-on experiences, they follow rote directions and procedures. In these cases, mathematics and science teaching appear to have changed, but in fact it is the old paradigm in new clothes. Greater attention should be focused on changes that will make differences in all students' lives.

WHAT CONSTITUTES APPROPRIATE MATHEMATICS AND SCIENCE CURRICULUM FOR LEARNERS WITH SPECIAL NEEDS?

Over the past 50 years there has been little progress in narrowing the gap between the grade level expectations of students with special needs and their actual performance (Cawley & Miller, 1989). Most current teaching practices, which try to alter children's thinking so they can be more successful, have not been fruitful. The most positive results were generated from short-term efforts focusing on the most basic of computational behaviors, for example, teaching multiplication facts to 16-year-old students (Mastropieri, Scruggs, & Shiah, 1991). In our increasingly technological society, this does not seem like a victory. In fact, one study found that students with learning disabilities typically reached a plateau in their mathematics knowledge after seventh grade and made only one year's growth in the entire period between seventh and twelfth grades (Warner, Alley, Schumaker, Deshler, & Clark, 1980). Usually, the average mathematics performance of such students in twelfth grade is only that of a fifth grader (Cawley & Miller, 1989). Some states already have raised high school diploma requirements to include completion of Algebra 1. How will this change affect secondary school students with special needs who are not ready for such abstractions, particularly if algebra is not taught in a more inclusive way?

New trends in mathematics education are reshaping and refining the priorities of what is taught. The "shopkeeper" mathematics of the past, which focused on speedy basic computation, is an anachronistic curriculum that will not open doors for students. Although we are unlikely to be able to accurately predict the types of jobs that will be available in the 21st century (as even 15 years ago, we would not have accurately envisioned the power of the computer over the lives of all citizens), we can forecast that tomorrow's jobs will require problem-solving and reasoning skills. As Berger (1989) noted, "We live and die on a technology that eats and sleeps on math" (p. A-19). Our expectation that providing computational skills alone will prepare students with special needs to be responsible citizens does those students a disservice.

Although math is a central part of the school curriculum, little emphasis is placed on science in elementary classrooms and in special education settings. Nationally, the average amount of class time spent on science instruction is 2.6 hours per week in grades 1 through 3 and only 3.1 hours per week in grades 4 through 6 (Blank & Gruebel, 1993). Another study found that only 30% of elementary teachers spent 2 hours or more on science instruction in a week (Huinker, 1996). Furthermore, science is rarely taught in self-contained special education classrooms, and because it is not specifically delineated in most individual educational programs (IEPs), it is often not assessed.

Problem solving should be the basis for the curriculum in both science and mathematics instruction. Students need to "problematize the subject," which Hiebert et al. (1996) described as "allowing students to wonder why things are, to inquire, to search for solutions, and to resolve incongruities"

(p. 12). Starting lessons with real-life, everyday situations that are ambiguous or that produce cognitive dissonance gets students actively engaged in seeking information, exploring options, and using their prior learning to process results. In this way, divisions between acquiring knowledge and applying it are blurred.

Science curriculum not only needs to include factual information but also must attend to the critical process skills that bridge content areas. Elements such as observing, classifying, experimenting, hypothesizing, predicting, inferring, measuring, communicating, and generalizing are components of any scientific endeavor. Children, particularly those with special needs, require a curriculum that centers on developing these thinking processes through engaging tasks on a variety of scientific topics. Clearly, a shift from lock-step, rule-based instructional practices to teaching methods focusing on understanding and meaningful concept development is needed. Curriculum should be reformed and refined to meet the broad needs of the society and the more specific needs of learners.

IEPs and the Inclusive Curriculum

Most IEPs of students with special learning needs focus on academic remediation, including lower level skills, and ignore the higher level learning strategies appropriate for mathematics and science learning (Lynch & Beare, 1990). Also, when NAEP test questions were compared with IEPs in grades 4 and 8, several differences were noted (Shriner, Kim, Thurlow, & Ysseldyke, 1993). While NAEP items had only one item requiring straight computation, 40% of the IEPs in fourth grade and 81% of the IEPs in eighth grade included only computational skills. Also, in stark contrast, none of the IEPs contained objectives incorporating application or problem solving in fourth grade, and only 12% did in eighth grade. A recent compilation of over 700 research studies showed that 80% of math instruction for students with special needs centers on arithmetical computation, emphasizing memorization and practice of routine procedures commonly referred to as algorithms (Cawley & Parmar, 1992). This focus leaves special education students ill prepared for productive careers where they must be capable of problem solving. Instead, they are being armed for the future with skills that can be more effectively carried out with a calculator. In reality, modifying instructional practice based on stagnant goals just reinforces an out-of-date curriculum. In this way, teachers prepare students for jobs that not only no longer exist but have not existed for over 2 decades.

What should be an integral part of IEPs and the curriculum for students with special needs is the core of mathematics that involves knowledge of geometry and spatial sense, data collection and analysis, estimation, measurement, number sense and computation, and process skills such as problem solving, reasoning, and communicating mathematically. In addition, these topics should be presented in a style that maximizes the connections and relationships among mathematics and other areas of study, such as science, geography, or literature.

WHAT PEDAGOGIES MATCH CURRICULAR REFORM AND BEST SERVE STUDENTS WITH SPECIAL NEEDS?

Beyond the issue of curriculum selection, traditional pedagogies need to be examined. When students have difficulty in mathematics, teachers often try to reexplain how to do problems using abstract algorithms (that previously failed for the student) and suggest more practice on the same. Teachers often assume that if they describe math and science concepts or formulas correctly and clearly, with plenty of symbols, they will necessarily be understood. Yet, "no matter how lucidly and patiently teachers explain to their students, they cannot understand for their students" (Schifter & Fosnot, 1993, p. 9).

Ineffective instruction remains a significant factor in the large number of students who face learning problems in mathematics. Methods traditionally used in regular classrooms and more specifically, with students with special needs often create situations where the teacher is the authority and dispenser of information. Students listen to teaching that centers on "telling" procedures and giving information. Dewey (1899/1969) vigorously opposed such methods, attacking what he called the "spectator theory of knowledge": Just as the biologist can take a bone or two and reconstruct the whole animal, so, if we put before the mind's eye the ordinary schoolroom, with its rows of ugly desks placed in geometrical order, crowded together so that there shall be as little moving room as possible . . . and add a table, some chairs, the bare walls and possibly a few pictures, we can reconstruct the only educational activity that can possibly go on in such a place. It is all made "for listening" (p. 31).

Learned Helplessness
Versus Independent Learning

Teaching methods based on "telling" promote prolonged dependency on teacher assistance, which may encourage learned helplessness among students. Learned helplessness is the perception that there is no connection between an individual's behavior and the onset or withdrawal of an aversive event. In a classroom setting, a likely consequence of this can be seen when a student encounters failure and views his or her own effort as irrelevant in affecting the chance of failing again. Students who develop learned helplessness have been found to attribute their problems to factors they see as either uncontrollable or unchangeable, such as ability, task difficulty, or attitudes of other people. An example that many can relate to is what happens when a person is working on a computer and reaches a barrier of sorts. Often another person with computer expertise is brought in, takes over the controls of the computer, "fusses" with the machine and software, and fixes the problem. Without really having the opportunity to do the work, the original user learns nothing more than who to call when problems arise. This is learned helplessness.

This helplessness response can be produced when teachers limit students' active involvement or their opportunities to respond, repeat students' responses, answer their own questions, write equations and record calculations for students, and spend extended periods of time with individuals during sessions of monitored work. Teachers could establish a model of student persistence by requesting elaboration after a partially correct response or by giving prompts at the point of an incorrect answer, but instead they often ask a question and then immediately respond with an answer. For example, a teacher might ask, "Can this fraction be simplified?" and then immediately state, "no, it stays the same." In another setting, a teacher might pose the question, "Is this item magnetic?" And almost instantly answer, "Yes, it is." This behavior teaches students that if they wait and remain passive, the teacher will give the answer. The science educator, Rowe (1969/1996), demonstrated that "wait-time", or the time teachers wait for students to answer questions, is particularly abbreviated for children with cognitive disabilities. Teachers in Rowe's study suggested that because they did not expect an answer, they quickly went on to another student when there was no immediate response. Yet, when teachers changed wait-time from an average of 1 second to 5 seconds, they increased the length and number of student responses, the degree of students' ability to speculate, the number of student-to-student interactions, the number of students who contributed (especially those children who rarely if ever responded), and the degree of flexibility in the responses they would accept. These were relatively large gains for a simple change in the teachers' verbal patterns.

Sometimes, in an effort to help, teachers take over tasks for some students while requiring others to do the identical tasks themselves. This differential behavior is often apparent in the practice of a teacher writing mathematical equations or procedures for a student. Sometimes the teacher takes away the student's pencil or uses his or her own to erase the student's work, rewrite an equation, or perform a mathematical process. This approach is also evident when a teacher helps carry out an experiment, asking a student to step aside so she or he can take over the situation. These actions are all performed with the teacher's best intentions. Yet, on a consistent basis, these behaviors suggest a message: The student is not able to independently accomplish the tasks. This encourages the student's view that when errors are made or barriers are reached, the teacher will take over, suggesting that they themselves need not extend themselves beyond their confidence level. When receiving such assistance from the teacher, not only are students deprived of the opportunity to practice the behaviors necessary for independent work, they practice dependent behaviors.

Challenging Goals and Expectations in Mathematics and Science

There is also a growing concern that the goals for students with special needs are too easy (Anderson & Pellicer, 1990). Learning activities involving risk taking and challenges lead to greater effort and performance than objectives that produce easy success (Locke & Latham, 1990). Many teachers even remind students to look for such opportunities by asking, "Did you challenge yourself today?" In mathematics, children can write their own word problems, choosing their own numbers at their own range of difficulty. In science, students can develop questions to research and experiment with. Teaching practices for all students should set high expectations and build independent, self-regulated learners.

Since the goal of many educators is to prepare students to be autonomous learners of mathematics and science, then instructional approaches that create and nurture independence are the approaches of choice. Yet, the appropriate choice of approach will differ depending on the individual student and the topic he or she is working on at a given time. Observing teachers in the Kennedy Project has revealed that there is no one right teaching model that should always be used, but the least intrusive method that meets the students' needs should always be preferred. Ultimately, effective teachers cannot simply choose to use student-centered instructional approaches; they must accurately select strategies that allow all students, including those with special needs, to meet the goals and objectives of their mathematics and science learning in the most independent way. The model that has been generated as a result of the observations and interviews of teams of teachers, referred to here as the "interwoven approach," is one that blends what teachers know as strategies for instruction and their keen ability to "kidwatch."

THE INTERWOVEN APPROACH

What seems to be most responsive to students' needs is a collection of teaching strategies that can be woven together to form a bridge beginning with students' current abilities and moving toward the realization of their potential. This reflects Vygotsky's (1978) idea of the zone of proximal development described in chapter 1 of this volume (see the "Cooperative Group and Project Learning" section). Thus, teachers try to match students' special needs with a teaching approach that is supportive and at the same time nurtures autonomy.

The interwoven approach respects the contributions of many paradigms. This model assumes no exact blueprint for effectively teaching all students, so any teaching strategy that produces positive student outcomes should be considered. Eventually, the approach must lead to the teacher fading from the equation. Rigid loyalty and allegiance to a particular teaching model are not compatible with the desire to help individual students grow in mathematics and science learning.

I am using the metaphor of weaving a pattern in a rug or piece of fabric to create an image of what happens when a teacher designs instruction for an inclusive classroom. Imagine, if you will, a large loom with the vertical threads in place. These threads represent the content of the instruction, and their position as the framework for creating the product illustrates the centrality of subject matter knowledge in teaching. This image represents the belief that a full understanding of and background in mathematics or science is essential in building an instructional experience. When those content threads are securely in place, then and only then, the teacher becomes the weaver, examining the array of colorful yarns hanging above the frame (see Fig. 2.1). The various yarns represent the repertoire of possible teaching strategies. In some cases, if only one strategy is incorporated, the piece may end up as a solid cloth with just a single colored thread or strategy used throughout. More often, though, the different colored threads are pulled individually, not necessarily in even amounts, creating bands of various sizes and colors in the weft. In other words, although the lesson may be based on a constructivist approach, at times one child or another may need other instructional techniques, such as explicit explanation, to best make meaning of the information. This results in a creation that has some solid space interspersed with patches and edges of other colors.

The instructional strategies (yarns) that comprise the weft threads of the model exist on a continuum. At one end are explicit strategies directly provided by the teacher. Then, moving in the direction of less teacher involvement, is coaching or the expert–novice learning relationship, which combines structured learning experiences with scaffolding. Toward the center, as students become increasingly independent, are collaborative designs involving peers or teachers. At the other end of the continuum are strategies that center on student construction of knowledge, where the student is most autonomous. Similar to Pearson and Gallagher's (1983) idea of the gradual release of responsibility (see chap. 1), this model represents

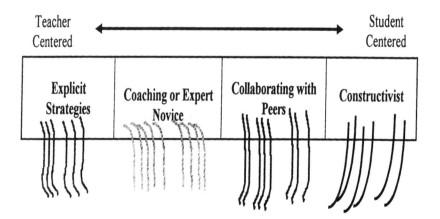

FIG. 2.1. *Continuum of yarns from which to choose in weaving a lesson.*

progression from high teacher responsibility for the learning to high student responsibility. The following sections of this chapter will discuss briefly the particular teaching strategies that are the components of the interwoven approach for mathematics and science instruction, in a sequence from the greatest amount of teacher intervention to the greatest level of student independence.

Explicit Strategy Instruction in Mathematics and Science

Explicit cognitive strategy instruction using self-instruction and guided or independent practice has been shown to be an effective intervention for teaching complex mathematical problem solving to students with special needs (Harris & Pressley, 1991). The self-instruction includes a structured, systematic set of procedures in question form. The questions guide students to read and restate the problem, draw a picture, develop a plan by identifying the type of problem, break the problem into smaller pieces, write the problem in a mathematical sentence, carry out operations, and check their work using a calculator. These self-instructive prompts guide the entire process from beginning to end.

In other uses of explicit strategies, mnemonics are incorporated into structured thinking processes, for example, solving word problems using FAST DRAW (Mercer & Miller, 1992), which represents:

Find what you're solving for.
Ask yourself, "What are the parts of the problem?"
Set up the numbers.
Tie down the sign.
Discover the sign.
Read the equation.
Answer the problem from memory, or draw, and check work.
Write the answer.

Unlike more inquiry-based instruction, the teacher or other students in the class model these steps and explain the components using terminology that is easily understood by those who have not discovered them independently. "Teachers promote students' internalization of cognitive strategies by modeling strategy use in authentic contexts, cuing students to activate and monitor strategy use, and gradually transferring control of the dialogue and strategies to students" (Englert, Tarrant, & Mariage, 1992, p. 73). Teachers' explicit modeling of cognitive strategies in solving word problems has produced very positive results with students with special needs (Mercer & Miller, 1992).

On the other hand, physical models can be used with explicit strategy instruction (Cawley & Reines, 1996). For example, in explicit strategy approaches, a teacher demonstrating multiplication concepts with cubes might say, "Watch me, and place your cubes just like mine. To show 4×3 we can make a rectangle that is four cubes long and three cubes wide." In contrast, a teacher with a constructivist perspective might say, "Let's see how you can show the multiplication problem 4×3 using cubes. I want you to be ready to explain your thinking to the class." Obviously there will be a distinction between the student who has only a rote understanding of the array and the student who can apply and talk about what the cube formation represents. Teacher scripts have been created to act as starting points for teachers new to this kind of explicit sharing of thinking strategies (e.g., Mercer & Miller, 1992). Sample dialogues are used until teachers can independently guide the discussion.

Modeling is a strategy that involves demonstrating the steps to accomplish a task while verbalizing the accompanying thinking process and reasoning, with students imitating these steps on a different, but parallel task. The teacher models the context in which the strategy is called for. For example, rather than merely demonstrating how to use a ruler to measure the distance across a room, the modeling strategy would involve talking through the process. As the teacher places a mark on the floor to indicate where the ruler ends after the first measurement, he or she states, "I am using this line to mark off where the ruler ends. How should I use this line as I measure the next section of the floor? I know I have to move the ruler, but should I copy what I did the first time?" This dialogue takes place prior to placing the ruler for a second measurement. Often teachers share alternatives: They point out other ways they could have carried out the task. They try to make their invisible thinking processes visible.

The skill of choosing the best models comes with what Shulman (1986) calls "pedagogical content knowledge." This is where the teacher hones the craft of instruction by selecting "the most useful forms of representation of those ideas (the most regularly taught topics in one's own subject area), the most powerful analogies, illustration, examples, explanations, and demonstrations—a word, the ways of representing and formulating the subject that make it comprehensible to others" (p. 6). Teachers decide the appropriate ways to experience concepts, working in the area between what students can handle independently and what can be achieved with assistance. Also at this time, teachers should discuss the rationale for learning the particular mathematics or science skill and the situations in which the skill is useful. Developing relevant activities makes this practice much easier. Then students concentrate on using, rather than remembering or memorizing, the necessary skill.

Coaching

Coaching is the term used to describe the support offered by the teacher on those aspects of the task the students cannot independently accomplish. This aspect of scaffolding has been referred to as "collaborating with a learner to provide exactly what is needed for meaningful participation" (Reid & Stone, 1991), or in some cases, as "elaborative interrogation strategies" (Pressley et al., 1992). This support includes teacher modeling of task steps that the student has not yet mastered or reformulating a question about a topic too complex for the student to answer. To use the previous example, the teacher might ask a student, "Why is it important to measure a room?" If the student fails to respond, then the teacher scaffolds the question by asking, "What are some things in your room that have to be measured to see if they fit into the space?"

The Role of Cooperative Learning

Cooperative learning, also known as "communities of practice," refers to learning situations in which students work together to enhance and expand upon what they could do on their own. Small group activity is considered an important instructional mode for most young students, including those with special needs. The social interaction among the students involved results in comparisons of multiple perspectives on a problem and appears to facilitate higher order thought. However, simply adopting the practice of putting students into groups will not achieve positive results. Teachers must bring an appropriate philosophy to cooperative classrooms. Without shifts in basic assumptions about what constitutes mathematics and science curriculum and how children learn, students in classrooms where cooperative learning is employed are not likely to learn anything new. The nature of the learning in these groups and the dynamics of the group interactions could foster individual learning not unlike that of students sitting at their isolated desks. The teacher must work to create situations, even by structuring them into the lesson, where students share thinking and problem-solving strategies. It is these interactions that transform the learning that takes place in these settings.

The more the "expert" can make his or her assumptions and knowledge explicit, the more the novice's learning is facilitated. Therefore, the more peers can talk with one another about what they are thinking and how they are approaching the problem, the better will be the chance that others in the group will benefit. This social role playing during instruction allows for practice, articulation, and evaluation of the knowledge to be learned.

Mathematics is considered a subject that is "conceptually dense" (Wiig & Semel, 1984). The kinds of context clues that enable students to comprehend a passage in reading without knowing all the words are absent in mathematics. Each symbol or mathematical term must be completely understood to solve problems accurately. Cooperative learning can promote the modeling of dialogue and oral language development necessary for successfully navigating the complexity of mathematical communication.

The think-alouds inherent in this interactive process are the verbalizings of what student mathematicians or scientists are thinking as they are doing mathematics and science. They consciously describe strategies and talk about the meaning they are giving to the task. These conversations become oral translations of thinking and understanding of inferences and sense making. One typical element of this thinking-aloud procedure is the practice of partner sharing, a common version of which is called the think-pair-share approach. For example, one teacher in a multi-age primary setting in the Kennedy project paired his students, mixing students with mental retardation and other cognitive disabilities into the pairs. Each pair selected a research question to ask the rest of the class. Each pair then made a joint decision about how to poll other students, record responses, and display their findings in a graph. The students were also asked to put into writing what they learned about their research question from looking at the graph they made. After children presented their results, the teacher remarked that "the use of this approach allowed all students to create meaning from the activity." In this way, students serve as role models or catalysts in the thinking process. Repeated exposure to these sharing sessions increases the likelihood that students with special needs will begin to think independently at higher levels.

The Role of Student Choice
in an Inquiry-Based Curriculum

In the constructivist model of learning, student choice and opportunities for leadership of their own learning are essential. In one of the classroom observations conducted as part of the Kennedy Foundation study, two kindergarten children with Down syndrome were brought into active roles in an exciting science lesson. The class was exploring which fruits would float in water and which would sink, to develop a basic understanding of the concept of density. Using cooperative working groups, the students teamed together at tables to color a prediction sheet with their choices on which items would float. One child with Down syndrome had the support of a teaching assistant, but the other child worked with teammates to complete the task. All students were busy discussing issues such as how heavy the fruit might be and whether its shape would make a difference. Then the experimentation took place. Each child came up to test a piece of fruit. All eyes were glued to the point where the fruit would be set free into the water in a large, clear plastic container. One of the children with Down syndrome was in charge of testing a kiwi. This fruit caused the greatest sensation. Many children had never seen a kiwi and were not sure, even after feeling it, what was inside. The child confidently predicted that the kiwi would sink. When he released the fruit into the water and it sank to the bottom, everyone cheered. It is unlikely that any child in the room will forget a kiwi after that experience.

While manipulative materials in constructivist mathematics and hands-on science can be powerful tools, "using them effectively is deceptively complex" (Leinhardt, Putnam, Stein, & Baxter, 1991 p. 97). The understanding of mathematical concepts does not go directly from the fingertips into the brain (Ball, 1992). On first glance, many teachers appear to be using the constructivist model, but under greater scrutiny, it can be seen that their prescriptive directions often give students little opportunity to explore real meaning. Using materials well takes reflective practice, particularly in connecting the concrete to the more abstract or symbolic representations.

On the other hand, there are very worthwhile mathematical and scientific activities that do not include manipulatives. Some instructional programs have been outright rejected because "no mention is made of hands-on manipulatives" (Carnine, 1992 p. 9), even though they have been shown to produce higher level cognitive performance in low and high achievers. Again, for most learners, the more concrete the representation used at the point of initial contact with a concept, the better, but that fact alone should not exclude other options that have proved to be successful. Blind and uncritical use of manipulatives is not the answer.

EVALUATING PROGRESS AND LEARNING

Part of the underlying foundation of special education is the focus on planning for an individual child. Regardless of where the program is delivered, goals and objectives are developed in response to a particular student's needs. In the past, teachers used a diagnostic-prescriptive approach, where diagnostic tests produced a profile necessary for determining the appropriate instructional program. Due to problems with the nature and validity of some of these tests, alternative assessment methods have become increasingly popular. These assessments are based on introducing instruction with an authentic approach, continuously observing and evaluating student performance, and using the results of the observations to improve instruction for that student. This model has resulted in more responsive programs that have a more positive impact on students with greater success (Fuchs, Fuchs, Hamlett, & Stecker, 1991).

Teachers find out about the learners in their classrooms through observations, diagnostic interviews, collaboration with colleagues, holistic scoring, checklists, portfolio items, student writing in journals, and more formal assessments, such as paper-and-pencil tests, before they know what and how to teach. Much can be gleaned from the use of richer assessments about the kinds of modeling and scaffolding necessary. A portrait of the students' learning, rather than the simple snapshot generated by most paper-and-pencil quizzes, provides guidance on subsequent instructional practices. Unless teachers move away from traditional assessment approaches, they will not be provided with opportunities to gain information on the students' metacognitive thinking. The particular danger of not examining the students' thinking processes in the case of students with special needs is that errors on even basic computational tasks can go undetected by teachers for years (McCarthy, 1991). If teachers depend only on examining student work for right or wrong answers, more subtle misconceptions rarely emerge.

Giving Students a Role in Assessment

Evaluation becomes part of the learning process when learners review the strategies they have used in their attempts to master tasks. This facilitates their awareness and control of what is learned. For example, after each child has an opportunity to measure the room and come up with results, the teacher might state, "I want each of you to think of one thing you did well when measuring and one thing you could do better the next time." Students volunteer responses and the teacher explores with them why they evaluated their performances as they did. In collaborative peer groups, these same strategies can be used by students to simulate expert and novice roles during task activities. Students take turns monitoring, evaluating, and discussing their performances using guidelines provided by the teacher. These meaningful tasks are designed to emphasize intrinsic motivation rather than external inducements. In the measurement example mentioned above, students were motivated to measure the room because they were going to be responsible for purchasing and applying wall paint. Their motivation was based upon being responsible for their own classroom rather than upon any rewards from the teacher.

This evaluation process also enables the teacher to interact more prescriptively and make modifications to his or her own instruction as students continuously recast their thinking. As students make known their misconceptions or gaps in knowledge, the teacher must rapidly make decisions, often returning to scaffolding behaviors to provide the spontaneous prompting and clarification necessary to help students reach full understanding. The teacher takes notes of his or her observations of students during these activities and keeps a narrative record that includes key responses indicating student growth or areas that need emphasis. This *kidwatching* improves teaching as well as the quality of student-to-student interactions.

CONCLUSION

As general education classrooms become increasingly populated with students with diverse abilities and backgrounds, teachers experience greater pressure to meet state and national requirements while teaching students with varying needs. The collaborative model, which this chapter and book embraces, organizes a team of professionals from general and special education who have unique skills and a common goal: to provide the best instruction to an increasingly heterogeneous group of students in general education classrooms. Through such collaboration, both general and special educators enhance their own abilities while developing specific strategies for students. It is important to note that as we hone in on ways to respond to students with special needs, we also connect with other students who are at risk or in need of support. Therefore, the aforementioned strategies benefit all students, not just those with special needs.

In the past, traditional special education programs in mathematics and science have encouraged teaching models that reinforce student dependency on the teacher or other supports. Students need to learn how to think, solve problems, and advocate for themselves in instructional settings. Self-regulated students, who have conscious control of their thinking, are the strategic learners needed for the future. Therefore, teachers of students with special needs can act prescriptively, but only insofar as deciding the best way to encourage student independence in learning. This may be through the teacher

- enabling students to discover for themselves,
- having students create engaging work with peer groups,
- asking the students questions,
- encouraging the students to challenge themselves,
- modeling critical concepts,
- providing a variety of examples and experiences,
- discussing students' own thinking strategies,
- sharing the relevance and usefulness of a topic,
- reflecting with the students,
- setting meaningful and challenging instructional goals,
- devising ways for students to transfer knowledge from the concrete to the more abstract,
- guiding instruction through scaffolding behaviors, and
- allowing students to be actively involved in their own learning.

Given the diversity of student ability in most inclusive classrooms, multiple learning models are useful. Teachers are weavers in the process of blending different instructional strategies for all students, but particularly for students with special needs. Adherence to any single approach will create an instructional situation that will leave some students unraveled and on the fringe. Consciously selecting fibers that create patterns of student success and independence is the goal of the teacher/artisan.

As teachers learn and practice these various teaching strategies, they expand the possibilities for weaving rich and meaningful lessons that are responsive to all students' needs. The underlying assumption is that instruction should be developed on a foundation of the teacher's strong content-area knowledge. Without fluent background information of the mathematical and scientific topics, the methods become weft threads placed on a loom without support. The combination of subject-matter knowledge and pedagogic knowledge gives strength to the weave. Then, as each individual student is considered, the pattern and texture of the cloth emerges.

REFERENCES

Anderson, L. W., & Pellicer, L. O (1990). Synthesis of research on compensatory and remedial education. *Educational Leadership, 48*(1), 10-16.

Anderson, R. J. (1992). Educational reform: Does it all add up? *Teaching Exceptional Children, 24*(2), 4.

Ball, D. L. (1992). Magical hopes: Manipulatives and the reform of math education. *American Educator, 3*, 14–18, 46–48.

Berger, R. (1989). *Teaching mild to moderately retarded students with computers.* ERIC Document Reproduction Service No. ED 322 650.

Blank, R. K., & Gruebel, K. (1993). *State indicators of science and mathematics education 1993.* Washington, DC: Council of Chief State School Officers.

Carnine, D. (1992). Expanding the notion of teachers' rights: Access to tools that work. *Journal of Applied Behavior Analysis 25*(1), 13–19.

Cawley, J. F. (1994). Science for students with disabilities. *Remedial and Special Education, 52*(2), 67–71.

Cawley, J., & Miller, J. (1989). Cross-sectional comparisons of the mathematical performance of children with learning disabilities: Are we on the right track toward comprehensive programming? *Journal of Learning Disabilities, 22,* 250–254, 259.

Cawley, J., & Parmar, R. S. (1992). Arithmetic programming for students with disabilities: An alternative. *Remedial and Special Education, 13*(3), 6–18.

Cawley, J., & Reines, R. (1996). Mathematics as communication using the interactive unit. *Teaching Exceptional Children, 28*(2), 29–34.

Dewey, J. (1969). *The school and society.* Chicago: University of Chicago Press. (Original work published 1899).

Englert, C. S., Tarrant, K. L., & Mariage, T. V. (1992). Defining and redefining instructional practice in special education: Perspectives on good teaching. *Teacher Education and Special Education, 15,* 62–86.

Fuchs, L., Fuchs, D., Hamlett, C., & Stecker, P. (1991). Effects of curriculum-based measurement: Helping general educators meet the challenge of students' diversity. *Exceptional Children, 60,* 518–537.

Harris, K., & Pressley, M. (1991). The nature of cognitive strategy instruction: Interactive strategy construction. *Exceptional Children, 57,* 392–404.

Heibert, J., Carpenter, T., Fennema, E., Fuson, K., Human, P., Murray, H., Oliver, A., & Wearne, D. (1996). Problem solving as a basis for reform in curriculum and instruction: The case of mathematics. *Educational Researcher, 25*(4), 12-21.

Huinker, D. (1996). Teaching mathematics and science in urban elementary schools. *School Science and Mathematics, 96*(7), 340-349.

Leinhardt, G., Putnam, R., Stein, M., & Baxter, J. (1991). Where subject knowledge matters. In J. Brophy (Ed.), *Advances in research on teaching* (Vol. 2, pp. 87–113). Greenwich, CT: JAI.

Locke, E. A., & Latham, G. P. (1990). *A theory of goal setting and task performance.* Englewood Cliffs, NJ: Prentice-Hall.

Lynch, E. C., & Beare, P. L. (1990). The quality of IEP objectives and their relevance to instruction for students with mental retardation and behavioral disorders. *Remedial and Special Education, 11*(2), 48–55.

Mastropieri, M. A., Scruggs, T. E., & Shiah, S. (1991). Mathematics instruction for learning disabled students: A review of research. *Learning Disabilities Research and Practice, 6*(2), 89–98.

McCarthy, D. (1991). *Young Native American children learn division.* Unpublished manuscript, State University of New York at Buffalo.

Mercer, C. D., & Miller, S. P. (1992). Teaching students with learning problems in math to acquire, understand, and apply basic math facts. *Remedial and Special Education, 13*(3), 19–35, 61.

National Committee on Science Education Standards and Assessment. (1996). *National Science Education Standards.* Washington, DC: National Academy Press.

National Council of Teachers of Mathematics. (1989). *Curriculum and evaluation standards for school mathematics.* Reston, VA: Author.

National Council of Teachers of Mathematics. (1991). *Professional standards for teaching mathematics.* Reston, VA: Author.

National Education Goals Panel. (1994). *The national education goals report.* Washington, DC: Author.

Pearson, P. D., & Gallagher, M. C. (1983). The instruction of reading comprehension. *Contemporary Educational Psychology, 8,* 317–344.

Pressley, M., Woods, E., Woloshyn, V., Martin, V., King, A., & Menke, D. (1992). Encouraging mindful use of prior knowledge: Attempting to construct explanatory answers facilitates learning. *Educational Psychologist, 27,* 91–109.

Reid, D. K., & Stone, C. A. (1991). Why is cognitive instruction effective? Underlying learning mechanisms. *Remedial and Special Education, 12*(3), 8–19.

Rowe, M. B. (1969/1996). Science, silence, and sanctions. *Science and Children, 34*(1), 35–37.

Schifter, D., & Fosnot, C. (1993). *Reconstructing mathematics education: Stories of teachers meeting the challenge of reform.* New York: Teachers College Press.

Scruggs, T., Mastropieri, M., Bakken, J., & Brigham, F. (1993). Reading versus doing: The relative effects of textbook-based and inquiry-oriented approaches to science learning in special education classrooms. *The Journal of Special Education, 27,* 1–15.

Shriner, J. G., Kim, D., Thurlow, M. L., & Ysseldyke, J. E. (1993). *IEPs and standards: What they say for students with disabilities.* Minneapolis: University of Minnesota, National Center on Educational Outcomes.

Shulman, L. (1986). Paradigms and research programs in the study of teaching: A contemporary perspective. In M. Wittrock (Ed.), *Handbook of research on teaching* (3rd ed., pp. 3–36). New York: Macmillian.

Sullivan, G., Mastropieri, M., & Scruggs, T. (1995). Reasoning and remembering: Coaching students with learning disabilities to think. *The Journal of Special Education, 29*(3), 310-322.

Vygotsky, L. S. (1978). *Mind in society* (M. Cole, V. John-Steiner, S. Scribner, & E. Souberman, Eds.). Cambridge, MA: Harvard University Press.

Warner, M., Alley, G., Schumaker, J., Deshler, D., & Clark, F. (1980). *An epidemiological study of learning disabled adolescents in secondary schools: Achievement and ability, socioeconomic status and school experience.* Lawrence, KS: University of Kansas Institute for Research in Learning Disabilities.

Wiig, E., & Semel, E. (1984). *Language assessment and intervention for the learning disabled child* (2nd ed.). Columbus, OH: Merrill.

3

Curricular and Instructional Considerations for Teaching Students With Disabilities in General Education Classrooms

Michael F. Giangreco
Mary Beth Doyle

For as long as she can remember, Ms. Brown has been told that she and other general education teachers were not appropriately trained or qualified to teach students with a wide range of disabilities. She was told, "That's why we have special education classes and schools where students with special educational needs can get the specialized instruction they need." This made sense to Ms. Brown; besides, she had her hands full with her students who did not have disability labels. Though she occasionally taught a child with mild learning disabilities in her classroom, for the most part, students with more significant disabilities were never placed in her class. If a student seemed to be having difficulty keeping up with the academic expectations Ms. Brown had established for the class, she felt she was doing the right thing by referring the student for special education. This approach was supported by her colleagues and school system as well. Recently, people started talking about educating students with more significant disabilities in the general education classroom; they referred to it as "inclusive education." Ms. Brown felt that she had never excluded children before because of their disabilities, but rather, was trying to help them by sending them to a place that would better meet their needs. Now she was about to have a student with more significant disabilities in her class. She wondered how this would work and what she could do to make sure it worked for her whole class.

We are in the midst of a major shift in educational service provision for students with disabilities in which they are increasingly valued and included in the same educational experiences that are available to students without disability labels. To extend the information presented in chapter 1 of this volume, we list seven characteristics of inclusive education (Giangreco, Baumgart, & Doyle, 1995), including:

1. All students are welcomed in general education classes in their local schools. The general education classroom in the school the students would attend if they did not have a disability is the first placement consideration, given individually appropriate supports and services.
2. Students are educated in classes where the number of those with and without disabilities is proportional to the local population (e.g., 10% to 12% have identified disabilities).
3. Students are educated with peers in the same age groupings available to those without disability labels.
4. Students with varying characteristics and abilities participate in shared educational experiences while pursuing individually appropriate learning outcomes with necessary supports and accommodations.
5. Shared educational experiences take place in settings predominantly frequented by people without disabilities (e.g., general education classrooms, community work sites).
6. Educational experiences are designed to enhance individually determined valued life outcomes for students and therefore seek an individualized balance between the academic or functional and social or personal aspects of schooling.
7. Inclusive education exists when each of the previously listed characteristics occurs on an ongoing, daily basis.

We will know that inclusive education has fully arrived when designations such as "inclusion school," "inclusion classroom," or "inclusion student" are no longer needed as part of our educational vocabulary because everyone is included (Giangreco, Cloninger, & Iverson, 1998).

As we usher in a new era of education in which children with disabilities are not summarily sent to special education schools and classes because of their disability labels, the roles of all professional staff who work in schools with students who have disabilities are evolving. Nowhere is this more evident or more important than when considering the role of the general education teacher.

Several myths surrounding the needs of students with disabilities have been used to perpetuate the status quo. Over time, what Ms. Brown came to realize was that she had unwittingly bought into some of the historical myths of special education. Some of these myths are:

1. General education teachers are not capable of teaching students with disabilities.
2. Only special education teachers know the specialized approaches that are effective for teaching students with disabilities.
3. Specialized instructional approaches are beyond the capability of general education teachers within the context of a regular class.
4. Special education is synonymous with a place, such as a resource room, special education class, or special education school.
5. Curriculum content and grade level placement are synonymous; in other words, all children placed in a fifth grade class must do "fifth grade level" work.

Nationally, numerous demonstrations have exposed these myths as false (Giangreco, Dennis, Cloninger, Edelman & Schattman, 1993; Hunt & Goetz, 1997; National Center on Educational Restructuring and Inclusion, 1995; Salisbury, Palombaro & Hollowood, 1993; Stainback & Stainback, 1996; Villa & Thousand, 1995; York-Barr, Schultz, Doyle, Kronberg, & Crossett, 1996). Increasingly, these myths and their corresponding practices are being replaced by new standards. While these newer standards of practice are not necessarily common across the country, they are present to some extent in every state and they represent a fundamental shift in how increasing numbers of educators, parents, consumers, administrators, and community members are thinking about the education of students with disabilities. Some of the principles underlying these new standards include:

1. Qualified general education teachers with inclusive attitudes and appropriate supports *can* successfully teach students with disabilities, including those with severe disabilities.
2. The principles of teaching and learning are the same whether a student has a disability label or not, although these principles may

need to be applied differently, adapted, or used more systematically for some students.

3. Just as many instructional approaches used by special educators are effective when used with students without disabilities, many instructional approaches that are effective within general education can also be effective for students who have special educational needs.

4. When general education teachers expand their skills to address the diversity presented by their students with disabilities, they often learn skills that improve their teaching for all students.

5. Special education, namely, specially and individually designed instruction, is a service, not a place. It is portable and therefore need not be bound by location.

6. Grade level placement and curriculum content need not be synonymous. Rather, grade level placement and curriculum content can be independent of each other. For example, in a fifth grade class, while most students might be pursuing what people think of as "fifth grade" curriculum (knowing that varies from place to place), some students will be pursuing individually appropriate curriculum content that is below or above that level through the use of multilevel instruction or curriculum overlapping (both are discussed later in this chapter).

7. We need to change the way we think about educating students with disabilities so that, regardless of what positive intentions we might have, our actions (e.g., to include or not) are not considered a "favor" to students with disabilities or their families. Appendix A to Part 300 of the Code of Federal Regulations (34, CFR 300) (March 12, 1999) states: ". . . IDEA presumes that the first placement option considered for each disabled student by the student's placement team, which must include the parents, is the school the child would attend if not disabled, with appropriate supplementary aids and services to facilitate such placement (p. 12471).

With the advent of inclusive education, a common scenario has been repeated nationally whereby special educators and parents ask administrators and general education teachers for access to the general education classroom for students with more and more severe disabilities. The promise is made that the general education teacher will not be inconvenienced or asked to do more. Initially, many general education teachers accept such invitations to participate in "inclusive education" based on the premise that they will function primarily as a "host" rather than as the teacher for the student with disabilities. In this "foot in the door" approach, general educators often are promised that special educators and others (e.g., paraprofessionals and related services providers) will attend to the educational needs of the student with disabilities. Additionally, many teachers are given the message that they have the option to accept or reject the student with disabilities in their class. Both premises, "hosting" and "the option to accept or reject," have conceptual, ethical, and legal flaws (Giangreco, 1996a; Giangreco, Dennis, Cloninger, Edelman & Schattman, 1993; Laski, 1991). In fact, the attitudes, decisions, and actions of general education teachers are critical factors in determining the success of a student with a disability in a general education class (Giangreco et al, 1993; Giangreco, Edelman & Nelson, 1998). The general education teacher may be the single most important school staff member in determining the success of a student with disabilities in the general education classroom.

Some people have suggested that in situations where paraprofessionals are assigned to a student with disabilities, the paraprofessionals are the key pieces in the personnel puzzle. While this may be true in some situations, recent research suggests that when the paraprofessional assumes the role of "teacher," a variety of problems can result that have an adverse, though unintended, impact on students with disabilities (Doyle, 1995; Giangreco, Edelman, MacFarland & Luiselli, 1997). For example, students with the most complex learning challenges inadvisedly may receive the majority of their instruction from the team member who typically has the least amount of training.

If you, as a general educator, are unaccustomed to having students with disabilities in your classroom, you are not alone in your anxieties, apprehensions, and even fears about inclusive education. These concerns are real and should be taken seriously by colleagues and families. The purpose of this chapter is to help you acquire the attitudes and skills that will assist you in successfully teaching your students with disabilities, rather than excluding them from the classroom or segregating them within it. Recently, we heard a teacher say, "I am concerned that inclusion takes time away from the regular education students because the teacher's emotional energies and attention are redirected toward the challenging student." Although we know that this sentiment may be shared by some general education teachers, it reflects one of the most basic problems facing students with disabilities and their families, namely, that they are considered to be in a different category than "regular" students. Embedded in that sentiment is the inference that the needs of "regular" students come first.

Almost every classroom has students without disability labels who sometimes need extra "emotional energy and attention" from their teachers for any host of reasons (e.g., impact of divorce, child abuse, challenging temperament, issues of normal adolescent development). The same holds for students considered "gifted." Someone could say, "Aren't those gifted students an emotional drain on the teachers because they require specialized planning to be sufficiently challenged and therefore they take teacher time and attention away from the majority of the class who are all at a similar level?" As teachers, we have to be prepared to offer differential amounts and types of emotional energy, attention, support, and individualization to our students, regardless of labels and needs. Good teachers build on the individual strengths of each student and recognize that *all* students have something valuable to contribute to the classroom community.

As you know, teaching takes enormous amounts of emotional energy under any circumstances. As many teachers who have taken on the challenge of inclusion have come to realize, the energy they put forth is often rewarded in their own personal and professional development as well as in the development of their students. We do not mean to present a picture of inclusive education as seen through rose-colored glasses. Can inclusive education be challenging? Sometimes it can, as can general education. Should teachers who work with increasingly challenging students, regardless of their labels, receive appropriate supports? Absolutely; such supports are essential to successful inclusion. We can start the process of giving each of our students an equal opportunity by considering all of them as our students who are welcome in our classrooms. As inclusive efforts begin, you can be on the lookout for common problems, such as having students who are physically placed in the general education classroom, but not really included as part of the classroom program or activities (e.g., students frequently separated with an instructional assistant). Another problem to watch out for is including students with disabilities in classroom curriculum, instruction, and activities, but without the necessary adaptations that will make participation meaningful.

One major goal of inclusive education is to provide shared meaningful learning experiences for students with and without disabilities within the context of classroom activities that address the individualized learning needs of each student. This is an important task that may take a bit of work to understand and implement, but is possible given support from a collaborative team (see chapter 4). This collaborative team comprises core members who spend time with the student daily, such as the teacher, parent, special educator, and paraprofessional, as well as the student, when appropriate. Extended members may include related services personnel who interact with the student less frequently and sometimes on an intermitant basis. Teams may also access other support personnel resources when it is situationally necessary. These individuals tend to have highly specific, short-term interactions with the team (e.g., a consultant who helps design or select a piece of specialized equipment). The one characteristic that brings all of these individuals together is arguably the most foundational characteristic of a collaborative team, namely, *having common goals* (Giangreco, 1996b). This is not to be confused with the common and unteamlike practice of group members agreeing to each have their own goals for a student which reflect the orientation of their particular disciplines (e.g., physical therapy, occupational therapy, speech/language pathology). See chapter 4 for more information on collaborative teamwork.

A competent, caring general education teacher who is effective with students without disabilities already possesses most of the critical skills necessary to successfully educate students with all kinds of learning challenges, including various disabilities (Giangreco, 1997). However, when teaching students with disabilities, you and the members of your collaborative team may need to apply the principles of teaching and learning in different ways. The remainder of this chapter addresses five of the most common questions posed by general education teachers who are interested in successfully including and teaching students with disabilities in their classrooms. These five questions, each related to curriculum and instruction, are:

1. What does a quality curriculum for a student with disabilities in a general education classroom look like?
2. How should the content of the curriculum be determined?
3. How can individualized curricular content be addressed appropriately in the classroom when students without disabilities are pursuing different curricular content?
4. How can appropriate learning opportunities to include students with disabilities in classroom activities be identified or adapted?
5. How can instruction be individualized within the context of general class activities?

What Does a Quality Curriculum for a Student With Disabilities in a General Education Classroom Look Like?

When considering educational curriculum content for students with disabilities, it is important to recognize that the population of students labeled "disabled" is enormously diverse. For example, when a student has a physical disability alone, with no concurrent cognitive disabilities, it is generally accepted that he or she should pursue the full general education curriculum established for students without disabilities. Similarly, students with mild learning disabilities also are generally expected to pursue much, if not all, of the general education curriculum. So, for many students with disabilities, the question is not what these students should learn, but rather how they will access the curriculum and what accommodations will be needed. Decisions about curricular selection become more complex and the curricular content tends to be more individualized when students have more severe disabilities or have combinations of physical, cognitive, sensory, or behavioral disabilities.

A quality curriculum for a student with disabilities includes learning outcomes that are at an individually appropriate level and are pursued within typical class activities (e.g., small cooperative groups, unit-based projects). Selecting appropriate learning outcomes has long been, and continues to be, considered a marker of educational quality for all students. Individually determined curricula for students with disabilities should include a small set of family-selected priorities to establish a focus for instruction, as well as a breadth of curricula that allows the student opportunities to explore many options that coincide with state or local standards.

As team members review general education curricula, they are often surprised to learn that many of the learning outcomes in them are applicable to students with disabilities, including those with severe disabilities. Although this core of curricular content should be reasonably attainable based on the student's current level of functioning and characteristics, a quality curriculum also should provide ample opportunities for students to surprise us with their capabilities. Therefore, we should never presume to know the upper limits on a student's abilities, especially if the student has never been exposed to something or received competent instruction.

We should expose students with disabilities to, and instruct them in, a full range of general education curricular activities to complement more traditional life skills. Too often we artificially limit curricular opportunities for students with disabilities based on our own preconceived notions. Because of this, few students with severe disabilities have had access to general education classrooms or curriculum until recently. As a student progresses through school, the emphasis placed on various curricular options can be adjusted based on actual experiences and evaluative data rather than on speculation based on disability labels or stereotypes.

How Should the Content of the Curriculum Be Determined?

Historically, determining curricular content has been the sole province of school professionals. This, too, has changed significantly. Increasingly, parents are involved in selecting priority curricular content for their children using any number of available approaches, such as MAPs (Making Action Plans), PATH (Planning Alternative Tomorrows with Hope; Pearpoint, Forest, & O'Brien, 1996), COACH (Choosing Outcomes and Accommodations for Children; Giangreco, Cloninger, & Iverson, 1998), and Personal Futures Planning (Mount, 1994). Such active solicitation of parent input can have a positive impact on relationships between families and professionals. Parental selection of priorities does not infer that professionals are nonessential, but rather that their curricular role has evolved from telling parents what is best for their child to assisting families in determining and articulating their own priorities based on their individual and cultural perspectives.

Important aspects of curriculum design today are choice and self-advocacy by students with disabilities (Nietupski, Hamre-Nietupski, Curtin, & Shirkanth, 1997). Such choice-making to select curricular content may coincide with the cultural norms of the family and/or the norms of the community. For example, young children may be given choices within the context of activities, while older students may select some or all of their own learning priorities. Professionals still retain an important role in developing the breadth of curricular content that is available to students in the school.

To augment the general education curriculum content, ecological analysis (Brown, Nietupski, & Hamre-Nietupski, 1976) has been used to select individualized curricular content. Using ecological analysis, curriculum is developed based on the real-life skills needed to function in current and future environments. While this approach remains eminently viable, a variation has been developed that shifts the context to current and desired future *valued life outcomes* (e.g., meaningful personal relationships, health and safety, meaningful activities in various places, choice, and control) as determined by the student with disabilities and or his or her family (Gian-greco, Cloninger, & Iverson, 1998). This approach is grounded in the life outcomes parents have said they value in helping their child pursue a "good life." By focusing on individually determined valued life outcomes, educational teams create a common denominator necessary to function as a team and provide meaning to their activities.

How Can Individualized Curricular Content Be Addressed Appropriately in the Classroom When Students Without Disabilities Are Pursuing Different Curricular Content?

One of the most common and anxiety-producing questions asked by general education teachers is, "How do you expect me to incorporate an individualized curriculum for a student with disabilities while teaching the rest of my class?" Unfortunately, all too often, the solution to this challenge is for a paraprofessional to operate a parallel educational program in the back of the classroom. For an example of this, see case 10 in this volume, titled, "Help, With Strings Attached." Such an approach is not an example of inclusive education and minimizes the potential benefits of participation in a general education class. Delegating primary instructional responsibilities to a paraprofessional also may relegate students with disabilities to receiving inadequate, unsupervised instruction. Two alternatives include multilevel curriculum and instruction and curriculum overlapping (Giangreco & Putnam, 1991).

Multilevel curriculum and instruction occurs when a student with disabilities and nondisabled peers participate together in a shared activity (e.g., science lab experiment) and students have individually appropriate learning outcomes at multiple levels, but all within the same curriculum area (e.g., science). While one student may be learning at a basic knowledge or comprehension level, another student simultaneously may be working on an application or synthesis level. For example, imagine second grade students playing a small-group social studies board game devised by their teacher to teach them about their neighborhood, town, and state. The teacher has prepared a set of 10 game cards for each student that target individual learning outcomes. For one student, the game cards require applying knowledge about the roles of community helpers (police, fire fighters, store clerks, postal workers) by moving game pieces to respond to scenarios on cards (e.g., "Move your player to the place where you might go if you wanted to send a card to your grandmother for her birthday"). Another student is learning to answer questions about where he or she lives (e.g., his or her street address, phone number, recognizing his or her neighbors). A third student is using map skills such as north, south, east, and west to respond to questions (e.g., "If you started at the book store, went two blocks north and one block east, where would you be?"). In this example, all the students have social studies learning outcomes that have been individually selected to match their level of functioning and needs.

Multilevel curriculum can include variations across subject content, level of learning outcomes pursued, or both. For example, in one seventh grade social studies class focusing on American history from the revolution through the Civil War, the topic would be the same for Joseph, a student with disabilities, as for his classmates, but the level of learning outcomes would be adapted. His studies would focus on American history but be adapted to an appropriate level (e.g., historical people, places, and events). In Joseph's algebra class, the subject content for Joseph would be different from that of his classmates, focusing on basic computation (e.g., adding, subtracting), and the level and quantity of the learning outcomes would be adapted as well. In both classes Joseph would be working on individualized learning outcomes within the same curriculum area as his classmates.

Curriculum overlapping occurs when a student with disabilities and nondisabled peers participate together in a shared activity (e.g., science lab experiment) and students have individually appropriate learning outcomes, but from different curriculum areas. Nondisabled students could have science objectives, while the student with disabilities might have communication or social skill objectives for the science lab activity. Imagine, for example, a high school biology class in which lab teams of three students each are assembling a model of a human heart. Two of the students have goals related to the identification, anatomy, and physiology of the human heart. The third student, who has severe disabilities, participates in helping to assemble the model heart but is working on communication and social skills (e.g., taking turns, following instructions, describing events, maintaining socially acceptable behavior).

Curriculum overlapping can also address other general education curriculum areas. You might recall Joseph, the seventh grade student with disabilities, who was participating in social studies and math via multilevel curriculum. His team agreed that his participation in French class would be through curriculum overlapping. He would be exposed to French words, language, and culture, but there would be no expectation of competencies in

French. The team viewed his participation in French class as providing him with opportunities to pursue learning outcomes that had been identified as important in his English class, such as listening, speaking, reading, writing, and spelling. For example, his spelling words from English class could be duplicated in French and he could practice reading and writing both sets, using them in sentences, and reading them orally.

Curriculum overlapping occurs when learning outcomes from two or more curriculum areas overlap within the same activity. Opportunities for both curriculum overlapping and multilevel curriculum and instruction are abundant in classrooms where students participate in active learning.

How Can Appropriate Learning Opportunities to Include Students With Disabilities in Classroom Activities Be Identified or Adapted?

All too often, school personnel expend significant effort developing an IEP that is not necessarily reflected in the daily schedule of activities for a student. Students may even be welcomed and included in general education activities, but not be pursuing the individualized learning outcomes that were selected as priorities in their IEP. Use of a Scheduling Matrix (Giangreco, Cloninger, & Iverson, 1998), is designed to prevent this from happening by explicitly comparing a student's IEP goals and additional learning outcomes to a list of the class's planned activities (e.g., arrival routine, opening routine, language arts, science, physical education). The scheduling matrix is a divergent activity where team members consider the possibilities for working on a student's learning outcomes within the various class activities. This process is aided by decisions made by the student's team about the nature of participation (e.g., multilevel, curriculum overlapping) in various class activities.

A student schedule is then developed, based on possibilities generated using the Scheduling Matrix. Deciding which learning outcomes will be addressed in which daily classes or activities requires team members to consider and balance a variety of issues (Giangreco, Cloninger, & Iverson, 1998):

- Are there sufficient opportunities for the student to work on identified learning priorities?
- Are there sufficient opportunities that pertain to the student's identified additional learning outcomes?

- Does the student's schedule follow the class routine as much as possible?
- Are learning outcomes and general supports addressed at the most naturally occurring times?
- Does the student have the same opportunities for breaks as students without disabilities, so he or she has time to just be a kid?

Answers to these and other questions that arise as a result of scheduling may lead your team to rethink the range of learning outcomes in the student's program as well as how to adapt instruction. A completed student schedule provides increased clarity to expectations for a student's participation throughout the school day. By looking at the schedule, a teacher or assistant would know what the instructional focus should be for a student with disabilities when he or she is in any class. Of course, each of the teachers should be involved in making such decisions. As the student progresses through the school year and as team members learn more about the student, the schedule should be adjusted accordingly.

The Osborn–Parnes Creative Problem-Solving Process (CPS) (Parnes, 1997) is a powerful tool to assist teachers as they create adaptations to their curriculum, instruction, and activities. Variations of the CPS process have developed specifically to address curricular and instructional adaptation issues as they pertain to curriculum-overlapping challenges that occur when students with disabilities are included in general education classes and activities (Giangreco, 1993; Giangreco, Cloninger, Dennis, & Edelman, 1994). Once a teacher or team has identified the general problem (e.g., "In what ways might we address Karen's individual education needs within the context of typical class activities with nondisabled peers?" they can use the remaining steps of CPS as a creative process to generate solutions. These include:

- fact-finding (gathering information),
- problem finding (clarifying the problem),
- idea finding (brainstorming a quantity of ideas in an atmosphere of deferred judgment, using idea-joggers),
- solution finding (selecting the best ideas based on criteria),
- acceptance finding (making a plan, refining it, and taking action).

An overarching characteristic of CPS is the alternating use of divergent and convergent thinking within *each* step. The divergent aspects encourage the teachers and teams to explore information and ideas broadly by extending in different directions from a common point (the problem to be solved). Convergent aspects encourage analysis of the divergent data to make decisions and select solutions. Most importantly, the steps of CPS assist teachers, support personnel, and students to develop a creative, optimistic attitude and a simple, effective process for solving problems.

How Can Instruction Be Individualized Within the Context of General Class Activities?

The vast majority of students with disabilities respond favorably to many of the same teaching methods that are effective with students who do not have disabilities. Some of these common methods include modeling and demonstration, class discussion, repeated exposure and practice, guided discovery, experiments, field study, participatory activities, use of multimedia technology, use of question-asking strategies, use of manipulative materials, educational games and play, use of positive and negative examples, corrective feedback, and individual or small-group projects. Many of these are described in chapter 1 of this volume.

Sometimes the adaptations that need to be made for students with disabilities are as simple as (a) changing performance expectations (e.g., different spelling words; 10 math problems rather than 20); (b) allowing students to respond in different ways; (c) changing the materials to match the motivational, sensory, or physical characteristics of the student; (d) providing additional time or task completion or responding; (e) providing assistive devices (e.g., tape recorders to take notes, computers); (f) preteaching or tutoring; or (g) modifying the rules of participation. Of course, to be effective, any such adaptations require a working knowledge of a student's characteristics and learning styles.

Challenges arise when students do not progress adequately using typical instructional methods. In such cases, instruction must be augmented using more precisely and explicitly applied methods. What follows (see Table 3.1) are some instructional methods that can be applied within the context of typical class activities (Alberto & Troutman, 1995; Snell & Brown, 1993). You will recognize that you have used many or all of these strategies before, though you may know them by other labels. Selection of methods should be based on (a) which method, or combination, is most likely to be effective based on your knowledge of the student's characteristics, (b) the characteristics of the learning outcome, and (c) which

TABLE 3.1. *Methods to Augment Typical Classroom Instruction*

Task analysis	Task analysis involves taking a skill and breaking it down into its component parts to facilitate learning. Sometimes these are fairly large chunks of behavior, at other times they are very small. Each step in a task analysis has a built-in cue that serves as a naturally occurring prompt for the next step. You may find that a student is having a problem with a particular part of a skill and that may be the only part that needs to be task analyzed.
Chaining	Chaining can be: (a) continuous (teaching all the steps of the task analysis); (b) forward (teaching the steps of the task analysis from the beginning until the student makes an error; instruction proceeds only after the step is mastered); and (c) backward (the teacher arranges the task so that all the steps are complete except the last one; the last step is taught until it is mastered and then the sequence proceeds sequentially backward until the beginning is reached).
Errorless learning	Errorless learning refers to guiding a student through a task using sufficient prompts so that the student can be successful at the task as quickly as possible while making as few errors as possible. Errors are interrupted as they occur and guidance is provided. As the student becomes more proficient, the guidance fades. Errorless learning provides more opportunities for practicing a skill correctly and is useful for tasks where errors just won't do (e.g., crossing the street).
Cue redundancy	Cue redundancy is when you exaggerate the relevant dimension of a cue to discriminate between it and other cues. For example, when teaching the difference between the hour and minute hands on a face clock, length is the relevant dimension (not color or shape). Using cue redundancy, you would exaggerate the difference in length by making the hour hand very short and the minute hand very long, then fade toward more typical lengths.
Shaping	Shaping is simply reinforcing increasingly proficient approximations of skill. For example, in composition, teachers expect increasing detail, description, spelling accuracy, and proper use of grammar. Shaping is by its very nature a developmental process of starting where the child is and moving forward at an individualized pace.

Prompts, cues, and fading	Prompts and cues include approaches such as full physical guidance, partial physical guidance, modeling, verbal directions, questions, reminders, encouragement, and visual clues. Prompts and cues can be provided prior to or following student responses. Prompts and cues should fade as quickly as possible. Using dotted letters in handwriting instruction is an example of a cue that eventually will be faded.
Time delay	Time delay refers to the pairing of two cues simultaneously (zero delay): one cue you know the student will respond to correctly, and the other cue, particularly a natural one, you would like the student to respond to. For example, when teaching a young child to say "Thank you" you want the child to respond to the natural cue of receiving something. You can start teaching this by simultaneously pairing the natural cue (receiving something) with the extra cue, "Say, Thank you," knowing the child will repeat, "Thank you." Once established, a time delay (e.g., a couple of seconds) is inserted between the natural cue and the extra cue and is gradually increased. When the time delay is long enough, the child responds "Thank you" before receiving the extra cue. Extra cues are often faded simultaneously as the time delay increases (e.g., "Say, Thank you"; "What do you say?"; giving an expectant look). Time delay can be especially valuable for teaching students who are not imitative.

method can be applied in the most status-neutral or status-enhancing way in typical settings.

Regardless of what instructional approaches you use to help students learn, most of them require frequent and ongoing opportunities to interact with content or to practice a skill in order to learn it. This is true for students with disabilities as well, and sometimes they need even more opportunities and consistency of instruction.

Any individualization of instruction would be incomplete without some form of evaluation. Teachers often have an intuitive sense of how their students are progressing, but in order to validate those impressions, it is important to gather additional information through some form of systematic data collection. Quizzes, tests, projects, observations, demonstrations, and work samples can all be used to measure progress. These various methods can tell you how accurate the student's responses are, how often the student uses a skill, how quickly the student accomplishes a task, the student's work quality, the amount of time (duration) a student's attention can be sustained, and the number of steps in a series (i.e., from a task analysis) the student can successfully complete. Ultimately, such information can indicate the student's growth over time and whether the student's quality of life has improved as a result of working on certain learning outcomes. The data collection methods you choose, and the information you look for, should be directly related to the student's learning outcomes.

CONCLUSION

General education teachers are playing new and important roles in educating students with disabilities with the support of special educators, related services personnel, paraprofessionals, and other school staff and community members. Though teaching students with more and more severe disabilities can present challenges, general education teachers can have a major, positive impact on the lives of students with disabilities. By helping to create these new opportunities, teachers will develop skills that improve their teaching of all children and will model many important behaviors for their students without disabilities. Teachers who successfully include students with disabilities demonstrate that they value the uniqueness of each child and model both problem-solving behaviors and coping strategies for dealing with change in constructive ways. In doing so, they help break down barriers that artificially limit students with disabilities and they help debunk stereotypes. As the role of the general education teacher continues to evolve in regard to educating students with disabilities, today's teachers have already demonstrated that inclusive education can be done successfully anywhere competent and caring people choose to extend their own learning on behalf of children.

REFERENCES

Alberto, P.A., & Troutman, A.C. (1995). *Applied behavior analysis for teachers (4th ed.)*. Englewood Cliffs: NJ: Prentice-Hall.

Brown, L., Nietupski, J., & Hamre-Nietupski, S. (1976). The criterion of ultimate functioning and public school services for severely handicapped students. In M.A. Thomas (Ed.), *Hey don't forget about me! Education's investment in the severely, profoundly, and multiple handicapped* (pp. 2–15). Reston, VA: Council for Exceptional Children.

Doyle, M. B. (1995). *A qualitative inquiry into the roles and responsibilities of paraeducators who support students with severe disabilities in inclusive classrooms.* Unpublished doctoral dissertation, University of Minnesota, Minneapolis.

Giangreco, M. F. (1997). *Quick-guides to inclusion: Ideas for educating students with disabilities.* Baltimore: Paul H. Brookes.

Giangreco, M. F. (1996a). Extending the "comfort zone" to include every child. *Journal of Early Intervention, 20,* 206–208.

Giangreco, M. F. (1996b). *Vermont interdependent services team approach: A guide to coordinating educational support services.* Baltimore: Paul H. Brookes.

Giangreco, M. F. (1993). Using creative problem solving methods to include students with severe disabilities in general education classroom activities. *Journal of Educational and Psychological Consultation, 4*(2), 113–135.

Giangreco, M. F., Baumgart, D., & Doyle, M. B. (1995). How inclusion can facilitate teaching and learning. *Intervention in School and Clinic, 30,* 273–278.

Giangreco, M. F., Cloninger, C., Dennis, R., & Edelman, S. (1994). Problem-solving methods to facilitate inclusive education. In J. Thousand, R. Villa, & A. Nevin (Eds.), *Creativity and collaborative learning: A practical guide to empowering students and teachers* (pp. 321–349). Baltimore: Paul H. Brookes.

Giangreco, M. F., Cloninger, C. J., & Iverson, V.S. (1998). *Choosing outcomes and accommodations for children (COACH): A guide to educational planning for students with disabilities* (2nd ed.). Baltimore: Paul H. Brookes.

Giangreco, M. F., Dennis, R. E., Cloninger, C.J., Edelman, S. W., & Schattman, R. (1993). "I've counted Jon": Transformational experiences of teachers educating students with disabilities. *Exceptional Children, 59,* 359–372.

Giangreco, M. F., Edelman, S. W., MacFarland, S., & Luiselli, T. E. (1997) Helping or hovering: Effects of instructional assistant proximity on students with disabilities. *Exceptional Children, 64,* 7–18.

Giangreco, M. F., Edelman, S. W., & Nelson, C. (1998). Impact of support service planning for students who are deaf-blind. *Journal of Visual Impairment and Blindness, 92*(1), 18–29.

Heumann, J. E., & Hehir, T. (1994). *Questions and answers on the least restrictive environment requirements of the Individuals With Disabilities Education Act.* Washington, DC: United States Department of Education, Office of Special Education and Rehabilitation.

Hunt, P., & Goetz, L. (1997). Research on inclusive education programs, practices, and outcomes for students with severe disabilities. *Journal of Special Education, 31,* 3–29.

Laski, F. (1991). Achieving integration during the second revolution. In L. Meyer, L. Brown, & C. Peck (Eds.), *Critical issues in the lives of people with severe disabilities* (pp. 409-421). Baltimore: Paul H. Brookes.

Mount, B. (1994). Benefits and limitations of personal futures planning. In V. Bradley, J. Ashbaugh, & B. Blaney (Eds.), *Creating individual supports for people with developmental disabilities: A mandate for change at many levels* (pp. 97–108). Baltimore: Paul H. Brookes.

National Center on School Restructuring and Inclusion (1995). *National study of inclusive education* (2nd ed.). New York: Author.

Nietupski, J., Hamre-Nietupski, S., Curtin, S., & Shrikanth, K. (1997). A review of curricular research in severe disabilities from 1976 to 1995 in six selected journals. *Journal of Special Education, 31,* 36–55.

Parnes. S. J. (1997). *Optimize the magic of your mind.* Buffalo, NY: Creative Education Foundation.

Pearpoint, J., Forest, M., & O'Brien, J. (1996). MAPs, Circles of Friends, and PATH: Powerful tools to help build caring communities. In S. Stainback & W. Stainback (Eds.), *Inclusion: A guide for educators* (pp. 67–86). Baltimore: Paul H. Brookes.

Salisbury, C., Palombaro, M., & Hollowood, T. (1993). On the nature and change of an inclusive elementary school. *Journal of the Association for Persons with Severe Handicaps, 18,* 75–84.

Snell, M. E., & Brown, F. (1993). Instructional planning and implementation. In M.E. Snell (Ed.), *Instruction of students with severe disabilities* (4th ed.). New York: Merrill/MacMillan.

Stainback, S., & Stainback, W. (1996). *Inclusion: A guide for educators.* Baltimore: Paul H. Brookes.

Villa, R. A., & Thousand, J. S. (1995). *Creating an inclusive school.* Alexandria, VA: Association for Supervision and Curriculum Development.

York-Barr, J., Schultz, T., Doyle, M. B., Kronberg, R., & Crossett, S. (1996). Inclusive schooling in St. Cloud: Perspectives on the process and the people. *Remedial and Special Education, 17,* 92–105.

4

Collaboration as a Tool
for Inclusion

Marshall Welch

Why does inclusion of students with disabilities work in some schools and not in others? This is a complex question without a simple or straightforward answer. Philosophically, most educators embrace the concept of inclusion. Pragmatically, many are resistant to the actual practice. Resistance and reluctance on the part of teachers and administrators are legitimate to an extent. Many teachers are concerned that they will bear the sole responsibility of providing an education to students with special needs despite the fact they have had little or no preparation.

Attitudinal research suggests that teachers are much more open to the integration of students with disabilities if adequate support is readily available and provided (Scruggs & Mastropieri, 1996). Teachers cannot do it all on their own. Returning to the question posed above, it would appear that inclusion has only limited success when educators do not share responsibility. Professionals must work together to make inclusion work. This, however, is based on the assumptions that educators understand collaboration and that they have the skills and resources to implement various forms of collaboration.

Collaboration requires that individuals interact and communicate with each other on an ongoing basis. There are many benefits of collaboration

71

for students, parents, and teachers. Increased interaction among school personnel helps develop an understanding of complementary roles. Greater communication helps expand perspectives, which in turn contributes to enhanced relationships between participants involved in collaboration. The collective efforts of administrators, parents, general educators, special educators, and special service providers in collaborative decision making enhance ownership and commitment to program goals (Duke, Showers, & Imber, 1980). In addition, the exchange of knowledge, skills, and resources from a range of professionals with diverse experiences helps conceptualize issues and goals. Because more dimensions of an issue can be explored, collaboration broadens a group's understanding of a given situation (Phillips & McCullough, 1990). Finally, collaboration generates a broader range and number of possible answers. This reflects the old adage that "two heads are better than one" when it comes to the quality of ideas generated. Furthermore, when all partners share responsibility, the range and diversity of expertise and resources available will be greatly enhanced (Curtis & Curtis, 1990).

This chapter has been written to assist educators in gaining an understanding of collaboration and its various forms as well as assimilating basic skills of collaboration. The chapter begins by defining collaboration and describing its key features. Building upon this definitive foundation is an exploration of some of the barriers to collaboration and how to overcome them. The chapter concludes with an overview of some of the various forms collaboration can take, as well as guidelines for implementation.

UNDERSTANDING COLLABORATION

The word *collaboration* is derived from the Latin *collabre,* which means to co-labor or to work together (Welch & Sheridan, 1995). Collaboration is a process that can occur at a variety of levels or degrees and settings. The duration of collaboration might be long term in some cases, whereas in others it may last only a few minutes. For example, a parent and a teacher might work together to reach a common goal for a student in a given classroom setting. Two teachers might team-teach in a mainstream classroom setting. A classroom teacher might consult with a specialist to learn of specific instructional strategies or methods of adapting instruction. At a schoolwide level, small teams of professionals might collaborate to develop innovative ways of incorporating new instructional techniques. At the community level, the entire faculty, staff, and student body might work with community organizations or businesses to enhance the educational experience of students. No matter who is involved or at what level, collaboration is a dynamic process designed to achieve a shared goal.

Within the context of inclusion, the goal of collaboration is to provide opportunities for students with disabilities to become meaningful members of their community. Collaboration is a fundamental key to the inclusion of students with disabilities. Inclusion cannot be effective unless educators, specialists, parents, and students combine their resources and efforts.

This brings us back to the question posed at the beginning of this chapter: Why does inclusion work in some schools and not in others? The answer is that inclusion is more likely to succeed when teachers, administrators, parents, and staff collaborate. In other words, the meaningful integration of students with disabilities is facilitated when parents and professionals work together. However, collaboration does not just happen by policy decree or by believing in it. Collaboration works when everyone involved understands its dynamic features and processes.

Collaboration Defined

Although there are many different definitions of collaboration in the literature, they all reflect the notion of working together. Phillips and McCullough (1990) suggested that schools must have and abide by an ethic of collaboration that consists of the following five basic tenets. First, all individuals within the school community must have common values and goals regarding the education of all students. This essentially means that everyone, including staff such as secretaries, custodians, and bus drivers, are responsible for the welfare and development of all children. Second, collaboration is valued and therefore sanctioned. Professionals and parents agree to expend time and energy to pool resources and talents in meeting the needs of students. Third, participants acknowledge that collaboration will generate side benefits, such as improved morale and cohesion, as participants acquire new skills and information through joint decision making. Fourth, collaboration requires structure and procedures. The school must allocate time and resources to facilitate collegial interactions. Furthermore, these interactions should follow the problem-solving procedures as a framework for decision making. Finally, all members share in the identification and solution of problems, thus making everyone accountable for services to students. In this way, the entire school community can celebrate the successes that would otherwise not have been achieved through autonomous or isolated efforts. When Philips and McCullough refer to shared rules, norms, and beliefs, they are describing cultural variables within schools that influence the collaborative process.

For the purpose of this chapter, collaboration will be operationally defined as a dynamic framework for efforts that endorses interdependence and parity during interactive exchange of resources between at least two partners who work together in a decision-making process that is influenced by cultural and systemic factors to achieve common goals (Welch & Sheridan, 1995, p. 11).

To gain a better understanding of collaboration, let's examine key features of this operative definition.

KEY FEATURES OF COLLABORATION

Common Goals

The entire process of collaboration is driven by goal attainment. That is, people work together to achieve specific shared objectives. It is assumed, therefore, that individuals do, in fact, share a common goal. In the context of inclusion, the goal for some educators is to allow students with disabilities the opportunity to be in the (last restrictive environment) LRE as meaningful members of their community. However, this goal might be in conflict with other goals sought by teachers and administrators. For example, the goal of many teachers is a pragmatic one: mere survival. Given the demands of teaching a classroom of students from various backgrounds with diverse needs, many teachers find the added responsibility of teaching students with disabilities overwhelming (Bullough & Baughman, 1995). Operating in this type of survival mode is legitimate unless professionals work together to provide support and resources. Unfortunately, in many cases, administrators' intentions in establishing inclusion may be merely to comply with federal policies and legislation rather than to broaden the educational experience of students with and without disabilities. When this is the case, students are included for the sake of inclusion, without the necessary support being provided. Therefore, inclusion cannot be undertaken only for its own sake.

Interdependence and Parity

Interdependence can be understood by imagining a spoked wheel. The functional use of the wheel is dependent upon the strength and utility of each individual spoke. If too many spokes are broken or too weak to carry the weight, the wheel will wobble. Similarly, the process of collaboration will "wobble" if individual members of the working team do not share the weight or responsibility of meeting a mutually defined goal.

Due to the reciprocal nature of working together, collaboration requires parity, which means that each individual member of the group is a meaningful and contributing member throughout the process. This is evident in case 12 of this volume, titled "Building an Inclusive School: Vision, Leadership, and Community," in which Bonnie, a first grade teacher, Lisa, a special education teacher, Sue, the school principal, and the other teachers in the school had equal input in problem solving. Together, they planned new programs and identified various issues and situations that could be potential problems. They then discussed what resources they could use with a variety of strategies to achieve their goals. However, parity does not imply that individuals have equal levels of knowledge, skill, and experience. On the contrary, the diversity of the group generates a greater variety of options, perspectives, and resources that can be used to meet a goal. We can see the advantages of diversity in the case just mentioned, in which individuals with three different backgrounds and areas of expertise shared their skills and knowledge.

Interactive Exchange of Resources

Collaboration also has been thought of as the process of sharing (Hord, 1986). By collaborating, we "extend the circle of ideas and contacts" (Fullan, 1993, p. 87). This involves sharing tangibles, such as materials, personnel, and funding, as well as intangibles, such as risk, control, and ideas, to meet a common goal. In a time of increased challenges associated with a diverse student body, sharing resources is more than just a philosophical ideal; it is a practical necessity.

It may be useful to think of resources as slices of a pie. The resource pie is composed of five domains: information resources, human resources, financial resources, physical resources, and technological resources.

In collaboration, the parties working together give each other one or more "slices" of the resource pie in order to reach their goal. In case 1, "One Parent's Struggle for Inclusion," one of the first steps Reed's mother took to achieve inclusion for her son was to establish a parent support group. This case illustrates how other parents (human resources) exchanged ideas (informational resources) in an attempt to help ensure that children with disabilities had successful schooling experiences. A small grant from the county social service agency provided financial resources to support the group. At first, the support group met in a condemned school building and eventually moved to a vacant dental lab at a nearby university. These sites represent physical resources that provided the parents with a place to meet. Any technological resources they might have had were the tools that they used to achieve their goals. These tools are not necessarily "high tech," such as computers. A chalkboard used to list ideas generated during a meeting might be one tool.

Inclusion will also require that educators share "slices" of the resource pie. This act of sharing resources reflects an important aspect of the concept of LRE from the federal statute known as the Individuals With Disabilities Education Act (IDEA). As you saw in chapter 1, the concept of LRE mandates the use of supplementary aid and services to ensure the success of students with disabilities in regular classes to the maximum extent appropriate. This use of supplementary aid and services in the general classroom reflects the practice of exchanging resources. In many of the cases in the casebook section of this volume, we see teachers, not just students, receiving support from specialists and parents, which is necessary for successful inclusion of students with disabilities. For example, specialists may assist teachers in adapting instruction, curriculum, and evaluation procedures to meet the needs of students with disabilities. Thus, classroom teachers need to be open not only to the idea of inclusion, but also to the idea of working with other adults.

Decision Making

Collaboration as a decision-making process is a common characteristic of all definitions of collaboration. Defining *process* as a verb "to move along" and as a noun "a series of actions in the production of something" (Robbins, 1990), collaboration can be thought of as making decisions to reach some type of mutually defined goal. Often, the goal is to solve a problem. Some forms of collaboration may have a highly structured series of steps to "move along," whereas others are fluid and less rigid. Decision making in collaboration involves two essential skills: problem solving and communication.

Problem-Solving Skills

Because the goal of collaborative decision making is often to resolve a problem, problem solving is a common theme in the various definitions of collaboration. Based on a review of the literature from counseling, psychology, education, and business, Jayanthi and Friend (1992) identified five common stages in problem solving. They are: (a) identifying problems, (b) generating possible solutions, (c) deciding on a plan of action, (d) implementing the solution, and (e) evaluating the outcomes. Although each step serves an important function (Fuchs & Fuchs, 1989), the stages need not be followed in a rigid or sequential manner (Tindal, Parker, & Hasbrouch, 1992). In fact, there is often an overlap between steps, and stages may reoccur.

The first stage, problem identification, typically involves defining a situation that is deemed a problem by reviewing factors that have contributed to it. If the situation is a recurring event, historical events such as what had been tried in the past are considered. Once a problem situation has been defined, a tentative objective to either resolve the problem or meet a need is established. It is important, however, to identify a situation that can, in fact, be dealt with. For example, teachers can do virtually nothing to minimize a student's disabling condition, such as hyperactivity or cognitive disabilities. They can, however, minimize the student's difficulties by adapting environmental factors, such as seating arrangements, duration of instruction, and the content and method of instruction. These kinds of adaptations are described in detail in chapter 3. In other words, the focus of problem identification should be on a situation that participants have some control over.

Once the problem has been identified, the next step involves generating possible solutions. This is a kind of collective brainstorming of strategies to achieve the objective or goal. Because the purpose is to come up with as many ideas as possible to serve as a menu of possible solutions, it is important to refrain from evaluating ideas during the process of brainstorming. Only after an exhaustive list of possible solutions has been compiled should participants constructively assess which ideas appear to be the most viable. Additionally, participants should avoid elaborating during the brainstorming session because this too impedes the flow of ideas. Clarification and details can be discussed after the menu of ideas has been generated.

The third stage of problem solving involves selecting an idea from the list of possible solutions. If the participants are members of a task force or committee, the selection process is conducted through discussion and consensus. In other cases, individuals seeking assistance with a specific problem might consult with a problem-solving group such as a teacher assistance team (TAT) (Chalfant & Van Dusen Pysh, 1989), which is described below. Yet, it will be the consultee who is ultimately responsible for selecting the strategy. Once a strategy has been selected, the problem-solving process continues by developing an action plan for implementation of the strategy. This can be an elaborate management blueprint or an informal, verbal agreement of who will do what, when, where, and why.

The fourth step is implementation of the strategic plan, accomplished by following the responsibilities outlined in the action plan. The process concludes with the fifth step, that of assessing the outcomes of the actions taken.

Effective collaboration is threatened when partners either are unaware of the problem-solving process or simply do not adhere to its general framework. Educators often have the illusion of working together to solve a problem or reach a goal when, in fact, their interaction could be characterized as a "gripe" session. Consider, for example, a team that meets with the goal of discussing curricula but usually only shares stories of students who are difficult to manage. This suggests that the team did not adequately define the situation or monitor its own behavior and procedures during its discussion. Team members must observe and regulate their actions throughout the decision-making process. This is facilitated by following an agenda or form that outlines the stages of the problem-solving procedures described above. Teams often adjourn only to flounder while attempting to implement the action plan. This is typically due to poorly defined objectives, roles, and responsibilities.

Communication Skills

Working with others during decision making and problem solving requires effective interpersonal communication skills. Communication is a reciprocal process of sending and receiving messages, both verbal and nonverbal, such as body language, facial expression, and eye contact. The key to communication is that the messages be interpreted correctly. A simple way of being aware of how one is sending and receiving messages is to monitor one's communication using the acronym CAPS (Welch & Sheridan, 1995), which stands for clarifying, attending, paraphrasing, and summarizing.

Clarifying is used to gain more information about a situation through the use of open-ended questions. This type of question requires more than a "yes/no" response. It requires elaboration with facts or descriptions that can be used to clarify what is meant. Clarification allows a listener an opportunity to gain additional information to understand a situation. For example, during a team meeting or consultation, a teacher may state, "Rebecca is just too hyper—she's too disruptive in class." To clarify what has been said, the listener might ask an open-ended question such as, "What do you mean when you say she's disruptive in class?" The teacher may then say, "Rebecca talks out without being called on and often gets out of her seat."

Attending is an active listening behavior that conveys a nonverbal message of interest. A speaker is more assured of being heard when listeners physically orient themselves to focus on the speaker. Other attending behaviors include looking at the speaker and making appropriate eye contact. It may also involve nodding the head to suggest an understanding of what is being said. Body language should be "open" and attentive by slightly leaning toward the other person. The arms and hands should not be crossed or clinched, which may suggest a "closed" or defensive position.

Paraphrasing is restating what another person has said. Paraphrasing is not simply "parroting" the exact words. Instead, the listener makes an attempt to understand what the speaker intended by using different words and phrases to represent the gist of what was just said. Unlike clarification, which uses questioning, paraphrasing involves statements. Let's return to Reed's situation in the case of "One Parent's Struggle for Inclusion" for an example. For years, his mother had tried to articulate what she meant by inclusion. She had specific objectives that were generally misinterpreted by teachers and administrators. However, one day, one of Reed's teachers called Reed's mother to say that he finally understood what she meant by inclusion. The teacher said, "You want me to have him in the regular class as much as I can, and just have him be part of the class with the rest of the kids. You don't want me to overwhelm him, or frustrate him, but you don't want me to underestimate him either." Reed's mother responded, "That's it! You've just spelled out inclusion. That's exactly what my dream is." It was only after this teacher's paraphrasing that the parent and teacher really began to work together.

However, sometimes what has been paraphrased may be inaccurate. When that happens, the communication process outlined in CAPS allows the partners to clarify with new information. In the earlier example in which a teacher described Rebecca's behavior, a listener might paraphrase the teacher's description of Rebecca's disruptive behavior by saying, "So you're concerned about the way she speaks when she's not called on and when she gets out of her desk to wander around the class. Is that right?" At this point, the teacher might rectify the listener's interpretation by saying, "She doesn't really wander around the class; she just stands up and bothers the person next to her." This response has provided new and clearer information as a result of the listener's paraphrasing.

Summarizing involves stating the themes and conclusions that have been drawn to make sure everyone understands and agrees with what has been said. Typically, summarization can also serve as a means of "tying up" all the details into one succinct statement. For example, the team might summarize the situation with Rebecca by stating, "OK, based on

what has been discussed in the last few minutes, it seems Rebecca has difficulty talking out during teacher-led instruction without being called on
and interrupting the work of her neighbors during individual seatwork."

CULTURAL AND SYSTEMIC FACTORS
THAT AFFECT COLLABORATION

All organizations, including schools, have a culture (Hanson, 1990). The
school's culture can both promote and impede collaboration. The school
culture is influenced by the general values and attitudes of the neighborhood, community, and society, as well as those shared by the professionals
in the building.

The cultures of organizations such as schools have four related func-
tions (Ott, 1989). First, culture consists of shared patterns and expectations that indicate how members of that group should think. This creates a
belief system within the organization. Second, culture provides a set of
values that shape how members feel. The set of values reflects attitudes.
Third, an organization's culture helps define membership in a group or
groups. This in turn helps establish the roles of groups and individuals
within the groups. Roles are assigned to or assimilated by individuals and
groups within the organization to facilitate social stability. However,
group members may not perceive a specific duty or behavior as part of
their role, which may result in role conflict. In essence, the belief that "it's
not my job" may undermine collaborative efforts. Finally, culture prescribes a set of expected behaviors that are based on beliefs, values, and
roles.

According to Kurpius (1991), the culture of an organization is the most
powerful factor determining the degree of collaboration that can occur in
it. The culture of an organization is analogous to the personality of an
individual: It is "a hidden yet unifying theme that provides meaning,
direction, and mobilization" (Ott, 1989, p. 1). The function and goal of
culture is to provide social stability and minimize social chaos. Thus, we
can think of culture as social management. Culture provides a structural
framework that helps members make sense of the world around them. In
other words, cultural factors indicate: "This is how we do things around
here."

Whereas culture can be thought of as a social management system to
ensure social order and stability, an organization such as a school is a formal system designed to meet specific goals or to create a product. This

formal system is represented by tangible objects and symbols, such as budgets, written policies, organizational flow-charts of administrative and staff duties, timelines, and structured divisions such as grades, academic departments, and general and special education programs. The combination of clusters of symbols, objects, and divisions characterizes patterns of activity within the system and has a profound influence on whether collaboration is possible. Schools are influenced by forces from both outside and inside the school building. Outside influences include state and district regulations, union contracts, and state and federal laws, all of which may mandate how educators within the school building work together to meet goals. A prime example is the federal law, IDEA, which mandates that schools must provide a free and appropriate education to students with disabilities.

Perhaps the most influential systemic factor within schools that affects collaboration and therefore inclusion is the bureaucratic structure of schools. Schools are divided into grade levels, academic departments, general education, special education, ESL programs, and Chapter I. Each of these divisions is governed by its own set of rules, regulations, and procedures that stem from governmental and societal mandates. These systemic factors within schools may impede collaboration in a number of ways, as we shall see in the next section of this chapter.

BARRIERS TO COLLABORATION

We have thus far considered what collaboration is and why it is important. Despite the benefits of working together to promote inclusion, educators and parents are doomed to failure and frustration in their efforts to collaborate unless they first understand the various barriers that may thwart their efforts. The diverse range of barriers can be grouped into four categories: conceptual, practical, attitudinal, and professional (Phillips & McCullough, 1990).

Conceptual Barriers

Conceptual barriers consist of expectations of "how things are done" in the school. This often reflects the school culture, which, as mentioned earlier, may actually impede collaboration. Role expectations are shaped through a socialization process that has developed over many years and is reinforced by individuals within and between various professions. Tradition is one of the greatest determinants of how others in a particular role will be perceived and utilized in the future. The traditional role of the special education teacher has been to provide special "treatments" or interventions to students with disabilities in segregated settings (Welch & Sheridan, 1995). Special educators were prepared for this role in their teacher education program. As a result, many teachers and parents believe that some special educators do not support the practice of inclusion. Consider, for example, Reed's resource teacher in the case of "One Parent's Struggle for Inclusion," who saw her role as working directly with Reed, rather than with his classroom teachers.

A common belief within a school culture is that students with disabilities do not belong in the mainstream of the school. Many people feel that these students are better off with their own kind. Because of the dual system of general and special education that has existed in schools, many teachers do not feel it is their role to provide an educational experience for children with special needs. Furthermore, many teachers believe they do not have the skills to teach these students. This assumption is based on history and tradition.

Pragmatic Barriers

Pragmatic barriers are often considered the greatest barrier to collaboration in school settings. These barriers are usually associated with systemic and logistical factors within the school, such as lack of time for implementing consultation and collaboration (Idol-Maestas & Ritter, 1985). Other pragmatic difficulties are associated with the large caseloads of specialists, scheduling problems, policies, competing and increased responsibilities, and bureaucratic structures within the school.

Schools have been described as "segmented, egg-crate institutions in which teachers are isolated" (McLaughlin & Yee, 1988, p. 40). Schools are organized as bureaucracies in which there is a division of labor that operates on rules and procedures (Mercer & Covey, 1980). The fundamental organization of schools seriously prevents professionals from working together. School schedules and the physical layout of buildings often perpetuate isolation of individuals and resources. This minimizes direct communication between professionals, limiting opportunities for them to interact and solve problems (Ware, 1994). Even just the mountain of paperwork that is required for determining eligibility and services reflects bureaucratic red tape that often tangles up the process of meeting students' needs. For example, many special education programs are located in what are known as "self-contained units" in secluded parts of the school, where students with special needs spend their entire day. Other districts have implemented programs that are centrally located in a specific school, requiring students to be transported across the district to attend a "special cluster" even when they live across the street from a neighborhood school.

Consider, for example, the case of Scott in "In the Best Interests of the Child" (case 11 of this volume), who had to ride the bus to attend a cluster school that was five miles away. What follows is an excerpt in which Scott's parents argue for his inclusion in his neighborhood school, while school administrators and officials provide a litany of reasons for why inclusion could not and would not work. The reasons revolved around policies, timelines, calendars, available resources, bus schedules, school boundaries, programs and departments: "We argued that although Scott was now in a restrictive environment . . . he had had many successes when he had been integrated. . . . But they said, "We can't do it, we don't have the support. We don't have the money or the space . . . Case 11, p.179).

Each of the "reasons" given by the school administrators reflect pragmatic barriers to collaboration. However, with a change in building principal, many of these obstacles were circumvented. A new principal came to Scott's neighborhood school who believed that students with disabilities should attend their neighborhood school with their peers from their own neighborhood (see Appendix to case 11, pp. 209–210, in *Inclusive Education*). This belief had a profound influence on the culture and systemic organization of the school. The driving force behind this was a belief that inclusion was valuable and possible. But it is not enough to endorse collaboration in a given school building. Adequate time and resources also must be made available to ensure that structured collaborative efforts be practiced formally and predictably. In other words, systemic structures must be modified to facilitate the occurrence of formal collegial interactions.

Attitudinal Barriers

Attitudes are affective responses associated with beliefs. In other words, individuals will feel positively or negatively about a situation based on what they think or believe. Educators' feelings and attitudes about working together will be based on what they know or expect to be a likely result of their behavior or actions. Also contributing to the status quo may be "fear of the unknown" and the rationale of "that's how things have always been done around here." Scott's parents describe Scott's experience when he was in kindergarten in the cluster school:

> During the morning session there was virtually no integration, even during recess. At lunch the students with disabilities all sat at the same table, with an assistant or teacher standing over them while they ate. On the few occasions when Scott was integrated with the kindergartners in the afternoon, there was always an assistant who stood by. The regular teacher made it clear to everyone that she did not want to have to deal with him if he acted up. . . . Needless to say, we weren't pleased with the situation. We were frustrated that Scott wasn't being integrated enough, but we felt we had no say. We were told, "that's just the way it's done here." When we talked to the principal about our concerns, we were made to feel that it was a gift to us that Scott was being integrated at all. He said, "Be happy with what you are getting." (case 11, p.176)

Professional Barriers

A major barrier to collaboration in promoting inclusion is the lack of or differences in training among various disciplines (Goodlad & Field, 1993; Pugach & Allen-Meares, 1985; Welch & Sheridan, 1993). Ware (1994) noted that professionals are "culturally isolated by long-established professional behaviors and beliefs" (p. 344). Differences in professional preparation programs across disciplines can result in disproportionate knowledge of and experience in collaboration. Although school psychologists and special educators sometimes receive preservice training in problem solving and communication skills (Phillips & McCullough, 1990), classroom teachers typically do not. Unfortunately, philosophical differences and the lack of knowledge and skills in problem solving frequently limit teachers' ability to participate fully in a collaborative partnership. Many teachers do not understand or value the role and talents of other school personnel, and therefore do not utilize them as a resource.

RESOLVING PROBLEMS
IN COLLABORATIVE PARTNERSHIPS

Professionals and parents can overcome many of the barriers that impede collaboration. A prerequisite step is understanding what collaboration can achieve and what it involves. In addition to valuing collaboration, participants must also acknowledge that it is a complex process that requires effort. Since collaboration is a process, participants cannot merely "plug in" a model and assume it will operate automatically. Rather, it is a dynamic operation that requires continued monitoring, as we have seen. In this section of the chapter, we will look at what you can do in collaborative relationships to prevent or resolve problems as they arise.

Collaboration is more effective when participants take a wide, ecological perspective. This promotes an awareness of the interconnections among various groups in the school, including a knowledge of various resources that might be utilized to reach a common goal. An ecological perspective enables participants to use human, technological, informational, physical, and financial resources within the building and community as they work to solve a problem or achieve a common goal (Welch & Sheridan, 1995).

Working together will inevitably result in some degree of stress and conflict. Collaborators must acknowledge this fact and agree to manage conflict when it is encountered. Therefore, partners in collaboration should focus their energy on how they deal with conflict rather than attempting to avoid it altogether. This is not to suggest that partners should actively seek or engage in disagreements, but rather that they agree to disagree and recognize the importance of working through the problem. Participants will only be disappointed if they equate collaboration with congeniality. Using the effective communication skills with the problem-solving process described earlier, participants will have the fundamental tools to constructively manage conflict. This may mean temporarily postponing pursuit of a targeted goal to discuss a problem that has arisen in group interactions. Although it is often a difficult process, acknowledging feelings and discussing them ultimately strengthens the group.

One tool that can be used to constructively discuss issues during conflict management is the "awareness wheel" (Miller, Miller, Nunnally, & Wackman, 1991). This technique focuses on observed behaviors, thoughts, and feelings, which are then translated into goals and action steps. The first spoke on the wheel involves an individual objectively stating what he or she saw or heard, as well as where and when. For example, a specialist might say to a frustrated music teacher, "During the faculty meeting yesterday I heard you sigh heavily and saw you slam your lesson plan book down on the table when the idea of having some students with disabilities in your choir was brought up." Hopefully, observational statements such as this will be taken as nonjudgmental and nonthreatening.

The second spoke on the wheel deals with feelings by stating how the person feels about the situation. The specialist might continue by saying, "I was a bit worried because I really value our relationship and the fact that you've been so gracious in the past about including my kids." Here, the specialist has expressed feelings of concern.

The process continues to the third spoke, where participants discuss their thoughts and interpretations of the observed behavior and feelings. In this case, the specialist might say, "Well, since yesterday's meeting, I began to think you weren't too thrilled about this idea." Notice the "I messages" (referred to as such because of the consistent use of the personal pronoun "I"), whereby an individual takes ownership of the situation.

At this point, the specialist must move to the fourth spoke on the awareness wheel by stating a possible resolution in this situation, such as, "I'd like to sit down for a few minutes and discuss this because I don't want you to be upset; I'd like to make sure I understand your concerns." At this point, the music teacher might indicate that inclusion of students with disabilities has never been a problem in the past; however, the choir is getting ready to compete in a choral festival and the music teacher is worried that students with disabilities might have a negative impact on their performance ratings. An empathetic response by the specialist would assure the music teacher that this type of concern is certainly legitimate.

This moves them to the final spoke on the wheel: considering actions to take. The specialist might continue by saying, "I understand your concerns and I certainly wouldn't want that to happen. I'm willing to work something out with you that would meet the needs of the choir, your needs, and those of the kids with disabilities. Let's see if we can brainstorm some ideas we're both comfortable with." At this point, the process moves to the problem-solving steps of brainstorming and developing an action plan, which were described earlier. As a result, two colleagues were able to objectively and constructively deal with the conflict they were experiencing.

FORMS OF COLLABORATION
IN THE SCHOOL

As indicated at the beginning of this chapter, collaboration can take many forms. Now that you have a better understanding of the benefits, complexities, and barriers to collaboration, as well as ways to overcome the barriers, the remaining portion of this chapter will examine common forms of collaboration within the context of inclusion. However, collaboration is not limited to these specific approaches to working together. The examples presented here are just the most common approaches to collaboration in the schools that are designed to promote inclusion. They are team-teaching, collaborative consultation, intervention teams, and multidisciplinary student service delivery teams. We will now examine each of these forms of collaboration and their challenges, as well as guidelines for implementation.

Team-Teaching

In team-teaching situations, two or more teachers work together in the same classroom, sharing joint responsibility for instruction (Bauwens & Hourcade, 1995). Team-teaching can sometimes be thought of as "pull-in programming" because a specialist is often providing both direct and indirect services to students with special needs in mainstream settings (Gelzheiser & Meyers, 1990; Meyers, Gelzheiser, & Yelich, 1991). Team-teaching has many advantages (Welch & Sheridan, 1995). First, it reduces the teacher–student ratio in the classroom. Second, individualizing instruction for students with special needs is more feasible with two teachers. Third, team-teaching allows educators an opportunity to develop their own professional skills by learning from each other. Finally, teachers broaden their perspectives and understanding of their partner's roles, responsibilities, and expertise.

Potential Challenges to Team-Teaching.   Despite the advantages of team-teaching, there are potential challenges that can undermine the efforts of educators. It is important to remember that collaboration is a dynamic process for achieving common goals. Unfortunately, many teachers go into team-teaching with neither a specific goal nor a carefully outlined plan of roles and responsibilities. Consequently, many specialists often become nothing more than glorified aides or they are simply relegated to pulling small groups of students into the back of the classroom and doing there what they probably would have done in a resource room. Other times, team teachers merely divide up responsibilities, each teaching different chapters, units, or lessons. When this happens, many teachers feel they are relieved of any instructional responsibilities and are free to do other tasks, which may even mean leaving the classroom altogether. These examples reflect neither the definition of team-teaching nor the shared responsibility of working together. Instead, they continue the isolation of teachers and students.

Guidelines for Team-Teaching. Some basic guidelines for team-teaching can help ensure success (Bauwens & Hourcade, 1995; Brann, Loughlin, & Kimball, 1991; Gelzheiser & Meyers, 1990; Nowacek, 1992; Walther-Thomas, Bryant, & Land, 1996; Welch & Sheridan, 1995). First, start small. Identify a subject area, grade, class, or group of students to start with, and allocate a specific amount of time, such as 1 hour a day, for team-teaching.

Second, have a specific objective, such as written expression skills in language arts, as the topical area for team-teaching. Then, establish some kind of measurable criteria that will help you identify what you want students to achieve at the end of your team-teaching efforts. For example, two teachers might decide to use students' assignment scores from a science unit to determine if their students had learned the material. These teachers may also develop a simple survey asking students to indicate if they enjoyed having two teachers in the classroom to teach the science lessons. In this way, the teachers are gathering academic and attitudinal data that will assist them in evaluating their collaboration.

Third, set aside a minimum of 30 minutes a week for planning, at either the beginning or the end of the week. During the planning meeting, you should carefully consider who will do what during the team-teaching for each day of the ensuing week.

Fourth, carefully define the roles and responsibilities of each teacher by answering questions like the following: Will one or both teachers develop the lesson plans? Will both teachers share instructional tasks for students with special needs as well as with students who do not have disabilities? What are the evaluation criteria and procedures? Will grading and evaluation be shared, divided, or the sole responsibility of one teacher? Will students be divided into groups? What kind of adaptations will be made for students with special needs and by whom?

Fifth, identify potential problems or challenges that may arise, particularly for children with special needs. Here, the background and expertise of the specialist plays an important role in the planning process.

Finally, explore how you will evaluate your efforts. To do so, you might look at student performance data or student and parent satisfaction surveys. Also, sit down together and honestly assess your own performance and satisfaction.

Collaborative Consultation

Consultation is defined as "a problem solving process in which two or more persons (consultants and consultees) engage in efforts to benefit one or more other persons (clients) for whom they bear some level of responsibility within a particular context or reciprocal interaction" (Curtis & Meyers, 1988, p. 36). Gallessich (1985) characterized consultation as having specific components common to all models. First, all forms of consultation have a goal that typically involves solving a problem. Second, the problem-solving process in consultation is a triadic or indirect process whereby a consultant, who has expertise in specialized bodies of knowledge and in problem solving, assists a consultee, who then works directly with a client. For example, a special education teacher might help a classroom teacher develop a plan for managing the behavior of a student who is acting out. The role of the consultant can shift, depending on the circumstances or situation. This means that specialists such as school psychologists or special educators do not always take the role of consultant.

Third, the interaction between consultant and consultee is based on role and relationship rules. Two of the most important rules are that the relationship be voluntary and that the consultee ultimately be in charge of the situation and therefore able to reject or accept any strategies proposed by the consultant. Finally, consultation is a temporary interaction in which the consultee receives assistance in dealing with an immediate problem or situation. Theoretically, however, the consultee will now be empowered to deal with similar events in the future and therefore may not need to rely on the services of the consultant.

Guidelines for Collaborative Consultation. Collaborative consultation will only be effective if both the consultant and the consultee follow basic guidelines (Welch & Sheridan, 1995). Following the problem-solving process and stages described earlier, the consultant works with the consultee to first identify the problem or situation with a client. Then, the partners analyze the situation to identify factors that may be contributing to the problem. Finally, they develop an intervention. The process then moves to implementation of the intervention, which is followed by an evaluation phase to assess the effectiveness of the intervention. Within this framework, the individual seeking assistance should be actively involved in the decision-making process. This means that a consultant must use effective communication skills described earlier to engage the consultee during the problem-solving dialogue. In this way, the process is a two-way exchange of information and ideas as opposed to the consultant imposing expert advice. The use of a structured interview protocol or set of questions reflecting the steps of the problem-solving process described earlier will facilitate an efficient interaction. This type of document tends to keep both individuals focused on the task at hand and serves as documentation of what transpired. Many forms of collaborative consultation include an action plan that outlines specific objectives, roles, responsibilities, time lines, and evaluation criteria. The consultee has an equal voice throughout the consultation, including, as mentioned earlier, the right to reject any ideas or suggestions presented by the consultant. A constructive relationship evolves only when the consultant is genuine and sincere, without passing judgement on the situation or the consultee.

Intervention Teams

Intervention teams consist of educators who meet periodically to discuss the behavioral or academic progress of a student who is not yet receiving special education support services. The goal of the team is to minimize the number of inappropriate referrals to special education by developing and implementing interventions through indirect service to meet the specific needs of a student in a mainstream classroom setting (Graden, Casey, & Christenson, 1985).

There are two major types of intervention teams which vary in their composition but not their fundamental purpose. One type of intervention team is the (TAT) (Chalfant & Van Dusen Pysh, 1989). The TAT is generally composed of three to four classroom teachers. Generally, specialists and administrators do not serve on the TAT so that a sense of ownership and responsibility for the student and the situation is created among the teachers. The other type of team consists of both classroom teachers and professionals such as school counselors, school psychologists, and special education teachers (Graden, Casey, & Christenson, 1985). Both types of teams usually have a team leader who schedules, coordinates, and facilitates team meetings. In addition, the team leader may assign a case manager to each individual case. The case manager usually conducts a premeeting "intake" of information that includes observations or interviews with the individual requesting assistance.

Regardless of the team's composition, the team typically goes through the collaborative problem-solving process described earlier. The intent is to use effective communication skills, verbal economy, and problem-solving procedures to address as many requests for assistance as possible. Meetings are usually held each week, often after school, for approximately 60 to 90 minutes to review as many as five or six cases. The team leader or case manager quickly reviews the background information with the entire team. The person requesting assistance attends the meeting and participates in the discussion. The team's first goal is to identify and define the situation. Following this initial step, the team develops a goal statement, after which the team collectively brainstorms possible interventions or strategies to achieve the goal. Because the individual seeking assistance is ultimately in charge, this person must either choose or reject any intervention plan developed by the team. If an intervention is selected, the team collectively develops an action plan that outlines roles and responsibilities for implementing the intervention. A follow-up meeting is scheduled to review the progress of the plan and to make any necessary revisions.

The research literature suggests that intervention teams are generally effective forms of collaboration because they appear to (a) reduce the number of referrals to special education, (b) improve student performance, (c) help teachers develop strategies to serve students with disabilities in mainstream settings, and (d) promote faculty morale and communication (Welch, Brownell, & Sheridan, 1999). Yet, despite the potential efficacy of a team approach to solving problems, a number of challenges and possible obstacles exist (Welch & Sheridan, 1995). For example, some teachers are reluctant to seek assistance from colleagues, fearing that they might be perceived as ineffective or incompetent as a result. Others do not perceive serving on the team as part of their teaching role, and avoid the added responsibility. Finally, some faculty members do not fully understand the role and function of the team. Consequently, they see the team as a bureaucratic "hoop" to jump through before referring a student to special education. To maximize the potential of intervention teams as a collaboration tool to promote inclusion, educators should consider the basic guidelines described next (Welch & Sheridan, 1995).

Guidelines for Intervention Teams. To ensure the success of intervention teams, administrators must provide philosophical and technical support to them. Building principals must publically articulate the importance and role of the team to the entire school, encouraging the faculty to understand and support the role of the team. Additionally, administrators must adapt the systemic organization of the school to facilitate the existence and functioning of the team. The entire faculty must also support and understand the role of the team. Team members' roles and responsibilities must be adjusted to allow them time and energy to serve on the team. Allocating the necessary time to team members may mean releasing them from other responsibilities. Team members must receive adequate training in the team process, effective interpersonal communication, and problem-solving skills to ensure effective and efficient team operation. Finally, teams should adhere to a regular schedule of meetings with an agenda.

Multidisciplinary Student Service Delivery Teams

The multidisciplinary student service delivery (MSSD) team is composed of teachers, administrators, specialists, and parents. This team reviews a variety of formal and informal assessment data to determine if a student is eligible for special education programs. Once eligibility is established, the team develops an individualized education program (IEP) consisting of specific goals and procedures to achieve those goals. The IEP serves as a blueprint, outlining who will provide specific services to meet the goals and where those services will be delivered. The decision-making process of the MSSD team is collaborative in nature, again following the problem-solving process described in this chapter.

Historically, it has been assumed that services outlined on the IEP would be provided in segregated settings by special educators. The practice of inclusion, however, is based on shared responsibility for service delivery in a variety of settings. With this principle in mind, educators should think of special education as a service, not as a place. As such, the role of the special educator might be reconceptualized as the coordinator of the IEP, rather than as the sole service provider.

Because the IEP serves as a tool to plan and implement services in a variety of settings, it is important that all stakeholders play a meaningful role in its development. In the past, teachers typically have eschewed any participation during the MSSD team meetings, assuming that service delivery was the sole responsibility of the special education teacher in a segregated setting. With the movement toward inclusive education today, however, the classroom teacher plays an important role by carefully articulating the demands and activities of mainstream settings during the team meeting. After all, it is the classroom teacher who knows this environment best.

As part of an IEP, a specialist, such as a special education teacher or school psychologist, might assist the classroom teacher in conducting an ecological analysis of the classroom setting (Welch & Sheridan, 1995). During this process, the instructional and curricular features of the classroom are identified, including types of instructional activities, materials used, student grouping, and evaluation procedures. Based on the information provided by the teacher, appropriate decisions can then be made regarding the kinds of supplementary aids and services a student with disabilities will need in order to be educated in the least restrictive environment. As a result of this information, the team can then determine to what extent a student with a disability can be included in the regular classroom and what kind of adaptations for instruction and curriculum might be necessary.

Parents also play an important role in the MSSD team. Just as the classroom teacher is an expert in the classroom setting, the parents of the student are in the best position to understand the goals, strengths, and needs of their child. Unfortunately, in some cases, parents have had very limited or peripheral opportunities to participate on the MSSD team. The case of the Bonn family is an example of how one team developed an IEP prior to the meeting and then attempted to coerce the parents into agreeing to it. As often happens, Scott's parents were seen as adversaries rather than partners. For their part, Scott's parents described IEP meetings as stressful and intimidating. This type of atmosphere hardly reflects collaboration and good will. Furthermore, the lack of effective interpersonal communication skills among some team members had a significant impact on the quality of interactions.

One way to promote active involvement of parents on the MSSD team is to use an advance organizer for IEP meetings (McKellar, 1991). An advance organizer outlines the agenda of the meeting and poses specific questions that parents can consider prior to the meeting, such as:

- What goals do you have for your child in specific academic and social areas?
- What lifelong or independent living goals do you have for your child?
- What strengths or interests does your child have that might help achieve these goals?
- What kinds of assistance or strategies have you used in the past to achieve specific goals, and how successful were they?
- What kinds of resources or assistance do you think your child will need to achieve specific goals?

These questions can be used as a basis for discussion as goals and procedures are developed. When appropriate, even the student with special needs can serve an important role on the team. Unfortunately, as Van Reusen and Bos (1990) noted, student participation in developing IEPs is usually passive, if not nonexistent. Therefore, to allow students greater opportunity to act as advocates for themselves during the IEP development process, Van Reusen and Bos developed a strategy known as I.P.L.A.N. Each letter of the acronym represents the following actions for students: Students are taught first to take an *in*ventory of their strengths and weaknesses, then to *p*rovide that information to the members of the IEP team. Following this, students *l*isten and respond to the comments. The response may include *a*sking questions. The objective is to ultimately *n*ame the student's goals.

Guidelines for Effective MSSP Team Meetings. One of the most important concerns in conducting a successful MSSP meeting is to make it as personal as possible. An easy way to begin this process is to introduce all the attendees by name and title with a brief description of their roles. It is also important to clearly state the objective of the meeting, which is to determine goals for the student and methods for achieving them. Educators might move the discussion by asking the parents to share their ideas from the advance organizer just described. When appropriate, the team might also consider beginning by allowing the student to use the I.P.L.A.N. method to articulate his or her strengths, weaknesses, and goals. Beyond the formal operation of outlining goals and services, Zins and Curtis (1984) suggested that IEP meetings can be improved simply by using the fundamental principles of interpersonal communication skills and problem-solving steps that have been presented in this chapter.

CONCLUSION

Inclusion is a complex process, fraught with many legitimate concerns and challenges. No one parent or professional can deal with the complexities of inclusion alone. Instead, it requires collaboration. Like inclusion, collaboration itself is a complex process, which professionals must understand in order to practice. It is not enough to merely "believe" in collaboration. One must have the tools, and the knowledge of how to use those tools. As seen from this discussion, collaboration can take many forms. It is not a static model, but rather a dynamic framework of procedures and principles that are influenced by both easily identifiable and subtle factors within the culture and organization of the school and community.

REFERENCES

Bauwens, J., & Hourcade, J. J. (1995). *Cooperative teaching: Rebuilding the school house for all students.* Austin, TX: Pro-ed.
Brann, P., Loughlin, S., & Kimball, W. H. (1991). Guidelines for cooperative teaching between general and special education teachers. *Journal of Educational and Psychological Consultation, 2,*

197–200.

Bullough, R. V., & Baughman, K. (1995). Inclusion: A view from inside the classroom. *Journal of Teacher Education, 46*(2), 85–93.

Chalfant, J. C., & Van Dusen Pysh, M. (1989). Teacher assistance teams: Five descriptive studies on 96 teams. *Remedial and Special Education, 10,* 49–58.

Curtis, M. J., & Curtis, V. A. (1990). The intervention assistance model. *Trainer's Forum, 10*(1), 3–4.

Duke, D., Showers, B., & Imber, M. (1980). Teachers and shared decision-making: The costs and benefits of involvement. *Educational Administration Quarterly, 16,* 93–106.

Fuchs, D., & Fuchs, L. S. (1989). Exploring effective and efficient prereferral interventions: A component analysis of behavioral consultation. *School Psychology Review, 18,* 260–283.

Fullan, M. (1993). *Change forces: Probing the depths of educational reform.* New York: Falmer.

Gallessich, J. (1985). *The profession and practice of consultation.* San Francisco: Jossey-Bass.

Gelzheiser, L. M., & Meyers, J. (1990). Special and remedial education in the classroom: Theme and variations. *Journal of Reading, Writing, and Learning Disabilities, 6,* 419–436.

Goodlad, J. I., & Field, S. (1993). Teachers for renewing schools. In J. I. Goodlad & T. C. Lovitt (Eds.), *Integrating general and special education* (pp. 229–252). New York: Merrill.

Graden, J. L., Casey, A., & Christenson, S. L. (1985). Implementing a prereferral intervention system: Part I. The model. *Exceptional Children, 51,* 377–384.

Hanson, E. M. (1990). *Educational administration and organizational behavior.* Boston: Allyn and Bacon.

Hord, S. M. (1986, February). A synthesis of research on organizational collaboration. *Educational Leadership, 43*(5), 22–26.

Idol-Maestas, L., & Ritter, S. (1985). A follow-up study of resource/consulting teachers: Factors that facilitate and inhibit teacher consultation. *Teacher Education and Special Education, 8,* 121–131.

Jayanthi, M., & Friend, M. (1992). Interpersonal problem solving: A selective literature review to guide practice. *Journal of Educational and Psychological Consultation, 3*(1), 39–53.

Kurpius, D. J. (1991). Why collaborative consultation fails: A matrix for consideration. *Journal of Educational and Psychological Consultation, 2,* 193–195.

McKellar, N. A. (1991). Enhancing the IEP process through consultation. *Journal of Educational and Psychological Consultation, 2,* 175–187.

McLaughlin, M. W., & Yee, S. M. (1988). School as a place to have a career. In A. Lieberman (Ed.), *Building a professional culture in schools* (pp. 23–44). New York: Teachers College Press.

Mercer, B., & Covey, H. C. (1980). *Theoretical frameworks in the sociology of education.* Cambridge, MA: Schenkman.

Meyers, J., Gelzheiser, L. M., & Yelich, G. (1991). Do pull-in programs foster teacher collaboration? *Remedial and Special Education, 12,* 7–5.

Miller, S., Miller, P., Nunnally, E. W., & Wackman, D. B. (1991). *Talking and listening together.* Littleton, CO: Interpersonal Communication Programs.

Nowacek, J. (1992). Professionals talk about teaching together: Interviews with five collaborating teachers. *Intervention in School and Clinic, 27*(5), 262–276.

Ott, J. S. (1989). *The organizational culture perspective.* Pacific Grove, CA: Brooks/Cole.

Phillips, V., & McCullough, L. (1990). Consultation-based programming: Instituting the collaborative ethic. *Exceptional Children, 56,* 291–304.

Pugach, M. C., & Allen-Meares, P. (1985). Collaboration at the preservice level: Instructional and evaluation activities. *Teacher Education and Special Education, 8,* 3–11.

Robbins, S. P. (1990). *Organizational theory: Structure, design, and applications.* Englewood Cliffs, NJ: Prentice-Hall.

Scruggs, T. E., & Mastropieri, M. A. (1996). Teacher perceptions of mainstreaming/inclusion. *Exceptional Children, 63,* 59–74.

Tindal, G., Parker, R., & Hasbrouch, J. E. (1992). The construct validity of stages and activities in the consultation process. *Journal of Educational and Psychological Consultation, 3,* 99–118.

Van Reusen, A. K., & Bos, C. S. (1990). I PLAN: Helping students communicate in planning conferences. *Teaching Exceptional Children, 22,* 30–32.

Walther-Thomas, C., Bryant, M. & Land, S. (1996). Planning for effective co-teaching: The key to successful inclusion. *Remedial and Special Education, 17*(4), 255–265.

Ware, L. P. (1994). Contextual barriers to collaboration. *Journal of Educational and Psychological Consultation, 5*(4), 339–357.

Welch, M., & Sheridan, S. M. (1995). *Educational partnerships: Serving students at risk.* Fort Worth, TX: Harcourt Brace.

Welch, M., & Sheridan, S. M. (1993). Educational partnerships in teacher education: Reconceptualizing how teacher candidates are prepared for teaching students with disabilities. *Action in Teacher Education, 15*(3), 35–46.

Welch, M., Brownell, K., & Sheridan, S. M. (1999). What's the score and game plan on teaming in schools? A review of the literature on team-teaching and school-based problem-solving teams. *Remedial and Special Education, 20*(1), 36–49.

Zins, J. E., & Curtis, M. J. (1984). Building consultation into the education service delivery system. In C. A. Maher, R. J. Illback, & R. J. Zins (Eds.). *Organizational psychology in the schools* (pp. 213–242). Springfield, IL: Charles C. Thomas.

II

THE CASEBOOK

An Introduction to Cases

Suzanne E. Wade

What you are about to read in this casebook are narratives, or cases, that describe in rich detail the actual experiences of students and teachers in inclusive settings. Each case is written from the perspective of the students, their parents, their general education teachers, special educators, and administrators—sometimes in collaboration. All of the incidents described in this casebook actually occurred, although names, locations, and identifying details have been changed for purposes of confidentiality.

WHAT ARE CASES AND WHAT CAN YOU LEARN FROM THEM?

Cases have long been a popular teaching method in medicine, law, business, and, more recently, education. Written in a narrative form, cases present real dilemmas and problems in rich detail. Learning with cases involves more than just reading narratives. It requires thorough preparation on your part before class, participation in class discussions, analysis, problem solving, and follow-up activities. As a result, these cases will enable you, as a prospective or practicing educator, to understand situations from the point of view of students, parents, and teachers. Cases also can make the information in assigned readings more meaningful, as you apply the theories you are learning to actual situations. Finally, cases give you a chance to work with your peers in class to analyze the problems teachers face in inclusive settings and to think through and evaluate possible solutions. Reading and discussing cases will give you the analytical and problem-solving skills that will make you aware of the needs of children and help you make good decisions. Here is how one teacher summed up her experiences with cases:

> I think [reading a case] can cause you to reflect more, especially those of us who have been teaching, on what you do. Do I do the same thing? Do I have the same reasons? Or, why do I do what I do? You tend really to internalize what you're reading. (Moje & Wade, 1997, p. 691)

READING THE CASES

When you read and discuss cases in class, you will be actively constructing knowledge. Instead of "just reading" a case, you will need to think carefully about the situation in the case, the case writer's point of view, and how the case is related to information in assigned readings and other sources of knowledge. You might ask yourself:

- Whose point of view does the case present? Whose points of view have not been included?
- How does the theory and information I am learning in this class help me make sense of the case and understand why the people in it act the way they do?
- How and why is this a case of inclusion?
- What do I see as the main problem in the case? Would the case writer be likely to view the problem the same way I do? If I could ask the different players in the case how they view the problem, what might they say?
- How is the problem posed in this case similar to and different from the other cases I have read and teaching experiences I have had?
- What ethical, curricular, pedagogical, policy, and legal issues are involved in the case?

As you answer these and similar questions, you are analyzing the case and framing the problems in it. This is important because it enables you to understand the situation from different perspectives, to examine it using a variety of theoretical lenses, and to think about how it is similar to and different from other cases and personal experiences. Then you will want to apply the theory and research presented in class and in your readings, together with your own experience, to think of possible solutions to the case. Always remember that there is no one "right" course of action in any teaching situation. So, try to think of several alternative solutions. However, not all solutions are equal—some may be better than others. Therefore, the next step is to evaluate each one. These questions might help you as you think of and evaluate various solutions:

- What would I do if I were the teacher in the case?
- Why would I do that?
- What are the assumptions, beliefs, and theories that guide my decision making?
- What are the possible consequences and risks of this solution? In other words, what might happen next?
- Would it be a fair solution to all involved?
- Would this solution achieve my overall objectives?
- What are some alternative solutions?

Now you should be well prepared for the case discussion that will occur in class.

PARTICIPATING IN CASE DISCUSSIONS

A good question is never answered;
It is not a bolt to be tightened into place
But a seed to be planted and to bear more seed
Toward the hope of greening the landscape of ideas.
(J. Ciardi, quoted in Christensen, 1987, p. 45)

Case discussions are different than most of the teaching methods you have experienced. There will be no lecturing, no instructor transmitting a prescribed body of information, no questions with one right answer. Instead, as the quote above suggests, you will be grappling with difficult questions that will help you analyze the cases from different perspectives and to understand all the issues involved. Sometimes, when you think you have understood a case or decided on a viable solution, someone may ask a question or offer an alternative interpretation or solution that will cause you to rethink your own. This is a process of collaborative inquiry, in which you are actively engaged in constructing and evaluating understandings with others.

You must be patient with the "disorderliness of discovery," as Christensen (1991) has put it, because "even the most steadfast explorer cannot march straight through a jungle" (p. 105). Sometimes you may feel frustrated about the time a discussion requires and the divergent directions it may take, but remember that you are examining complex issues and situations that may be like the ones you will face as a teacher. Fruitful discussions will take time, hard work, and critical reflective thinking.

Another thing that makes a case discussion successful is creating a *learning community* in the classroom. In a learning community, everyone feels that they have something valuable to contribute. As a result, everyone feels safe enough to take risks, which makes learning possible (Christensen, 1991). Creating a learning community is everyone's responsibility. Your job is not only to offer your own carefully thought-out ideas but also to listen actively with an open mind and to acknowledge the ideas of your classmates. For example, you might say something like, "Related to the issue that Jane brought up. . .," or "Jeff brought up an interesting point that. . ., but I think there's an another way to look at it," or "Just to play devil's advocate. . . ." By carefully listening to what others have to say and building on their contributions, you are being supportive of others (even when you disagree), as well as helping to add some coherence and direction to the discussion.

RELATED CASE ACTIVITIES

Your instructor may ask you to write a case analysis either before or after the case discussion. Writing will help you think through and integrate your ideas, and will often lead to the discovery of new understandings. As you write a case analysis, make sure that you relate the information in your texts and other assigned readings to the case. In addition, you may be asked to engage in any number of follow-up activities. These might include small-group work to decide on a course of action to solve the problem or dilemma in the case, role-playing activities that place you in a similar situation, cross-case comparisons, or research activities in which you further examine a problem or issue.

ON TO THE CASES

This casebook is designed to prepare you for the real world of teaching in inclusive settings. You will hear and come to understand the perspectives of the students, their parents, and their teachers who have worked successfully with students who have not been successful in school for various reasons. Someday you may think back on these cases as you seek to understand and solve the problems you may face as a teacher.

REFERENCES

Christensen, C. R. (1987). *Teaching and the case method.* Boston, MA: Harvard Business School.
Christensen, C. R. (1991). Every student teaches and every teacher learns: The reciprocal gift of discussion. In C. R. Christensen, D. A. Garvin, & A. Sweet (Eds.), *Education for Judgement: The artistry of discussion leadership* (pp. 99–119). Boston, MA: Harvard Business School.
Moje, E. B., & Wade, S. E. (1997). What case discussions reveal about teacher thinking. *Teaching and Teacher Education, 13,* 691–712.

Case 1

One Parent's Struggle for Inclusion

as told by Karen Hahne

This case chronicles a mother's efforts to secure an inclusive program for her adopted son with Down syndrome, their experiences at a neighborhood school where inclusion is attempted, and her son's involvement in their community. The focus is on the parental role in promoting, shaping, and coping with the attitudes and expectations of those who work with children with disabilities in different contexts.

THE EARLY YEARS

I was just a mom who wanted a program for my son. That really is the whole story. Eleven years ago we adopted a little boy with Down syndrome. We were excited and nervous and overwhelmed. He was our sixth child, the fourth one we adopted, and the only one with disabilities.

Before we brought him home at six weeks of age, Reed had been in the hospital since birth. He weighed about four pounds, had had surgery, had a feeding tube, and had very low muscle tone. He had lots of strikes against him. We took him to a center for children with disabilities in our county, where the director said, "Love him, but don't expect much." That bothered me. If the people who were providing the services expected so little of these children, then how could parents expect much?

Fortunately, I met other people who had received services in other places. One woman I met had a 7-year-old daughter with Down syndrome who had great language ability and had never been in a segregated setting. I met other people at a summer workshop on Down syndrome. Seventeen years ago I had been a special education teacher, and I was thrilled to find out that what I had learned long ago was changing. There was a new expectation that children with disabilities didn't have to be institutionalized or segregated—that they could learn to read and to live relatively normal lives.

I went back to the center where we were taking Reed, all fired up. I said, "I'll volunteer my time. I'd like to involve parents and move in some different directions." I think the administrators were threatened by that because they said, "No, you can't do that." So I went to the school district and said, "I'd like to start an evening program for parents of children with Down syndrome." They agreed to let us use several rooms in the local high school. We found a couple of therapists who really valued the parents' role and were willing to donate their time. We had about 10 sets of parents who would come with their children, mainly infants and toddlers. The children got therapy and the parents got a support group. If the baby was sick, the parents would get a sitter and come anyway. We needed to be together to end our isolation. This program grew to three nights a week.

Then the center where I had been taking Reed since he was little was put on probation because of program problems. The State Department of Social Services sent out a "request for proposals" for new programs in our county. Even though we really didn't know how to do it, another mother and I wrote a proposal for a grant to fund a program for kids with all kinds of developmental and physical disabilities. We named our program "Kids on the Move." And we got the funding.

We started with about 30 families in an old school building that had been condemned many times. It was an inclusion project—we called it reverse mainstreaming—to bring children with and without disabilities from the community into our preschool. Then, when Reed was four, our building was condemned and we had to move the school. The only space we could find was a vacant dental lab at the local community college. It was a much smaller space and, unfortunately, we didn't have the room for the full inclusion project. A few brothers and sisters could still come, but I wanted more of a neighborhood situation for Reed. If he was in a segregated setting at school, I wondered how he would ever fit into a community. So I approached the local university preschool about taking Reed into their program. At the time, they had a policy against taking kids with disabilities. I went to the administrators and said, "This kid will not hurt the other kids. He is not contagious." They said the only way they would do it was if special education sent somebody over to be with him. I said, "I don't want somebody with him the whole time. You'll really find that he can do most things himself." Eventually, they took him and it worked out well.

The university preschool was a lab school where college students majoring in early childhood did their student teaching. Many of the student teachers came up to me later and said, "I'm so glad Reed was here this past year because I learned that he's just a kid. He's not that different. Even though he didn't have a lot of language, he could do it. And I could do it." Having Reed in that preschool gave those teachers the courage and the confidence to have kids with special needs in their classrooms.

The next year, when Reed was five and ready to start kindergarten, we had a series of IEP meetings to decide where to place him. The district wanted to send him to a special school for kids with disabilities, saying that's where their services were. Of course, I said, "No. The law says you can't segregate based on disabilities." So they looked at his IQ test and saw that he had scored 81, which put him just barely within the normal range. Then they said, "Well, we don't even have to deal with you because he has a normal IQ." In other words, they were saying, "Let's just dump him in a neighborhood school without any services." I said, "Even with that IQ, he still has Down syndrome. You'll have to come up with some other options."

One of the options they proposed was something they called a "transition kindergarten," which was basically a self-contained unit within a regular school in the district. When we went to look at it, we saw that there was absolutely no inclusion going on. We said to the transition teacher, "When are these children with the other kindergarten kids?" She said, "Oh, once a week we go down for singing time." I said, "Oh, so it's like, 'Here come the retards to sing!'" I was good at offending. I didn't mean to be; it was just the passion I felt.

Another thing that troubled me was the big bulletin board where the principal had listed all the classes. The "transition kindergarten" was designated as "THE HANDICAPPED CLASS." At the next IEP meeting, I told the principal of this school that a lot of things about his program offended me, especially this label on the bulletin board. A district person turned to him and said, "Well, obviously, this mother hasn't accepted her child's disability."

"Yes, I have," I said. "I'm perfectly fine with it, but I know he is also a great kid. All you want to do is focus on his deficits. I want to look at his strengths and his needs, and his greatest need as a five-year-old boy is to be around typically developing five-year-olds."

At that time, we were part of a group of parents, all from "Kids on the Move," who were pressuring the district to come up with other options. The district called us "adversarial" right to our faces, but we insisted we were just being assertive. Eventually, they said they'd start a new program in a cluster school where kids with behavior problems that weren't severe enough for the self-contained unit were sent. I agreed to send Reed there for kindergarten. We parents thought we'd be patient and see how things went.

Well, they didn't go very well. There was not a lot of inclusion going on. But it wasn't by design; it was just because the principal hadn't thought things through. We parents went to him and said, "You know, our kids could have recess with the regular kids their age, they could go to lunch with them, and they could do opening exercises." We asked him why our kids went to computer class with sixth graders with behavior problems.

"Don't you want them going to computer class?" he asked.

"Of course we do. Is your goal to have the sixth graders tutor the younger kids?"

"No, not really."

"Well, I want Reed to go to computer class with the kindergarten kids."

"Well, then he'll have to share a computer."

"Wonderful," I said. "That would be great: to have him sitting there with a typically developing kindergarten kid, learning to use the computer together. Reed will learn much faster that way."

The next year, for first grade, we moved Reed again, this time to another new program—what the district called an "inclusion unit"—in a school closer to our neighborhood school. The district had hired a special education teacher to work with the regular education teachers. That first year was great. The regular educators saw that Reed really had a lot of skills, and they wanted him in their classes for more of the day. The special educator that year was receptive to the idea, too. Unfortunately, the one they hired the next year wasn't.

This next special educator had worked at the state institution for children with severe disabilities. Her favorite saying was that kids with disabilities had to "earn" their way into the regular classroom. They had to prove themselves good enough: that they could read, were potty trained, and had language. In IEP meetings, I heard this sentiment echoed among district officials and I said, "Whoa! Wait, I think that it's more that they have to earn their way *out*. The law's on our side on this one, and we will have to see more kids with disabilities in regular classrooms."

"No," they said, "the pendulum has swung way, way over, and it will swing back, and then you parents will come crawling on your hands and knees begging for self-contained services."

"No, that will never happen," I said. "Maybe the pendulum will swing back a little, and there will be some redefining, but you will never see parents begging for self-contained schools—never."

At the same time, I know that there are those parents who have children with learning disabilities, autism, or extreme behaviors who may want a self-contained classroom in their neighborhood school for their children, where their needs would be met and they would have lots of opportunities for inclusion.

I saw this same attitude on the part of special educators working in self-contained units. It was like they were always apologizing that the kids they worked with weren't like all the other kids.

The responses I've seen among regular educators have been different. I think every regular education teacher Reed has ever had has started off afraid because, after all, the district says he's "severely, multiply handicapped." But pretty soon they arrive at a stage where they say, "Wow, this kid is great. He's not any lower than some of the kids in my class. He's got a lot of capabilities."

Anyway, between that special educator in second grade and the 45-minute bus ride to and from school for Reed, we decided, "Enough. Let's just send him to the neighborhood school." There was a wonderful resource teacher there who said, "Bring him." But the principal was another story. I called him up and told him Reed would be coming and he said, "Don't do it. We're not ready." And I said, "He's coming. He'll be there tomorrow!"

THE NEIGHBORHOOD SCHOOL

The school wasn't ready to have Reed in a regular classroom, but they got ready. We decided to have him repeat second grade in the neighborhood school. He was small for his age and the second grade classes had fewer children in them. Reed has been in the neighborhood school for five years now. We've had our ups and downs, but we've worked things out. The resource teacher when he first started there was wonderful at working with the regular education teachers. For instance, Reed's second grade teacher did creative writing for part of the day. But Reed wasn't at the point where he could sit down and compose something on his own. So his resource teacher had Reed dictate something to her in the morning (she found out all our family secrets!). Then in the afternoon, when his regular class did creative writing, he would take what she had written down and copy it. They adapted the curriculum like that throughout the year.

In fourth grade, I thought Reed was going to have a real problem. At the beginning of the year, I took some information and materials to his homeroom teacher, who said, "I'm too busy, Karen. Don't worry. I've taught for a long time." In other words, he said, "Buzz off." I thought, "Well, maybe I need to buzz off and see what happens." I told him I was just trying to support him and if there was any problem, I just wanted him to know I was concerned.

One day that year, I overheard Reed talking to one of his friends. His friend said, "I did really good on my test today." Reed said, "I didn't. I don't do good on tests." So I went back to talk to his teacher. Apparently, every Thursday they had a multiple-choice and fill-in-the-blank history test that was about six pages long. I told the teacher that Reed didn't do very well with that format. The process of reading and understanding the questions and filling in the bubbles and blanks just took him longer. I also told his teacher that I was really concerned about Reed's self-esteem because he feels he doesn't do well on tests. "I know what we can do," he said, "We can send the test home on Wednesday night and he can do it at home." I thought, "Oh, great! One more thing to do with everything else." But I wanted it to work, so I said, "Let's try it." So Reed started bringing home his history tests. Often when we were in the car going somewhere, he would read the test aloud and fill in the blanks and the bubbles. It blew me away how much of the stuff he knew! I knew that he wasn't just guessing because he got so many of the questions right. He had successes in science that year too. His teacher told me, "I'm delighted with what he knows. He raises his hand to answer just about every question, and even if he doesn't know the right answer, he knows the context. He knows how to make the experiments work. He figures things out faster than some of the other kids."

His homeroom teacher called me after a few weeks and said, "I figured out what you want."

"What's that?" I said.

"You want me to have him in the regular class as much as I can, and just have him be part of class with the rest of the kids. You don't want me to overwhelm him, or frustrate him, but you don't want me to underestimate him either."

I said, "That's it. You've just spelled out inclusion. That's exactly what my dream is."

Some other teachers are receptive as well. For instance, his fifth grade teacher this year takes Reed and four others aside and reads their test questions aloud because they can show what they've learned better that way. But then there are those teachers who aren't receptive. We have a new resource teacher at the neighborhood school this year who believes in a self-contained program. She doesn't see her role as supporting the regular classroom teachers. Reed is in resource for math; that's his choice. He has friends in that class, and he wanted to be with them. So in resource math, he just works through the third grade math book. The teacher sends him home with all the multiplication facts to memorize—the 0 through 12 times tables. I told her, "He will never memorize these. He has poor short-term memory skills, and he is so compulsive he will make us drill him anyway. Do you know how long that takes? Do you know how much good that doesn't do?" I told her, "Let him use the calculator. We want him to work on telling time and understanding money." But she has a hard time with that because that's not what she does.

THE NEIGHBORHOOD AND COMMUNITY

It's nice that Reed is so fully accepted socially. Of course, it wasn't always that way. When he first started in the neighborhood school, there was a group of older kids, fourth graders, who targeted him. It was a "kick the dog" kind of thing. They were hurting and they wanted to hurt somebody else. They would taunt him, "Oh, you are so retarded, you are so retarded." When my older sons heard it, they were going to beat those kids up. I said, "Oh super! Are you going to do that every day?"

"Well, no."

"What's going to happen on the days when you don't beat them up?"

So we came up with another plan. During Christmas vacation, we invited a couple of these boys over with the promise of hot new games to play. While they were there, I said, "What if something happened to you, an injury or something? What if because of that injury you did things a little differently, so they wouldn't let you go to the school in your neighborhood anymore?"

"Oh, that would be terrible," they said.

"Well, this is Reed's first year at this school. He has always had to go far away to school just because he has Down syndrome." And I explained what the syndrome was. "Do you think it's fair that he has to go far away to school for that?

They just said, "No, it's not fair."

So we talked and they came over every day that Christmas vacation and played games. When school started they didn't play with him that much because they had their own fourth grade friends, but those two have been his advocates, kind of his body guards, ever since.

We've kept Reed really involved in the community and in extracurricular activities. He's done well and been so accepted. He's played on soccer teams since he was five. He's gone from knowing nothing about the game—you know, scoring points for the opposite team—to having pretty good soccer skills. We've also had him on the local university youth gymnastics team. He is a lot more flexible than some of the other kids because of his low muscle tone. It's a trade-off for what he lacks in strength. Last year, we let him go to a basketball camp where, again, he was the only kid with a recognizable disability. But his team won the competition. Now, it wasn't because of his efforts; everybody was a lot taller. But, everybody got to play, so he was included in the games. Three hundred kids at a basketball camp, and he has a shirt that says, "THE WINNER!" You know, he feels that he can do anything. He has so much self-confidence.

Sometimes, though, that can get him in trouble! A year ago at Christmas time, he and two of his friends were throwing rocks at the school and broke a window. Then they went into the school and knocked over some garbage cans. The principal called the police. Reed's two friends denied everything, saying, "We didn't do it, we didn't do it!" Reed piped up and said, "Yes we did, yes we did!" The principal was wonderful. He said, "I had to give up a night of vacation to come over here because of you guys. Do you think that's fair?" They realized that it wasn't fair and that they were in pretty serious trouble. They had to stay after school for the month of January and help the custodian.

Reed was grounded from playing with those boys for a while, and we wondered if we should let him play with them at all. But the experience gave us the opportunity to talk to Reed about what to do when his friends are acting inappropriately. He doesn't know that intuitively. And that's what we have to relearn every time too. We can't take anything for granted. Still, we have to be willing to risk and to pick up the pieces. And we *have* risked, and we've worried. Reed has gone on overnighters with the Boy Scouts in blizzards and come back as grubby as anyone. He's in a performing group of kids with special needs who travel all over the state; all of those kids are in inclusive schools. We try to get the kids who are in the self-contained settings involved too, but their parents are afraid. They say it's too hard: "It may be fine for Reed. He's gifted." Gifted? This is a kid with trisomy 21, not mosaic, not normal chromosomes.

Reed's teacher this year called us a while ago and said, "When I first knew I was going to have Reed in my class, I figured I could do a good job preparing him for the community. But I need to tell you that I'm preparing him for college just like the other kids in my class. He's got the potential. He's got the ability." So when people tell us, "Oh, you are so lucky! Reed is so gifted," I have to think, he was the most low tone, failure-to-thrive baby that you have ever seen. At 9 months he weighed 7 pounds. He was so delayed he had almost no motor development. He's still missing a third of his immune system, so he's really prone to respiratory ailments and the like. But now people look at him and say, "He's gifted." Well, the gift has been inclusion; the gift has been the typical kids in the classroom and the opportunities in the community. I look at the neighborhood school as the microcommunity. If Reed can make it there, he can make it in the larger community when he gets older.

THE FUTURE

It won't be long before Reed moves on to the neighborhood junior high, which has just started integrating their resource kids into regular classes. Reed will be the only student with Down syndrome at this junior high. It seems that everywhere he has gone he has paved the way, been the first kid in that category. We're lucky that the kids who have known him at the neighborhood school will be there too. They'll be his advocates.

But what will the future hold?

Case 2

The Dialogue That Might Be Silencing

Janine T. Remillard

This case focuses on issues of race and culture in mathematics education reform. Set in the author's first grade classroom, the case raises questions about students' cultural differences in a discussion-intensive mathematics class. While most of the students were from White working-class families, three were African-American students bused to the school from the inner city. Even though the other students seemed to gradually appropriate the tools that allowed them to participate in class discussions, the three inner-city students struggled. The author's concerns for these three students were further heightened when she read "The Silenced Dialogue" by Lisa Delpit (1988) in a graduate course. Delpit's claim that teachers must explicitly teach African-American children the cultural tools for participating in mainstream society led her to question the appropriateness of her social constructivist-oriented goals for her students.

Janine looked up from the pages of the article she had just finished and out the window at the quiet neighborhood street. It was a sunny mid-fall afternoon. Brilliant red and orange leaves dropped from the arms of the giant oak tree that shaded her yard. Janine did not see the leaves; instead, she saw the faces of Jackson, LaTisha, and Dante, three students in her first grade class. Her mind raced between the words she had just read, her students, and her goals as a math teacher, as she wondered whether she was making a tragic mistake in her teaching.

Although math was the only subject she taught to this class of first graders, her teaching frequently occupied her thoughts. Even though she had given up full-time teaching to become a graduate student in mathematics education, she wanted to maintain contact with children and schools. Furthermore, her graduate studies had prompted her to consider new goals and approaches for teaching math, and she believed it was important to try them out in a classroom. So she arranged to take daily responsibility for math in a first grade classroom in a local public school.

The school was situated in a working-class neighborhood in a city dominated by manufacturing plants. Only a third of the students, however, came from the immediate neighborhood. Because the district had instituted a busing program in order to desegregate the schools, about a third of the students rode buses to school from a low-income, inner-city neighborhood. These students were predominantly African-American. Another third of the students lived in a trailer park a few miles from the school. The students in the neighborhood and those from the trailer park were mostly Caucasian and came from working-class families.

In her dual role as math teacher and graduate student of mathematics education, Janine was very deliberate in her choices. She wanted to establish a community of learners in which the students' knowledge really counted. She hoped that her students could develop what she called "authority for knowing"; that is, she did not want them to look to her for right answers. Rather, she wanted them to think their answers through, themselves, and with others to decide whether they made sense. Thus, she knew it was important to establish particular routines in the class for how she and her students talked to one another and for the roles that each played. For example, she did not want to be the one asking all the questions. If she gave the students a problem to work on that had many possible solutions, and two students were sharing their solution with the class, it was her goal that classmates would ask them questions about their solution. Perhaps they would even disagree or suggest an alternative way to look at it. Her role, as she saw it, was to facilitate discussion by posing problems and asking questions that continued to push the class in mathematically productive directions.

Janine knew that establishing these norms in the class was likely to involve a lengthy and careful process. She was certain that she could not just "tell" these six-year-olds the new norms and have them comply. Although they were relatively inexperienced school-goers, they already had firm ideas about what math should be like and how teachers and students should interact that conflicted with her ideas. Her plan was to cultivate a collaborative, sense-making environment by subtly communicating the message that doing math was a group process and that she did not have all the answers. For example, after a student shared a solution to a problem, Janine planned to ask the class if anyone had comments, or to ask who agreed, who disagreed, and who was not sure. She planned to get other children to explain why they agreed or disagreed and to ask the question "why" a lot.

She started the year by giving the students a fairly open-ended problem to work on in their notebooks each day. While the students worked either alone or in pairs, Janine walked around the room, interacting with them about the problem. After giving them a substantial amount of time to work, she led a whole-class discussion, during which she called on students to share their solutions. She intentionally called on students who she knew from observing their work had different solutions. While she wanted her students to arrive at an answer that was defensible and accurate, her main purpose was to use these discussions to help them learn to reason for themselves.

Although it was slow going, these norms did gradually become part of the class culture during math. Some students readily embraced them. Anxious to contribute, these students became good at providing reasons for their answers and scrutinizing the approaches of others. Other students were reluctant for the first few months. It seemed to Janine that they understood the norms, but that they—mostly girls—were afraid of being wrong, so they only raised their hands when they were as close to certain as they could be. Much to her delight, even these students began to participate more consistently in the class discussions as the weeks wore on. It seemed that she could almost see the confidence of the students grow as they ventured into the class discussions and met some success.

Overall, Janine was impressed with how seriously this group of six-year-olds took their responsibilities as members of the class and with how sophisticated their conversation became. She was not surprised that a few students, whose behavior was inconsistent during the class, tended to float in and out of the discussions, being highly engaged one day and crawling on the floor or scribbling in their journals the next. She also had two students who wanted to be in control of the conversation all the time. She made efforts to help these students participate in the discussions productively—sometimes helping a student prepare a solution to present to the others, other times explicitly reminding a student that "an important part of doing math in this class is figuring out whether other people's solutions make sense." She found that many problems with student behavior could be addressed by taking the students and their ideas very seriously, as they, in turn, seemed to take themselves and their work seriously. She viewed these problems as a matter of helping the students learn new classroom norms.

About eight weeks into the school year, Janine began to notice that three students were not picking up on the class norms as well as the others. They seemed to be confronted by barriers that she did not understand. They paid attention during class and worked hard on individual tasks, but could not seem to figure out how to contribute to the discussions. All three frequently raised their hands in response to Janine's questions or invitations to respond to other students, but when she called on them, they sat silently. It was as if they could not find the words to explain things that Janine thought they understood from having worked with them one-on-one. They had the most trouble responding to "why" questions. Even when they could give an answer or say that they disagreed with someone else's answer, they could not say why.

These three students perplexed Janine. She believed that they were as capable as other students in the class. But they did not seem to be catching on to how to participate in the mathematical conversations. Their lack of progress concerned Janine because she believed that communicating one's ideas was an important mathematical ability that they needed to develop. Furthermore, the mathematical conversations the class had were a primary vehicle for the students' mathematical learning. The more they were part of the conversation, the greater number of opportunities they had to learn. What made Janine even more uneasy was that these three students, Jackson, LaTisha, and Dante, were all African-American children who were bused to the school from the inner city.

Janine had been trying to figure out new ways to help these three students for a few weeks, but now, as she gazed outside, she was struggling in her mind to justify her efforts to Delpit, the author of the article she had just finished. In the article, "The Silenced Dialogue: Power and Pedagogy in Educating Other People's Children," Delpit (1988) suggested that progressive pedagogical approaches can be disabling to African-

American students. She contrasted teaching approaches that are very directive and behavioral to those in which the teacher's control is less explicit and the children are given more intellectual autonomy. She acknowledged that many White educators saw the latter, "progressive" approaches as ways to empower students as thinkers and learners. However, Delpit was concerned that such approaches tended to leave Black children even further out of the picture because they required patterns of interaction that were unfamiliar to them. She referred to these patterns of interaction as the language of "the culture of power." These patterns included ways of communicating shared by the dominant culture that most White, middle-class children learn in their homes but that most Black children from lower economic classes do not. As Delpit put it, "adherents of process approaches to writing create situations in which students ultimately find themselves held accountable for knowing a set of rules about which no one has ever directly informed them" (p. 287). Reading these words made Janine stop short. She saw the faces of Jackson, LaTisha, and Dante, hands raised, but not knowing what to say.

As she looked out the window, Janine began to question her own pedagogical stance. Was she one of those liberal educators Delpit's argument implicated? Looking back down at the page, she reread: "Many liberal educators hold that the primary goal for education is for children to become autonomous, to develop fully who they are in the classroom setting without having arbitrary, outside standards forced upon them" p. 285). This description seemed to fit perfectly with what she was working hard to do in her class. What made her question these goals was Delpit's claim that this was not enough for children of color. Parents of these children, the article stressed, "want to ensure that the school provides their children with discourse patterns, interactional styles, and spoken and written language codes that will allow them success in the larger society" (p. 285), and it is the responsibility of the teacher to explicitly teach these to students who don't learn them at home. Janine fully agreed with the idea that she needed to help her students learn how to participate in the culture of power. In fact, her aim in fostering mathematical discussion was to help all of her students learn to think and develop ways of communicating about their ideas. What made her uncomfortable was that Delpit seemed to be saying that she needed to help African-American students develop these abilities through direct instruction.

The idea of directly telling students how to act or what they needed to do made Janine uncomfortable because it seemed opposite to what she believed about learning. She was convinced that students learned through using prior knowledge and experience to make meaning of new experiences. It seemed to her that students would gain more meaning of ways to participate in conversation through taking part in them than they would through being told how.

But, what about her three African-American students? They did not seem to be learning these skills through doing. Janine began to wonder whether the learning theory that guided her teaching was culturally grounded. Did it only apply to White middle-class people? Although she did not explicitly address theories of learning, Delpit had something to say about culture and the role of the teacher. Delpit provided several examples from research and her own experience that indicated that Black children learn in their homes to look to teachers as authorities and are much more accustomed to receiving direct instructions from authority figures. She contrasted this to the "veiled" commands used in middle-class, White cultures where a child might be asked, "Would you like to sit down now?" when the intent is to communicate to the child to sit down. Children in this culture know how this language works. But African-American children who are not part of this culture generally do not. Reading this prompted Janine to wonder whether these three students did not have the cultural tools to make sense of how or what she was asking them to learn. Perhaps these students did not have the interpretive tools they needed.

Janine took a deep breadth and sighed out loud. Once again, her eyes dropped down to the page. After reading and rereading this article, she was convinced that she needed to do something differently. But what? Did Delpit have a valid argument? Should she change her pedagogical approach for the entire class? If so, in what ways and to what extent? Or should she provide Jackson, LaTisha, and Dante with some form of direct instruction on these cultural norms? If so, when and how? How would doing so affect the community she was trying to nurture? Were there other students that she had not noticed who may have been facing similar struggles? Janine felt she had a new perspective on her teaching and her students, but no answers.

REFERENCE

Delpit, L. (1988). The silenced dialogue: Power and pedagogy in educating other people's children. *Harvard Educational Review, 58*(3), 280–298.

Case 3

Teachers' Attitudes Toward ESL Students and Programs

Mary Anne Schmidt

The primary aim of teaching English as a Second Language (ESL) is to give students a linguistic foundation for successful inclusion in mainstream classrooms. This case summarizes the dilemmas confronting Sarah Townsend, an ESL teacher at Hawthorne Jr. High, and describes her efforts to get ESL students fully incorporated into classrooms as accepted participants. While the case is based on interviews with Sarah and her faculty peers, some of the information is also derived from the author's observations. Part A presents background information about Hawthorne and about Sarah as well as different teachers' beliefs and attitudes toward the students in ESL. Part B describes the attitudes of two groups of teachers toward the ESL program: those who did not want an ESL program and those who thought the program should be self-contained. Part C describes a group of teachers who were somewhat receptive to working with Sarah to accommodate ESL students in their classes, but who saw it as a struggle.

PART A

Hawthorne is located in a highly diverse, working-class, urban neighborhood. About 20% of the school's population is non-English speaking or limited English speaking. ESL students attending Hawthorne live within the school's boundaries; no students are bused into the program. Classes in ESL were initiated in the school district about five years ago, so the program at Hawthorne is fairly new. Mechanisms for identifying, testing, and providing services for the students are still being developed. The school district is currently being audited by the Office of Civil Rights, so Hawthorne is under pressure to correct any problems in its ESL program.

Sarah began her career as a social worker in a small school district in the Midwest. She worked mainly with children with learning disabilities and emotional problems. After five years, she moved to the West coast and earned her teaching certificate in elementary education. There, she taught in a bilingual setting; instruction was in Spanish, with ESL taught three times per week. When she moved to her present location, Sarah started teaching ESL classes, which emphasize learning English rather than retaining the student's native language. Sarah finds that her various professional experiences have helped in dealing with diverse student populations.

When Sarah first arrived at Hawthorne over a year ago, there was no full-time ESL teacher. Students wandered in the halls and were tutored by untrained college students. Sarah organized ESL classes in science, social studies, and English. Students currently attend a maximum of four ESL classes per day; the remaining three periods must be in mainstream classrooms. This year, each ESL class averages about 10 students, with 34 students in all who are registered in the program. Because parents change jobs frequently or move due to rent increases, Sarah's program experiences a 50% turnover rate each year. Sarah estimates that she serves only 75% of the eligible students.

This year's ESL program consists entirely of students who are Mexican American or recent immigrants from Mexico. Since students in an ESL setting usually represent diverse nationalities and languages, this situation is atypical. The majority of Sarah's students this year have difficulty reading and writing in their native language as well as in English. According to Sarah, "the majority of students have come from situations where they have not been in school full time. As a result, their academic skills are not strong, even in Spanish. When these students are asked to do grade level work in English, the situation is ripe for failure. Most teachers, however, don't even realize that the students can't read because they assume that at this age students can read. There is a certain amount of hiding the students do because they don't want to be thought of as dumb."

Sarah also describes the students this year as unfamiliar with the procedures and expectations of the school's culture. Because copying another student's paper isn't prohibited in the cultures of many of the ESL students, she said, one person will often do the class work and pass it around. Students do not view their actions as cheating, although that is how the school culture interprets it. Teachers also complain because the students' behavior isn't "age appropriate"; for example, teachers complain that the students have difficulty remaining in their seats or concentrating for more than a few minutes.

Sarah notes that since all the students in the ESL program this year speak Spanish, they have formed a strong group identity. She says that they find it difficult to relate to people who don't speak their language. Sometimes it feels like a betrayal to speak English or to like someone who hasn't learned their language. Feelings of alienation and discrimination in mainstream classes exacerbate the group dynamics. According to Sarah, because the students feel most comfortable in the ESL classes, they resist full inclusion, even to the point of purposefully failing exit tests from the program.

PART B

Classroom teachers have widely varying opinions about what to do with ESL students. On one end of the spectrum, teachers think the ESL program is totally unwarranted. Two teachers that think students should be immersed in mainstream classes without any accommodation are Ted Hale and Denise Carter. Although neither one has students from Sarah's program in their classes, they strongly believe that the ESL program is detrimental to second language students. Mr. Hale asserted the following:

> These students should be immersed in English so they are forced to learn it. Letting them speak too much Spanish means the students won't work in English. ESL students shouldn't be allowed to speak Spanish in school at all, even in the halls. I think ESL students understand and speak more English than they admit. Once I was in the hall during class time and came across a group of ESL students talking to some other students. I heard these kids speaking in English. But when I asked everyone which class they belonged in, the Spanish speakers

pretended they didn't understand me and ran off laughing. These kids are getting special breaks because they pretend they don't understand English. Then they're disrespectful. They should just be put into regular classes and treated like everyone else.

Ms. Carter believes that some ESL students try harder than others to succeed:

A student from Poland, who had attended a Catholic school in his native country, moved into the school two years ago. When he began taking classes in the ESL program, he noticed how similar English is to the Latin he had taken in the Polish school. After a year, he started speaking English fluently. Now he's enrolled in the honors program. Teachers don't mind this kind of ESL student. It's the ones that don't try to learn that we object to.

Along with Mr. Hale, Ms. Carter believes that ESL students belong in regular classes and shouldn't be "pampered" with special programs. When asked how they would handle immersion students in their classes, both teachers replied that they would probably never see them since they only teach honors classes.

At the other end of the spectrum are faculty members who want ESL students segregated in a self-contained unit. Jeanne Dawson, a special education teacher at Hawthorne, is one of these. She has three students in her cluster unit who also attend Sarah's classes. Ms. Dawson has consulted with Sarah several times about providing appropriate material for the ESL students, but, according to Sarah, she is reluctant to reciprocate with information about how Sarah can deal with the behavioral disorders she encounters. Ms. Dawson explained her attitude as follows:

I'm not sure you want to know how I feel about ESL. I occasionally consult with Sarah to get materials my students can understand. But I don't see the need to help her because I'm not sure her program is useful in its present form. Yes, we need more ESL classes because these students aren't receiving adequate service; but mainstreaming ESL students isn't effective. Nonnatives can't learn English in school because they have no English skills in the first place. Besides, the students sluff and goof off in class when they don't understand. They should then be in their own class the entire day. After they can speak well, students should be put in regular academic classes full time. We need to work with the home environment as well. Most of these kids come from dysfunctional, illiterate homes with nonsupportive parents, and that translates into absenteeism, poor performance, and possible gang involvement. Students should also be taught English with their parents after school, using bilingual textbooks and materials.

Sarah reports that other teachers actively attempt to get ESL students out of their classrooms. She says that teachers make fun of the students' accents, refuse to allow them to speak Spanish, accuse them of cheating, and complain to the administration about their behavior problems. Sarah does acknowledge that ESL students can be challenging, but she is sympathetic to them when they're in classes where teachers do not want them and are unwilling to make any accommodations:

If I were put in a class where they were speaking a language I didn't understand and there were no clues to help me understand it, I would tune out, go to sleep, write letters, or see what kind of entertainment I could create for myself in the classroom. That's what happens in many of the classrooms where the students don't understand English. Even students who understand English but who resent the class or resent the teacher tend to be troublemakers and get into all sorts of things. They feel that the teacher is picking on them, and they end up with a lot of referrals to the office for behavior, a lot of detentions, and often are suspended or excluded from the school. Even a student who's really motivated and wants to do well has to struggle very hard to be successful. There isn't enough support in the other classes for them; they really have to put in the extra effort if they want to succeed.

These teachers have made Sarah's professional life more difficult. Last year, they persuaded the administration to move the ESL students to a smaller room with no windows. They also pressured the administration to take ESL students out of the mainstream classes and keep them with Sarah all day. Sarah reminded the administration that it was unlawful to discriminate against ESL students through inadequate facilities or limited opportunities. Faced with the legal ramifications of their actions, the administration restored Sarah's classroom and suspended plans to segregate ESL students. However, Sarah's forceful stand earned her political enemies on the faculty.

PART C

Three teachers on Hawthorne's faculty are receptive to mainstreaming ESL students and have included them in classes with varying degrees of success. Ellen Cook, who teaches English, shared the following observations:

> I try a lot of different things to help ESL students in my class. First, I talk to Sarah to find out what I can expect of a particular student. Then, I will let a student do his or her book report in Spanish. Sarah grades it since I don't speak Spanish, and I put the grade in with the others. I like to take advantage of the diversity of my classes. I let the students tell about the countries they come from. Sometimes the other students make fun of their accents, but I won't allow that. I also come from a different country, so I know what it's like to speak differently from the majority.

> Sadly, I think hiding behind the ESL program becomes like a game. I'm not sure it's helpful to treat the students differently. I wouldn't do away with the program—especially for monolinguals—but maybe we've swung the pendulum too far in order to avoid lawsuits. Students seem to know all the ways to get something for nothing. I think there needs to be stricter guidelines for mainstreaming these students. In the long run, they'll have an advantage by being bilingual speakers.

> I'm frustrated with several aspects of teaching ESL students. The success of students in my class depends on their motivation. Some of the students really try: They participate in class and do their homework. I won't neglect a student who will work. Others don't bring anything to class and do nothing, no matter what I try. They have a high detention rate because of tardies, absences, and behavior problems. I can tell that some students understand what's going on, but they manipulate the system. They won't do the work if they can get other students to do it for them. You have to look at ESL students as individuals, but generally they try to get away with not understanding, even though they do.

Jacqueline White is a veteran teacher at Hawthorne. She currently has several ESL students in her Family Studies class:

> I don't mind having ESL students in my classes. That's a good thing since many of them end up here because I don't have what's considered a strictly "academic" curriculum. I set up my classes so that I

can give a lot of individual help to those who need it. I pair up English speakers with non-English speakers so they can help each other. I also let the students work in groups. This can be hard on the students who want to work. The ESL students can get pretty noisy when they're together. That's a little uncomfortable for me, but if I don't let them work together, they don't work much at all. They usually want one student to do the work, then they'll copy from that paper. I don't grade ESL students any differently than the others. By the same token, I won't fail any student unless he or she doesn't put forth any effort. ESL students tend to get restless when I lecture. Sometimes I think that's due to behavior disorders rather than language difficulties. I just deal with it. For me, getting material that the ESL students can understand is my biggest problem.

We need an ESL program for students to get basic English skills, but they should be mainstreamed as soon as they understand any English. But please don't put them in the system until they're ready. Ideally, ESL students would have an aide with them in the classroom like the special education students have. We also need more teachers for ESL—Sarah is expected to do too much by herself. I know we need to find a way to educate ESL students and get them into regular classrooms, but the current programs seem pretty ineffective the way they're carried out.

Sarah thinks that Jill Finch, who teaches reading and English, is the most successful example of how ESL students can be included in a mainstream classroom. Ms. Finch described her approach this way:

I cut ESL students a lot of slack. I let them work with students who speak their language. My curriculum is oriented around projects that involve a variety of successful outcomes. I try to make my classroom a safe place to learn. I also give students a break on their grades when they're trying to achieve. For example, if a student is close to monolingual and earns a "D" in my class, I'll usually give him or her a "B." As students become more proficient in English, I determine their grade accordingly. I recognize that most ESL students come from the lowest socioeconomic class and therefore lack some of the advantages available to other students. Many of them have had few previous educational experiences, either because of a scarcity of money to send them to school or because they have had to quit school to find a job and help support the family. When you're illiterate in both a native language and in the school culture, you lack many of the skills that would make learning a second language easier.

When Sarah first came to Hawthorne, I questioned her about her curriculum and methodology. I was concerned because there wasn't a good program for the ESL students, and they were really suffering. Sarah knows what she's doing, and I support her efforts in the school. Of course, each student determines his or her ultimate success. Students who just don't care won't succeed in any program; but those who are motivated will benefit from this ESL program.

Because of the initial chaos in the ESL program, teachers had originally refused to discuss ESL issues or consider ways to better accommodate ESL students in their classrooms. Now that the program is more orderly, teachers come to Sarah for help. Some are looking for bilingual materials that ESL students can complete during their classes. Others want information about specific students. A few ask for suggestions that will include ESL students in more active learning. As Sarah explains:

It would have been impossible to come in as a new person and tell teachers what to do because it would not have been received well. When they saw that the program was better organized and that students were under control, some became more willing to talk about the students and to seek some help with teaching them. Now, giving suggestions is easier to do because the teachers know me better and they're more familiar with what's happening in the ESL class. Many teachers have seen a lot of progress in their students, so they're more open to looking at how they can be more helpful as well.

Case 4

Overcoming Cultural Misunderstandings

as told by Sione Ika

This case explores a Pacific Islander's life in the United States. His experiences as a college student and as a high school teacher afford insights into cultural assimilation. Part A recounts Sione's college experiences and his first few years of teaching in a rural village in the western part of the United States. In Part B, Sione describes an experience he had when he was a high school band teacher with an American Indian student. In Part C, Sione discusses why Pacific Islanders can have a difficult time adjusting to American culture, especially school culture. He also describes what he has done as a teacher and as member of his community to help students from minority cultures succeed in school.

PART A

Eighteen years ago, I left the Pacific Islands to come to the United States to attend a university because there was no college in my homeland. I came with the idea that to gain an education is a great thing. Anybody with a degree from a university, especially an American university, was expected to come back and do just about anything. In fact, I was not thinking of going back to teach. I was thinking of going back to help my village in any way I could.

At the university I spread myself a little too thin. Part of my problem was that I was interested in a lot of things and, to be most useful back home, I thought that I should know a little bit about everything. So I did not have a focus. I majored in political science and minored in English, and because I was not particularly strong in math, I took a lot of math classes. My last two terms I took music classes. I knew that when I went back to my village they'd expect me to know everything. They'd have me teach the choir and the band, as well as English, math, and science. You see, I would be the only person with a degree in the village.

I finally graduated, but I did not feel ready to go back. I did not feel confident. I decided to go to graduate school and was accepted into a master's program in political science. I also took band, basically because I love football. I couldn't afford the tickets, so this was a way to see the games for free. After I took my first graduate political science class, I knew that I was in the wrong field. So I changed my degree to music. I studied music for about four years and got certified to teach it. Somehow I felt natural in that field, especially when I was conducting.

At the university I was different in a lot of ways from the other students. When I started the master's program I was still learning English and I had three kids and a wife. Also, the cultural thing was still very difficult for me, even though I did not see it at that time. I think some of the things I did back then were probably not acceptable in the dominant culture. I look back now and think, "Oh I did that, oh my gosh." If someone did such things in front of me now I would be offended. I remember thinking, "If only I knew what should be the right thing to do." I did such things out of ignorance. I did not know. Maybe people were offended, but they tried not to show it. They tolerated me somehow. I remember many professors who reached out and really helped me.

After graduation I was ready to go back to my village. But there was a monopoly back there—they would pick and choose the people they wanted and tell you when you got there what you would teach. I asked them for more specifics about what I would do in the high school that I was going to teach in, but they only said, "Oh, just come on back." I did not like this situation. Then, a couple of my university professors helped me locate a job here. Even though they knew I was not at the top of the class, they had a lot of confidence in me. That was something that really touched me. They knew I couldn't speak the language well—I still can't, I'm still working on it—and they knew that I was struggling because I had to switch majors and had a family, but at the end of the year they told me they would recommend me for a job. In fact, it was just one phone call to a principal who had an opening, and I had a job.

I taught band in a small high school in Hillsdale, a rural village a few hours away from a city. I stayed there for three years, and then I saw on TV the gang problems among Pacific Islanders in the city. There were no Pacific Islanders in Hillsdale, so I decided to move to the city. I wanted to help my people out and I had overextended myself as a teacher. In Hillsdale I said yes to everything. I said yes to every parade, even in the winter. I said yes to every football and basketball game, even when it meant 7 hours of traveling after school on weeknights. Sometimes we would not get home until 2:00 in the morning, and school started at 7:30.

It was only during my last year in Hillsdale, when I was preparing to lead the summer band, as I had every year, that they asked me what I wanted for teaching in the summer. I was too shy to ask for anything. I said, "You just give me whatever you want." They gave me more than I would have ever expected; it was beyond my imagination. Only later did I find out that other teachers who did the same thing were getting three or four times as much money as I was. I had never asked for anything extra because in my culture you just said "yes," even if you didn't get paid for it. If I'd known this culture better, I would have asked to be paid from the beginning and probably would have gotten it. In my culture I was taught to be thankful for whatever I get, which is okay. It has helped me, but yet I look back now and say, "Well, I could have had this or that if only I had asked."

In my culture you are taught to be very humble. Where I come from, a king is in charge, and whatever he says is always right, and the nobles are always right, and the church leaders are always right. We were born to be commoners and always say yes to the nobles. As children we are taught to obey always. Other adults, besides our parents, could discipline us. A good example of this happened when I was young. A bus would drive by every day and I'd cross the street very close to the bus. One day the bus driver stopped the bus and got out, found a stick and whipped me three times. My mother stepped out and said "Thank you" to him. I still remember that. Even now I'll never cross too close to a bus. The whole idea behind what happened is that the community works together. The Pacific Islander kids here in the States are having trouble, I think, because all of a sudden they have so much freedom to do what they want compared to what they were used to. Here in the States I still struggle a lot if I disagree with something. Because of my upbringing it will take a lot of courage for me to complain about something.

When I moved to the city, I took an ESL job that had just opened up in a high school. For the last five years I've been teaching ESL and social studies, and last year I taught a music class. Sometimes I have students from four or five different cultures and languages all in the same ESL class. I can't speak their languages either, and I am learning English just like they are.

PART B

Although it was a long time ago, I still think back to my three years in Hillsdale. There's one student I will never forget. He was the only American Indian in the band. I still feel guilty about him. He was the best in the band the year before I taught it, and he knew it. I could see the happiness on his face when the year began. He loved the fact that he was number 1. He didn't say anything, but on the first day of school he grabbed his horn and he sat where the number 1 person would be sitting. I would never have done that. Even if I was number 1, I would wait.

In my experience, in band, you try to compete with each other. I thought that was the only way to get kids to go home and practice. In school back in my village it was all cooperation. But when you step into school here, it's competition from the very first day. When I took band in college, they challenged me and I became number 1. The band teacher was so impressed with me and I felt so good. I've never felt so good ever in band.

Well, in Hillsdale, I had all the students take a test. He was the best, so he stayed in the number 1 seat. Then, after a month, I said, "Okay, let's have a challenge. You challenge number 1, and if you do better, then you'll move up and number 1 will move down." Then I tried to have the rest of the group beat him, and one of them did. So the American Indian student moved down to the number 2 seat. I can still see his face. I realized that he didn't like that. I thought, "He's not happy, so he'll go home and practice." But with each challenge he went down some more in the seating. He didn't show that he was upset about it, but you could tell that he was not happy. He would start coming late, and his interest in band in general just kind of dwindled. After a couple of weeks he quit the band. I saw him later, but I didn't know what to say. I felt really bad and then I kind of thought, "Well, I blew it, so just be quiet and don't do it again." If I knew then how he felt about competition—knowing then what I know now—I would have done things very differently. He would have been a very valuable member of the band. But I didn't know, and I wasn't sensitive enough to find out, and I didn't have the training in multicultural education to help me.

I was devastated when he dropped out. I could see myself in him. We were the only minorities in the band, he and I, and I had lost him. I still blame myself for that. Later he moved to another school in the next village, so I never saw him again. I don't know where he went, or whether that made a difference in his life. He was very smart. I think he'll survive.

PART C

When I moved to the city, the first thing I did was take a multicultural class, the first one offered in the district. I've learned a lot since then. Now everything I do is to help the minority kids and their families to at least know what is expected of them in the United States. This is, I think, my biggest challenge. I'm also a licensed realtor because I've heard of many Pacific Islanders who have suddenly lost their homes. The bank had been writing to them, reminding them of their obligations, but they did not always understand the language or the ramifications of bills because where we come from, there are no bills. I think my house in the village was the only one that had electricity and therefore bills, but that was only the last year I was there. Here there are all these new things going on, and I think that's why a lot of the minorities are struggling. A lot of their homes are lost because they don't know beforehand about things like bills. So even when I teach, I try to give some information to the students to take to their parents. I didn't lose a home, but it's hard to see your people get smacked in the face before they learn.

In the schools here, most of the teaching advocates individualism. The teachers discourage group work. I suspect that that is why some Pacific Islanders join gangs. They want to form groups because they think they are becoming part of a trusting community. This is a big part of our culture. We were taught early on to rely on each other. The American concept of standing on your own is totally different. In my culture, people would be willing to accept any offer of help from anyone. It would be very tacky to refuse an offer. Such a person would be considered too proud.

As a teacher, I have learned that it is important to accept new students the way they are, especially when it comes to language. It is from their first language that students learn a second language. Sometimes in this culture, students go to a classroom, and the message they get on the first day is, "Change to English, which is better." Some students are confused when teachers send messages that English is the best language and at the same time tell the class, "We have a person from another culture in our class so now we'll learn about that culture." I would suggest that teachers use volunteers to authenticate the child's first language. Students will feel better about school instead of feeling inferior because they grew up in a "wrong" culture.

When ESL students are encouraged by the school system to change their language in order to survive, the relationship can deteriorate between the parents and the child. The children start taking charge. They are the ones communicating at the grocery store and with the dentist, doctor, and others because their parents cannot. When the parents lose control of their children at home, there are more problems at school. Teachers must let the children know that even though they speak English, there is still a place for their native language in their home and that their native language is valued.

What I've learned is that if I speak a little bit of somebody's language, they'll feel more accepted. That's one of the things I've tried to do now as a teacher. I've tried to incorporate some of the different languages into the curriculum to help students learn the lesson I am teaching. My students are very responsive to me that way. Part of the reason why I felt bad when I was going to school is that my language was never accepted: "It is too bad you have a different language. Now learn a better language."

But it still hurts to think back to the American Indian student in Hillsdale. My university professors approached things differently with me than I did with him. Those professors reached out, and I think that made a difference in where I am now. I didn't reach out to him. It is a good reminder to me.

Case 5

Tragedies and Turnarounds

as told by Linda Nesi

"Tragedies and Turnarounds" takes place in an inner-city Chapter I school, where classrooms are seriously overcrowded and where most of the students come from low-income homes. Many of the students have reading difficulties and some have been identified as having behavior disorders, learning disabilities, or mental retardation, and are eligible for special education or Chapter I classes. The case focuses on one student who had been considered a behavioral problem throughout his schooling. As you read the case, you will see what his fifth grade teacher, Linda Nesi, did to enable him to succeed in her classroom. As a result, he became a peer helper in cooperative groups and a valued student in the gifted and talented program. But, unfortunately, good beginnings do not always end well.

I came to West End Elementary after my first teaching job, which was at a residential school for juvenile delinquents called Canyon School. I guess you could say that at West End I taught earlier versions of the students I had encountered at Canyon. Poverty, neglect, and abuse will do that to kids. Anyway, I came to love the troubled kids at Canyon, and I brought that love with me to West End.

West End was average in size for an elementary school, with a population that was ethnically diverse. The students' families were overwhelmingly low income and single parent, with a high transient rate. When moms couldn't make the rent, they moved. Often they moved back in a few months when they couldn't make the rent again. So some kids went in and out of the school four or five times a year, in a revolving door fashion. Their comings and goings really had an effect on the classroom dynamics. We also had a lot of mothers with drug problems who, when they came to the school, were incoherent when we tried to talk to them about their children. So we did a lot of referrals to protective services, which meant that some of the kids would be pulled out of school and placed in foster care for a week at a time. Then they would be returned home and back at school. So you can see that our kids were either survivors or wrecks.

The classes at West End were always large, so having 39 students in my fifth grade class was not unusual. We started out the year with about 26 students per class, but in January the district cut back on teachers and combined grades. As a result, I had a lot of concern about classroom control and was able to do less in-depth teaching. In addition to my 39, I also had 3 students with mental retardation, who came into my room for reading from the self-contained unit. Of my 39 students, about 10 had learning disabilities and were pulled out for portions of the day for reading and math in the resource class. Another 10 were Chapter I students, who got pulled out for reading during science and social studies. Chapter I and resource both supplemented and supplanted what I did in the classroom. The teachers would come and say, "What are you doing at this point? How can we help you?" They would find materials on the same topic, but at a lower level. In reading, I'm not sure what they did, but I assume it was basic phonics.

The kids really didn't like going to resource or Chapter I. I think that's because they felt labeled. The teachers in these programs would stand at the door to get the students' attention and somebody else in the class would say, "Hey, so-and-so, your resource teacher is here!" or "There's your Chapter I teacher!" The kids would slowly and reluctantly get out of their seats and get their things. I think inwardly they felt inferior. Lots of times, they'd say, "I don't want to go," or "Can I just stay here?" I'd say, "Just be glad you are getting some extra help. Not everybody is going to get it." I'd try to turn it into a positive thing, but really I think it's better for everybody's self-esteem if you just have inclusive education.

I like to think that the way I teach fits with inclusion. I like to do cooperative learning. I like to experiment with alternative assessments because sometimes kids will look at a paper-and-pencil test and not know what it's saying. So instead, I'll have them work in pairs and put everything we've learned on a game board. Or, we'll play "Jeopardy," or they'll set up experiments as a group and I'll walk around and quiz them. I don't like to use the content-area textbooks. They are the most boring things in the world to me. And, if they are boring to me, can you imagine what they must be like for students? I like to do hands-on learning. I want kids to do the things the kids in the pictures in the science textbooks are doing. I want kids to have choices.

There was one student, Tommy, who really sums up the challenge—and the rewards—of reaching these goals. Tommy was a very bright kid who, I think, was never challenged in school. So he became a real behavior problem every year at West End from first grade on. He would bother other kids, get into their business, get physical with them. Of course, he did hardly any class work, and he was lucky to get Ds. The administrators tried to refer him to the behavior disorder program in another school, but it was full and they had to wait for an opening. The teachers really didn't like him, except for his third grade teacher, who just loved him to death. She really loved those kinds of kids. She tried a lot of interventions with him, but still nothing worked.

In fourth grade, his teacher put him in a carrel—like the ones in the library. Basically, it was a big wooden box with a chair pulled up to one side. But that didn't work either. He'd be popping up, reaching around, touching kids, and getting into their stuff. He drove everybody, including the teacher, crazy. Now in that class, they did worksheets and workbooks, and read round-robin style from their textbooks and basal readers. So putting Tommy in that carrel probably sounded like a great idea to that teacher because everybody was supposed to be separated anyway. Then, in fifth grade, he was assigned to me.

When Tommy came into my room the very first day, I said, "Hey, I'm really glad to have you here." And I meant it. I had gotten to know him a little over the last year, when his fourth grade teacher would kick him out of the room. He'd come to my classroom for time out. He'd sit in the back of the room, and try to get everybody's attention. But I'd tell everyone to ignore him, and for short periods, we'd do all right. That first day, I told him, "I'm glad to have you in my room, but I don't want you in a carrel. In fact, I'm going to refuse to put you in a carrel."

"Well, I want one," he said.

"Well, you aren't going to have one in here. We sit at tables of four, and you'll be part of a group. You have to be a team player when you come in here. That's just the way it is. That's the way I set up my classroom."

"Well, I'm not going to be a team player," was his response.

"Let's give it a try."

It lasted about a week. He was into everybody's business at his own table, the table behind him, and the table to the side of him. With his mom's support, I tried different interventions over the next few months. I allowed him to think of plans of how he could get along in the class, and I was clear and consistent in my expectations. At first nothing seemed to work, but eventually, after the other students wouldn't talk to him when he was disruptive and made it clear that they would not accept his behavior, he came to me and said, "I like this class. You do some fun stuff. I wouldn't mind working if I could do more writing and if I could draw sometimes."

"Okay," I said. "There's lots of time for writing. You do everything that's asked of you and when you have free time, you can draw too."

Well, it was like a whole turnaround. He ended up that year writing and illustrating probably the best stories I've ever seen. His mom was just thrilled. She would come in for conferences, or she would just drop in, and say, "I can't believe what you've done for him."

I said, "I didn't do anything. He chose. It was his choice to do this."

The turnaround also came in his relationships with the other kids. For example, as the year progressed, Tommy became a real help to Carlinda, a very low achiever who was a real social butterfly, always off talking and not working. He got frustrated with her sometimes though, because I think he saw a lot of himself in her. It was as though he felt, "Hey, I've turned myself around here. You can too." Tommy also worked with another boy at his table, Jose, who wanted to learn and tried so hard, but really struggled. Jose would come up to me and say, "I don't get this." I'd sit down and try to explain it to him, and he'd walk away saying, "Okay, I understand." But I knew he didn't. So I would pull Tommy up to my desk and say, "Look, this is what Jose is having a problem with. Can you think of a better way to explain it to him? Evidently, I'm not doing a very good job." Tommy would go back to the table, and I'd see those two getting their little heads together and pretty soon, Jose would say, "Oh, that's how it works!" It didn't happen every time, but enough times that Jose was starting to catch on. The other little girl at the table was homeless, living out of a car with her mother. Many times she wouldn't show up for school. Tommy didn't have a chance to get to know her well because she was gone so much.

So, all three of the other kids at Tommy's table were very low achieving. With a class full of low achievers, I really came to rely on his help there. Of course, every once in a while, he'd still have his moments and I'd have to remind him of the deal we made. But overall, he was the glue that held that table together. I would see him working with the kids, listening to them, commenting back to them. He became like another teacher in my classroom.

For example, we did a lot of cooperative learning in science. Because it's important to me that all the kids get their hands on the equipment we're using, I spend a lot of my own money. For the electricity unit, I hand each kid a battery, a light bulb, and a wire. I show them how to strip both ends of the wire, and then I say, "Okay, now make this bulb light up." "How?" they'd say.

"You're going to have to show me how. You're going to have to be the scientist and figure it out. Try something, and if it doesn't work, try something else. It's called trial and error."

Well, of course, Tommy quickly figured out how to do it. The kids at his table were all looking at him, asking, "How did you do that?" He said, "I'm not going to tell you, but I'm going to watch you. If you are starting to do it right, I'll let you know."

So he made them work through it, just like I was working with the other groups. He was listening to me, and saying the same things I was saying: "You have to make a complete circuit. You have to make it so it all hooks together so it's one thing. Nope, you're on the wrong track. Start off doing what you did before. That's it, now you are on the right track." There was just a lot of support and encouragement going on, and everyone in the group was happy when they all finally got it.

Tommy's grades went from Ds to As and Bs. One day, I said to him, "You are so talented. How would you like to go to the accelerated learning program once or twice a week?"

"Me! Go there?" was his response.

"Sure, you have everything you need to be there. Do you want to try? Shall I talk to the teacher?"

He said, "Yeah."

So I talked to the teacher and she said, "Oh, I know about him. He's a real behavior problem."

"You know what?" I said, "If it doesn't work, send him back to me. But just give him a chance." As it turned out, he was probably the best kid in that pull-out program. The teacher just loved him. He had all these great ideas. He kind of ended up being the class leader. Well, he certainly ended up being *my* class leader.

EPILOGUE

I left West End Elementary the next year, and I haven't seen Tommy since. Things might have been different if I had stayed, but I chose to leave. I saw a teacher I had worked closely with at West End the other day, and I asked about Tommy. She said in sixth grade he went into a classroom where there was no discussion, no cooperative learning, no direct teaching. It was, "Here is your book, do your page." The classroom was always very quiet. The kids would just do their work, and then they would go up and get it corrected. Then they would go on to the next worksheet and get that corrected. That was for all the subjects, all day long.

She said, "You know, after you left the school and Tommy went into sixth grade, it was the worst year he ever had."

Case 6

Small Victories: Pedro's Story

Carminda Ranches, with Judy Zone

Carminda, a preservice teacher, tutored Pedro, a 14-year-old eighth grader, as part of a college course on the assessment and instruction of reading and writing difficulties. The case is based on her work with Pedro and her interviews and observations in his home and school. Her reflections (Part A) capture the life of an adolescent who reads at the second grade level and spends most of the school day in a resource classroom. In Part B, Carminda describes her approach to teaching him reading and the small victories possible through careful instruction, even in a difficult situation.

PART A: PEDRO'S BACKGROUND
AND SCHOOL EXPERIENCE

When I talked to the head resource teacher at Van Buren Middle School about finding a student to tutor, she recommended Pedro. She told me that he was a good kid who could use some help. He was also a student who never handed in any homework. His mother had once told the teacher that

Pedro was embarrassed and ashamed, almost to the point of tears, because he couldn't read his science book. When I first met Pedro, I had a hard time imagining him crying over science. He's such a tough-looking kid, with slicked back hair and long baggy pants. He kind of struts when he walks and he writes in "gang script," the kind of writing you see in graffiti on walls. His teachers told me he was a real troublemaker last year, but they'd gotten him into a program for at-risk youth and now he really seems to be avoiding the gang scene. Because Pedro doesn't want his little brother involved in a gang, he's trying to stay out of one himself.

Pedro, a Chicano, lives with his mom, her boyfriend, and his little brother, who is seven. His parents were separated when Pedro was five, and his mom says that was really hard on him. She says Pedro would like to spend time with his dad, but his father is never around, and that really frustrates Pedro. She also says she doesn't allow him to express his anger at home, so she thinks sometimes a lot of what he does at school reflects his anger. Pedro doesn't seem so angry this year at school, though. His teachers say he is much more personable than last year, but that he is also very withdrawn. He won't participate in class unless the teacher pushes him to say something. I think he thinks participating isn't in keeping with his cool image. For example, he refuses to read out loud in class. Granted, he reads on the second grade level, but there are lots of kids in his resource class who are equally poor readers. But I believe Pedro thinks that if he stumbles over a word, the other "wannabe" tough kids will laugh at him. So most of the time he sits slumped at the desk with his head in his hand. Once in a while he's on task, if it perks his interest, like working on the computer.

Pedro tells me that he doesn't like school, that it is boring to him. But considering his classes, I don't blame him for feeling this way. Except for science, which includes students from all the tracks, he's with the same students in resource classes for English, reading, math, and history. From what I've seen, there's not a lot going on in the resource classes, and the teachers' expectations of the students are really low. For example, in his English class, they do spelling workbooks and copy vocabulary words and definitions from the board. Occasionally, they do some writing. Once they were doing an acrostic poem for Halloween. The teacher had written the word "zombie" vertically on the board and was asking for student input to fill out each line. When they got to "O," somebody said, "Old Billy's face." She asked, "Do you want 'face' or 'fate'?" "Face! Face!" they all called out. She put "fate" on the board. She's a nice lady, but she wants to be in control. This story is ironic because when you talk to her, she insists that she wants to build the self-esteem of her resource students and to give them successful experiences. She gave this example of what she considered a successful experience for Pedro: The class was assigned to write a report on an endangered species. Pedro's was on the bald eagle. They were both very proud of the paper because it was so long, a full page in length. But most of it was plagiarized, straight out of the encyclopedia.

Then there is his reading class. Occasionally, the teacher will bring in short expository pieces for students to read in class with comprehension questions at the end. One time the teacher took students to the library and said, "Everyone pick out a novel." But, Pedro hasn't read any of his novel for months, except for what we've read together in tutoring. Another time, they had a lesson on apostrophes. I knew Pedro had done really poorly on it because the teacher had asked me to give him the test during our tutoring time. When I talked to her about it, she said, "Oh, Pedro did pretty well on his test. He didn't get many answers right, but his handwriting was much neater."

His resource history class doesn't have a set of texts, so the teacher photocopies each chapter from a history textbook for the students. The problem is that the students don't receive most of the text aids, like the table of contents, the maps, and the glossary. Once, in a tutoring session, I showed Pedro the actual text. He was amazed by all the parts he had never seen. In class, the history teacher goes through each chapter and tells them what to highlight on their copies, gives them a set of questions, and tells them where to find the answers in the chapter. Then she tests them on the questions and is astounded that they do so poorly.

Science, Pedro's only regular education class, is really hard for him. The content is difficult and there's a lot of homework. To make matters worse, he has to miss this class every Friday afternoon. His little brother has a half-day of school on Friday and Pedro's mom needs him at home to baby-sit because she can't afford to pay someone.

So basically, Pedro just scrapes by, lucky to get a C even in his resource classes. I'd like to believe that Pedro would be happier in an inclusive classroom because, in my opinion, the curriculum of the regular track at Van Buren Middle School is more interesting and the students are treated more like people who can think. Last year, in fact, the school attempted to integrate all the resource kids into all the content area classes. When I asked one of his teachers how Pedro had done in that program, she said, "Well, he didn't flunk out, but he wasn't a superstar either." Frankly, I think it's great he didn't flunk out. And I don't think he should be expected to be a superstar in regular class if he's been in resource since second grade. The school scrapped the program after 1 year because the teachers complained so much. They hadn't received any training in inclusion, and it was just too hard for them to accommodate the needs of the resource students in the regular classroom.

PART B: PROGRESS IN READING

Based on an informal reading inventory administered at the beginning of tutoring, I estimated that Pedro was reading at about the second grade level. The few answers he got correct on the comprehension questions came pretty much from his background knowledge rather than the text. When I preview the hard words with him before he reads a passage, he often miscues on them when he's reading. But, then, he also miscues on words I know he knows. His miscues are mostly whole word substitutions or nonsense word substitutions. It's like he sounds out the first letter of a word and makes the rest up.

I think that Pedro reads too fast. When he reads out loud for me during tutoring sessions, he never pauses at a period. And, when he comes to a word he doesn't know, he just says anything so he doesn't have to break his pace to figure it out. However, once in a great while when he miscues, he does go back and reread and self-correct. And once, when I was using a cloze procedure with him, he found a typo and said, "This doesn't make sense." So, I know that sometimes he does try to read for meaning. Pedro hasn't done much reading in his life. He has little idea how text, especially expository text, is structured. In his classes his teachers do nothing to prepare students to read, to activate their background knowledge, or to help them monitor their comprehension. Pedro needs all of these things. He also needs more experience with writing. The most I've ever seen him write was the top third of a page about a fight he almost got into over a jacket. But mostly, I want to keep Pedro interested. I'd like him to feel some control over his own learning.

One of the first things I did with Pedro in tutoring was to show him the actual history text. As I mentioned before, his resource teacher makes photocopies of the chapter they are studying because they don't have a classroom set of books. Pedro really liked looking at all the pictures and the maps. At the time they were studying the Revolutionary War, so we looked at a picture of the Boston Tea Party. "Tell me about this picture," I said.

"Well, there are people, and they're in a boat in the water. They are Indians," he volunteered.

"Well, they're not real Indians. They are White people dressed like Indians because they don't want their identities known."

"Why?'

To answer his question, I explained how the colonies were trying to break away from England. I told him that it was like when I went away to college—I wanted to break away from my parents. Finally he said, "Oh, I get it. They just wanted to be free." Then, we talked about some of the things that angered the colonists, such as taxation without representation, which he found interesting. His history teacher doesn't connect anything to the students' background knowledge or experiences. There are no discussions like that in his classes. All they do is highlight the photocopies of the text and answer the worksheet questions.

We also work on decoding by analogy (Cunningham, 1995), on building up experiences with texts, and on reading strategies. In the beginning, I would model this process for him a lot. We started with one-syllable words and he got those pretty well. Then one day, when we were reading his history text, we came upon the word "independence." I said, "Well, here's the first chunk. What's that say?" He said, "in." We chunked the whole word through, and at the end I said, "So what's the word?" "Independence," he said. I looked at him and saw that he had a big smile on his face. Another time he came upon the word "resurrected." He tried to chunk it in his head, but he couldn't. So I handed him a pencil and asked him to write the word and to split it up into chunks. That worked pretty well for him. I think it's important that he knows it's okay to pause for as long as he needs to figure out a word or to understand something he is reading. I've been trying to get him to stop during his reading and have him ask himself, "Did that make sense?" A lot of the time, he admits he doesn't understand what he's reading.

His motivation to comprehend has a lot to do with his interest in the topic. During one tutoring session, Pedro asked a question about the Bermuda Triangle. I decided to just let him research it. We went to an atlas to find it on a map and we looked it up in the encyclopedia. Then we found a book in the library about it. He was so excited about the subject, we must have spent five tutoring sessions on it. He was reading material way above his grade level—words like "atmospheric disturbance" by chunking them out. And I was so excited for him. I'd say, "You're doing so great! Don't you ever let anyone tell you you can't read, Pedro, because you read fine. You're reading so much better than when we first started." And he'd just grin and say, "Yeah."

So, there are conditions under which Pedro can learn and grow. If his teachers just did simple things, like previewing text and activating background knowledge, he could make some progress. And if they gave him some tools and strategies for making sense of his reading, and let him have some control over what he learned, that would be good, too. It would also be good if Pedro were in classes where students got to share their viewpoints. Because of his ethnic background and family situation, he has a really different view of the world than the majority of Anglo kids who go to Van Buren Middle School. There are a number of Hispanics, American Indians, and African Americans who go to the school, but they are socially isolated from the White kids. They all hang out in a hallway by the resource room. Pedro has talked to me about how he and his friends are blamed for everything that goes wrong in the school. If the Anglo kids could hear from Pedro and his friends, I think they would learn a lot from them. For example, we were working on his review questions for history and one of the questions was, "What were William Penn's beliefs about Native Americans?" To find the answer, we searched through the text until we found a section that said that Penn was a Quaker and that he believed everyone was equal under the eyes of God—that we were all children of God. It said that because of this belief, Penn bought land from the American Indians instead of just taking it like everyone else did.

"So what does that tell you about William Penn?" I asked him. "Is he prejudiced against American Indians?"

"Well, he could be," he said thoughtfully.

"How can you tell?" I said, a little bewildered. "I mean, if someone treats you equally, doesn't that mean they're not prejudiced?"

"No, not necessarily."

So Pedro has a lot of insight he could share if he had the opportunity. He's a great kid. I know now that he can read. And I know he can succeed. Right now he's registering for high school next year. He wants to take a computer class and a woodworking class, and maybe get into playing the saxophone again. These are things he likes to do, and he's good at them. But as far as academics go, I just don't know. I'm afraid he's going to be even more lost when he gets to high school because there are so many more kids. I'm really nervous about it for him.

There's so much more that I wish I could teach him: how to learn and how to figure out what the teacher wants him to know. But the short time I've spent with him doesn't really compare to what he gets all day long, what he's gotten his whole life long. I just hope I am making some impact. Lately, when he's been able to figure out really long words, words that he wouldn't even have attempted before, I'll just sit back with a big smile on my face and say, "You know, Pedro, that was great. That was killer. That was really awesome." I hope he knows that I'm totally excited for him and the stuff we've been doing. I think he does.

REFERENCE

Cunningham, P. M. (1995). Phonics they use: Words for reading and writing (2nd ed.). New York: HarperCollins.

Case 7

Reading in Biology Class

Elizabeth B. Moje

This case is built around the experiences of Elizabeth, the case author, when she was a first-year biology teacher. It describes what happened when she encountered resistance both to reading the course textbook and to her lectures that covered the material presented in the textbook. The case is constructed in the following manner. First, the classroom participants and the context of the classroom and school are described to provide the reader with background for examining the events that occurred in the case. Second, the events of the case are described, including Elizabeth's reflections later.

THE CONTEXT OF THE BIOLOGY CLASS

When the principal at Light High School, Rick Kraft, showed Elizabeth her new biology classroom for the first time, her head began to spin. "What have I gotten myself into?" she thought, as she looked at the double-sized classroom with several 50-gallon fish tanks that were coated with slimy green film after a summer of neglect. "What will my students

149

be like?" "And what am I going to teach them?" Elizabeth consoled herself with the knowledge that she had been able to choose the textbook she liked. "At least I can use that as my guide," she thought nervously.

Elizabeth had graduated the previous spring from a small liberal arts institution in the Midwest. She felt prepared to teach a variety of classes, having obtained a B.A. in history, political science, and biology. Her student teaching in U.S. history, government, biology, and chemistry had been a successful experience as well, so she wasn't prepared for the nervousness she felt when she looked around the large biology classroom and realized that she was on her own now. After a few weeks of looking through the textbook and beginning to plan lessons and laboratory experiences, however, Elizabeth's nervousness began to subside. She thought back to her biology courses in college and to what she had done as a student teacher in biology. "I can do this," she thought confidently, as she prepared her lectures.

Elizabeth had been told a great deal about the school, her class, and her students. The school was located in the Southwest and, although privately funded, had a diverse student body. Most of the students were European Americans, although several students were Latina/o or Mexican American. In addition, because biology was a required class, Elizabeth had a range of abilities, personalities, and cultural and home backgrounds represented in her class.

Although biology class was required, students were not encouraged to take biology until their sophomore year because it was considered a challenging class that freshmen might find difficult due to the note taking, reading, and writing demands of the content. Most students took an introductory science class such as physical science or earth science during their freshman year. The few freshmen who were allowed to take the class had demonstrated superior science ability or aptitude in eighth grade science classes. In addition, many sophomores who weren't interested in science chose not to take biology during their sophomore year; they waited until their junior year to take the class. Consequently, the class comprised primarily sophomores, with several juniors, a lesser number of freshmen, and even two seniors making up the balance of students.

Elizabeth's class rosters indicated approximately 30 students in each class. With a total of five biology sections, Elizabeth taught roughly 150 students a day. She also had study hall duty, a task assigned to her specifically because she was a new teacher, and the study hall would presumably give her extra time for preparations and grading. Another of Elizabeth's responsibilities included being one of the senior homeroom teachers; the workload of this responsibility was minimal, but it allowed her to get to know some of the seniors with whom she normally wouldn't have much contact. In addition to teaching biology, monitoring study hall, and serving as one of the senior homeroom teachers, Elizabeth had been hired as the drama director for the school. Her drama responsibilities included directing three productions: a dramatic play in the fall, a touring children's theater in the winter, and a full-scale musical in the spring. Elizabeth looked forward to the challenges of casting, coaching, and directing the plays, and had begun to work on her first play even before school began in the fall. During the second week of school, Elizabeth had scheduled auditions for the fall play and had begun to work on developing the set and costumes for the play. Several of Elizabeth's biology students became members of the cast, and Elizabeth met several other students in the school through this extracurricular activity.

THE CASE EVENTS

After several weeks of teaching biology, Elizabeth had settled into a comfortable groove with her students. She learned names easily, so she had quickly developed friendly relationships with most of her students. And she had developed a teaching routine as well. Each day, Elizabeth prepared lecture notes that she outlined on an overhead projector. She provided students with a full outline so that they could copy all of the information easily as she embellished on the points in the outline. She often showed a page of the outline at a time so that she could move around the room, up and down the rows, as she lectured. Elizabeth liked this style of lecturing because she felt that it helped move the teacher out from behind the podium (or in her case, the lab demonstration table) into closer contact with her students. She believed that such a move afforded her better classroom control and also allowed her to develop more personal relationships with her students.

Approximately three weeks into the first semester, one student, Larry Hall, asked Elizabeth a question at the end of the lecture period, "Why do you just lecture on what's already in the book? Why should we read it if you're just going to tell us what's in it?"

Elizabeth was floored, not so much because Larry had asked what seemed to be a somewhat impertinent question, but because his question indicated that he had read the textbook assignments she had been giving. In her student teaching experience, it had appeared that none of her students ever completed the reading assignments they were given, even when they had been asked to define vocabulary words or answer questions. More often than not, students simply skimmed the readings to find the words in the text and copied the definitions verbatim. Or, to answer end-of-chapter-questions, they simply skimmed until they found some text wording that was similar to the question wording and copied what they thought might be an answer. Elizabeth's cooperating teachers had simply lectured over the material, telling her that the students never read. In addition, her cooperating teacher in biology had believed that even when students did try to read the assigned material, they couldn't make much sense of it without the teacher's interpretation of the concepts through lecture. Consequently, Elizabeth had adopted the same techniques she had seen used in her student teaching classrooms.

Moreover, when she had asked students questions about what they remembered from the reading during the course of her lectures in the biology class, students could rarely answer questions. To Elizabeth, this indicated that students had either not read or not understood the material they had been assigned. Larry's question to Elizabeth had been somewhat challenging, and Elizabeth responded accordingly.

"Well, Larry," she said, "When I ask you questions about the readings, you can't always answer. You don't always understand what you read, so I have to go over it again. I add bits and pieces of information along the way, but the book represents the information that you need to know, and not everyone understands it."

Larry didn't respond except to shrug his shoulders as he gathered up his books to leave class. Elizabeth thought that she had answered his challenge quite well, but she should have known better.

Two weeks later, at the annual Parent–Teacher night, when parents visit each of their children's classes, Elizabeth had to face Larry's question again, this time from his father. Mr. Hall raised his hand, and in front of all the other parents from sixth-period biology, he asked Larry's question.

"My son Larry says that all you do is lecture from the textbook. Why do you do that?"

Elizabeth had become somewhat defensive when Larry had asked the same question; that question coming from a parent, however, in the context of Parent–Teacher night, represented the ultimate challenge. Elizabeth's response was brittle.

"Mr. Hall, Larry raised that same question in class two weeks ago, and I explained to him that not everyone in the class read the material or could read the material and understand it completely. What's really interesting, though, is that I later asked Larry a question based on the reading, and he couldn't answer it. That tells me that I need to explain the textbook readings to everyone in the class."

Mr. Hall simply nodded his head, as if he understood, but was somewhat skeptical. A few moments later, the passing bell rang, indicating that parents should proceed to their child's next class. As the parents were leaving, one woman approached Elizabeth and said, "Don't worry about what he said. That was inappropriate. He's a high school teacher, and he thinks he knows everything."

The woman, Mrs. Marvin, was a teacher, too, and Elizabeth felt somewhat vindicated, although the episode had really begun to make her think. "What could I be doing differently?" she asked herself. "Most of the kids won't read the textbook even when I assign homework, at least judging by their responses in class; how else will they learn this information? And what about the ones who try to read but just don't get it? Am I supposed to ignore them because of this one kid who thinks he knows everything?"

Larry's question (and his father's) haunted Elizabeth for the rest of the school year. She believed that she *had* tried to encourage students to read the textbook, but that they simply weren't going to read or that they couldn't understand the reading. Elizabeth also argued with herself that her lecture style was interesting and engaging; her students seemed to like coming to class and seemed to be learning, if the multiple-choice, short-answer, and fill-in-the-blank tests she gave were any indication. "And," she thought, "I'm keeping the students involved in learning biology by engaging them in lots of laboratory activities. We've studied cells under microscopes; burned sugar to create carbon; tested different substances for starches and sugars; dissected frogs, pigs, and cats; and typed our blood. It's not as if all I do is lecture! What else could I do?"

In the months that followed, after several observations with glowing comments from her colleagues and the principal, Elizabeth began to believe that Larry's comments were unjustified. She felt that Larry wanted special treatment because he was a better reader and had more understanding of biology than other students. Elizabeth consoled herself a bit by rationalizing that Larry was just a bit arrogant and that his father didn't help matters by supporting Larry's negative thinking about the class. Although she continued to think about Larry's question, especially in the following years when she began teaching history classes and wanted to foster discussions of the readings, Elizabeth believed that Larry had been asking for too much, and that her biology teaching methods were good. But still, what if Larry had a point? What else could she have done?

Case 8

When She's Ready, She'll Catch Up

Wendy Besel Hahn

In this case, Sue, a high school student with a learning disability, struggles with reading and writing assignments in her regular education classes. The case was written by Sue's tutor and is based on reading assessments and on interviews with Sue, her mother, and several of her high school teachers.

At the beginning of the first grade, Sue's mother began noticing problems with her daughter's progress in learning to read. She noticed that Sue read across the page from right to left and often reversed the letters in words, for example, reading *and* as *nad*. But the first grade teacher was reassuring: "No, Sue doesn't need special resources, she just needs time. When she's ready, she'll catch up."

Sue hadn't caught up by the end of the year, when her teacher expressed concern for the first time and recommended that she repeat first grade. Sue's mother strongly opposed this idea, believing that more of the same would not help her. Instead, she decided to carefully pick Sue's future teachers and asked that she be tested. Diagnostic testing by the special educator revealed that Sue had a learning disability, and she was placed for part of the day in the resource room. By fourth grade, however,

Sue's mother asked that she stop going to resource and instead spend her entire day in the regular classroom. Her mother felt that because resource was a pull-out program, Sue was missing out on the regular curriculum. Sue remembers that while resource classes were easier, she was glad she was no longer in them. She didn't like being pulled out and having to leave her friends. However, at her mother's request, Sue continued to receive help in reading in the resource classroom as she needed it, usually after school.

Since the discovery of Sue's reading difficulties, Sue's mother has her tested every couple of years by a neuropsychologist. Recent results suggest that Sue's comprehension skills and short-term memory continue to be fairly poor. Results also indicate that Sue has great difficulty understanding directions. Her strengths are her motivation and artistic ability.

Today, Sue is a ninth grade student at Forest Hills, a large high school with 2,000 students, serving both the wealthiest and some of the poorest sections of a medium-size city in the western part of the United States. Sue says that she still finds reading difficult, especially when it comes to reading her content area textbooks. Her teachers report that her main difficulties involve a very limited vocabulary and difficulty connecting information across and within paragraphs. To work on these skills, she receives help from the special education teacher, who has been designated as her case manager. Sue meets with her on a "consultant basis," that is, whenever she feels she needs it. Her special education teacher follows her progress, keeps track of her test results and her IEP, and acts as an advocate, making sure that she is placed in the most appropriate classes. However, her mother is not satisfied with the amount of help Sue is getting.

Sue is very insightful about her reading strengths and difficulties. She considers herself a fairly good reader but recognizes that it takes her much longer than her classmates to read and comprehend. Sue describes herself as a phonetic reader, who reads and spells according to sound. But she's also aware that she still reverses letters in some words, and she says that she has the most trouble reading and spelling smaller words with silent letters.

Sue studies for long hours each night, rereading the assigned sections of her textbooks three times, and struggling to write out answers to end-of-the-chapter questions. She usually reads aloud because she feels she has a better auditory memory, and this helps her concentrate. Drawing on her artistic ability, Sue keeps a notebook in which she often draws illustrations of a story or the content of paragraphs in her textbooks to help her remember them. If she has to memorize a speech for debate class, she copies it out three times and draws an illustration. She feels that this process enables her to present her speech without jumbling up the words.

For leisure-time reading, Sue has occasionally attempted to read very long, difficult novels, which are at her frustration level. She likes these books because they "grab her attention" and keep her "in suspense." She has expressed a sense of accomplishment at having read such long books. But the ease with which other people read often frustrates Sue. Although her strategies work for her, she says that if she could change anything, it would be the amount of time and effort she has to expend in order to understand her textbooks and the novels she chooses.

Sue likes to write, especially stories, and believes that the content of what she writes is good. However, she feels that she is not a good speller and has difficulty with punctuation and "spacing" between words, citing those problems as the reasons she gets Cs on her papers. She feels much freer in her writing when she doesn't have to worry about the mechanics. Sue works hard on revising her writing and following her teachers' feedback, even though she's not always sure what the teachers are asking her to do.

Much of the writing she does in her high school classes is no longer than one to two paragraphs in length and contains many spelling and punctuation errors, including some capitalized words in the middle of sentences. She says it sometimes takes her as much as three hours to write two paragraphs. However, she was disappointed with her grade on a speech she had written for debate class. The teacher had given her a C, commenting that she had few connecting ideas and transitions between paragraphs, that the speech consisted of bits of information from different sources and lacked direction and elaboration, and that she had relied too much on quotes, which had not been tied together well.

Sue feels the most frustration in her history class. She finds the history textbook especially difficult because "the topics jump around from paragraph to paragraph, making it hard to know what will come next." As a result, she has to struggle to make connections among the concepts within paragraphs, although her memory for details is impressive. She knows that the subheadings usually tell what the passage will be about. But it is inside the paragraphs that it gets very confusing for her. She also finds that the text is very dense and full of sophisticated vocabulary. The problem is not so much understanding isolated concepts once they have been explained to her, but tying them together. The same problem can be seen in her writing for this class, too.

Almost all the reading in history is done outside of class: She's sent off with her textbook and expected to make sense of it on her own. Only after the reading is supposed to be done and the writing assignments turned in does the teacher go over the material by outlining it on an overhead projector. This doesn't help her much, Sue says, in "trying to find the really important information—things that might be on tests." So, she tries to commit everything to memory when she studies. Her special education teacher is concerned that she's not acquiring a large vocabulary because she's reading at such a frustration level without help and she's limiting her writing to what she can spell and punctuate.

To make matters worse, she frequently doesn't know what her history teacher wants in writing assignments or on tests, including multiple-choice questions. The teacher is unable to give her much help. Sue recalls one time when she showed him what she had written. He quickly looked it over and said only, "Oh, no! This is wrong." Besides having 35 other students in the class who demand his attention, he can't understand what Sue's "problem" is, believing that his directions are clear enough. As evidence, he notes that most of the other students seem to grasp the instructions.

Sue wants to go to college after high school to get a degree in a field related to children or child care. Her teachers describe Sue as a very hard worker who always gets her homework done on time and participates fully in class. But Sue is frustrated that she isn't achieving grades higher than C in school. Lately, she has been having severe migraine headaches, which her mother attributes to the stress and anxiety Sue is experiencing in her school work.

Case 9

"We Are Chauvinists": Sexual Entitlement and Sexual Harassment in a High School

as told by Karen Jones[1]

In the late 1980s, the overwhelmingly White, upper middle-class high school where Karen worked as an English teacher was integrated when a lower income, predominantly minority high school was closed across town. As students from a range of ethnic minorities began to attend school in a wealthy section of this metropolitan area, racial tensions were expected. The school was unprepared for conflicts of another sort that developed, centering around issues of sexual harassment. Part A of the case describes incidents that were the source of the controversy and explores the reactions of the administration, faculty, and students. Part B of the case traces Karen's personal and professional involvement as she attempted to halt the stereotyping of women and peer-to-peer sexual harassment.

---

[1]Karen Jones is a pseudonym.

PART A

When the district decided several years ago that urban flight had left our city with too many high schools and not enough kids, they closed Crosspoint High, a school attended by low-income students and students of color. Crosspoint's students were distributed among three other area high schools. Roosevelt High, where I work, went from being a White, upper middle-class school to one with ethnic and socioeconomic diversity.

The school began to hold all kinds of meetings and to develop plans and programs to prevent the racial conflict that everyone anticipated. The principal at the time asked several of us to go to a training program designed to prepare teachers to spot ethnic and gender inequity in schools, bring it to the attention of the administration, and educate other teachers on these issues so that they could eliminate them from their classrooms. I returned to the school after the program and did some in-service workshops, but the response was typically, "Okay, fine. Just hurry up and get this over with, so we can get out of this meeting."

Surprisingly, as the school year began and the school was integrated, racial conflicts didn't seem to surface. But issues of gender equity, which perhaps had always been there, seemed to reach a fever pitch. I'm not quite sure why that happened, but things got really ugly. To me, it appeared that Roosevelt was run by a small group of White, upper middle-class boys and their parents. The events that occurred that year seemed to reflect issues of income and gender more than race. If there were wealthy male students of color, I think they would have been accepted by this group. It just so happens that the rich and elite happened to be White, too.

At the beginning of the first year of integration, a group of these boys started a club. It was approved by the administration, which just meant that some students went into the office, filled out a form, and an administrator signed off on it. There were no guidelines for clubs then, except that they had to have a faculty advisor. I can only hope the advisor of this particular club was clueless about what this club was really about. The boys called their club "WAC." If you asked them what WAC stood for, they told you, "Women are C___s."

WAC had posters advertising their club all over the school. One pictured a caveman dragging a smiling Betty Boop cavewoman with huge breasts by her hair. Others showed pictures of women in chains with men dominating them. There were also pictures of women as slaves walking behind men, and women in Middle-Eastern chardors. The captions read, "We can teach our women to behave properly. All men join WAC."

As soon as the first posters went up, many teachers, including myself, went screaming to the administration. Both the principal and vice principal were men. There were men teachers as well as women teachers who were upset, but the most vocal were women from the English Department. We said, "This is a real problem. You've got to address this. Do you even know what the name of this club is?" And this is exactly what they said: "Oh, lighten up! Get a sense of humor!" They basically just patted us on our heads and sent us out the door. The one thing they did do was go to the boys who started this club and tell them that their name was offensive to a few people, so they would have to change it. They changed it first to "Women are Cuddly" and then to "We are Chauvinists." And that was that.

WAC was just the beginning of the madness that year. There was also another club called RAM, which stood for Roosevelt Associated Men. RAM had an initiation ceremony at the beginning of the school year, held in the courtyard during lunch. Any male student could join RAM as long as he went through an initiation rite. This involved being blindfolded, finding the way over to a naked mannequin, and unsnapping a black lace bra on it with one hand. We were especially outraged that the mother of one of boys, a religious leader in the community, had provided the mannequin and the bra. She thought there was nothing wrong with what she had done or with what the boys were doing, although lots of other people thought there *was* something wrong. Several of the teachers went straight out to the courtyard when they heard about what was happening and confiscated the mannequin. They put it in the English Department office, which created even more hostility on the part of the boys against the women English teachers.

Other teachers went screaming to the administrators, again saying, "How dare you allow this?" Their response again was, "Where's your sense of humor? You feminists don't know how to take a joke." Although they said they'd talk to the boys, all the administrators told them was, "We want you to have your club, but these women in the English Department don't want you to."

This attitude was picked up by the kids, and pretty soon our own students were spouting the administration line to us, the teachers. We would say, "We're going to study a great author, Virginia Woolf," and the students would say, "Oh, is she another one of you feminists?" It would bring the whole class to a standstill. So the teachers who were really visible and vocal in the battle were being ridiculed publicly by the students.

But not all the students felt that way. I have my students write journals, and lots of girls wrote private messages to me. They'd say, "I'm so glad you're fighting this." Or, "I really hate how what's going on makes me feel." The majority of girls were embarrassed or upset, but they blamed themselves. They would write about how they felt it was their fault because if they had a good enough sense of humor, they wouldn't find it so offensive. But some of the girls stuck up for their boyfriends and told me to back off: "If we don't mind, why should you?" I'd say, "Well, excuse me, but I do mind, and if I mind you should mind also."

The sexism and the general attitude that it was okay was so pervasive that even school assemblies were affected. Occasionally, the whole school would come together for an assembly put on by a student group or a class, or for a particular occasion or holiday. That year, the assemblies were the most obscene things. The students had started a new sport called "pole clumping." It went like this: A boy would run up to and jump on a pole, climb up, and writhe on the way down in a sexually suggestive way. The crowd would go wild while the boy did this. They'd do it during lunch too, on the columns in the hallways downstairs in the building. I saw other students gather around and cheer them on, calling out things like, "If he can clump that pole that well, I bet he could clump his girlfriend real well, too." The students even videotaped the pole clumping and showed the tapes at several of the assemblies. The faculty advisor and vice principal who were responsible for assemblies saw nothing wrong with it whatsoever. They just thought it was funny and said to us, "Come on, boys will be boys!" Eventually, though, they did ban the videotapes of pole clumping from the assemblies.

Pole clumping was only one of the mind-boggling activities that went on in assemblies. For example, when the dance club had a concert one evening, the girls came out in skimpy costumes in one dance number and writhed around on the stage in what was a lewd dance. The boys in the audience just shrieked and hollered. In another assembly, the Pep Club did a skit in which the girls dressed up as pregnant women and lay writhing on the stage floor while boys stood over them doing a bump and grind. It was astonishing. WAC continued to be allowed to have skits, even after it was outlawed by the administration and was therefore an illegal club. In this skit, the boys dressed up as cavemen, dragging off giggling cavewomen by their hair.

After every one of these assemblies, some of the teachers would march out of the auditorium down to the principal's office, and scream bloody murder. "Did you see this? Did you approve this?" More and more teachers were getting angry, and by mid-year, about half the faculty was really up in arms. In response to this growing force, the principal would say, "I'll look into it. Yes, you are absolutely right, it's disgraceful." But then someone else, a teacher or an administrator, would say, "Get a life." "Worry about something that matters. This is so petty." "Lighten up." "We need to let the kids have freedom of speech." And so, nothing was done.

PART B

The situation came to a head in March of that school year when student body elections were held. There are some stipulations about what you can put on a poster for display in the school, but basically they have to do with cost and size and where the posters are allowed to be hung. The content matter was never addressed. That year, poster after poster after poster showed men brutalizing women and women in submissive roles. It was really bad.

I had had enough, so I called the ACLU and told them what had been happening and how the administration hadn't done anything about it. They said it sounded like I had a case and told me to call the State Labor Commission. I did, and the man there told me to write a letter explaining my concerns and detailing what I wanted the school administration to do. He told me to send him a copy, to give the principal a copy, and to send a copy to the district personnel director.

I drafted the letter along with another teacher, a man who was very conservative and religious. I wanted to be sure the letter was not too emotional: I wanted it to be a letter he would feel comfortable signing as well. Well, we spent a few days drafting the letter and other teachers heard about it and wanted to sign it. Out of our faculty of 120, 57 teachers signed the letter. Our major request was that the administration establish some guidelines for club charters, school activities and assemblies, and posters that were displayed on school property. These guidelines would prohibit discriminatory or degrading content based on gender as well as ethnicity.

I went to the principal and told him who I had called, showed him the letter, and told him who I was going to send it to. I said I wanted to be up front and honest with him about it. He said, "Great. I support you. But I'd like you to take this letter to the School Improvement Council before you send it to anyone and see if the situation can be resolved there." This ugly mess had been going on all school year and I—and others—had been in his office about it countless times, to no avail. I really didn't want to wait another two weeks before the Council met to take any action, but I reluctantly agreed.

The School Improvement Council is comprised of teachers, administrators, and parents. On the afternoon of their meeting, I was actually hopeful as I went before them. A few of my colleagues went with me to present the case. As I began to discuss the situation, I could see that I would get nowhere with these people. I was getting the brush-off. "There's no problem at Roosevelt," they told me. "There's no need for guidelines. But, if you want, you can bring it up again next year." When I left the meeting I was furious. I walked up to the first mailbox I saw and deposited the letter.

That evening, I went to dinner with another teacher from the school. Coincidentally, at the restaurant we ran into a mutual friend who worked for a local TV station. "Hey, you've got to hear what's been going on at Roosevelt," my colleague said. Of course, our reporter friend wanted to put this story on the news. The following Monday, the reporter showed up at school, got copies of the videos of the assemblies, and aired segments of them that evening on the news. Another teacher and I were asked to go down to the station and make comments, which were aired later that same evening.

Half the community was outraged by what they saw on TV. Many parents called the administration in outrage saying, "How dare you let my children see assemblies like that! What's going on? Who's in charge over there?" But, the other half was outraged that two teachers would dare say bad things about Roosevelt. Even though 57 other teachers had signed the letter, I became the problem: "If she was not such a feminist, we wouldn't have this problem."

The next day when I came to school, I stopped by the main office to pick up my mail. The principal came flying out of his office, screaming at me. Many other teachers were standing around as well as students and the secretaries. He was screaming so loud that a lot of what he said was incomprehensible. He kicked me out of the office and told me never to come back. He did not speak to me for the rest of the year, and someone else had to go down every day to the office to pick up my mail for me.

Because there had been students in the office when the principal was screaming at me, the incident quickly got around the school. Some of the more concerned students asked me if I was going to get fired. But, there were also boys who stood just outside my classroom and called me a "f__ing b___h," "lesbo," "Nazi," and "man hater" through the door. Those first few days, right in the middle of lessons, on anything from Herman Melville to editing a passage, students—both boys and girls—would raise their hands and say, "Why do you hate men so much?" So a lot of class time was given over to fielding their questions and explaining my position. I was worried about spending time in that way because I'm an English teacher and it really isn't subject matter. And, I felt the administration was scrutinizing every word I said and every move I made. But still I felt I had to answer their questions, even the silly ones like "If you sued, would you get a million dollars?" They really wanted to understand, and in the end it was a good social studies lesson for them. This was something I had done because I felt strongly about it.

In addition to these conversations with the students, the notes from some of the parents sustained me those first few days. I started getting handwritten notes from parents, which the students brought in. I never got a note from a parent who thought I had done anything wrong. Rather, I got notes that said, "Thank you very much. I'm glad my daughter has a teacher like you." Whenever I was feeling shaky and scared, I'd pull the notes out of my desk and read them.

The situation had become extremely divisive in the school, with teachers taking sides for and against what I had done. For the first few days after the letter was mailed and the TV station aired the segment, I was terrified to step out of my room. I thought, "I'm going to lose my job. I've only been here a few years. I just know that somehow the principal will figure out a way to get me out of here."

There was a lot of discussion among the faculty about whether I had a right to speak up. Had I broken some unspoken bond by bringing shame to the school, by airing our dirty laundry in public? The teachers who had signed the letter were in shock those first few days, too, especially when the principal began going in and out of classrooms, screaming at people. In fact, one of the teachers in the school put a sign up on his door that said, "I stand in solidarity with Karen Jones and the teachers who signed the letter." The principal came screaming into his class one day, ripped the sign up, threw it on the floor, and stomped on it in front of his class of students.

But after a few days, many of the teachers rallied and said, "Gosh, she is carrying this weight for all of us. We believe in what she did. We all signed the letter, too." And they started coming into my room to give me hugs and say, "You hang in there. We're behind you 100%." And when the principal would stop someone in the hallway and say, "That d___ Karen Jones, she started all this trouble." They'd say, "No, you're the administrator. You need to do something about these problems." They were standing up to him.

A couple of months later, toward the end of the school year, a group of faculty got together and put a lot of pressure on the principal to apologize to me. We hadn't spoken since that run-in in the office in March. On the final day of school, when I had to go in and have him sign me out for the year, he said he was sorry things had turned out the way they had, that he was looking forward to working with me again in the future, and that he hoped that "our communication would be better enhanced." It was a round-about apology. But his approval wasn't really what I was looking for.

I was actually feeling pretty good about how things had turned out by then. However, there still aren't any guidelines. To this day, five years later, we still have inappropriate clubs. For instance, last year, the boys had a "Hooters" club and they elected one girl a week as an honorary member for her "enthusiastic spirit." Of course, these girls were always very large chested. This club even put their honorees on the school television network. The club was eventually banned.

But some things are different. Parents who didn't feel they had any power in the school feel differently now. You know, there was always that group of parents—the parents of the most popular boys—who seemed to run everything. Those wealthy parents all stuck up for their sons in this controversy. They were the ones who didn't see any problems at the school. But a lot of the other parents were on my side, and they were saying, "Boy, we wondered when someone was going to do something about that. That was pretty disgusting." So when this all happened, those parents were happy to support me because it was also a retaliation against the very powerful parents.

I think the whole experience was also good for the teachers because they gained a voice they never had before. They are more vocal and more confident now. The year after all these incidents, when they went into the principal's office to complain about inappropriate activities, they would say, "Have you learned absolutely nothing from what has happened? We have the government and the parents behind us now." One group of female teachers actually held a retreat and discussed filing a sexual harassment suit. The administration doesn't dismiss us so readily anymore or tell us to learn to take a joke.

It has also been good for the students. They've found out, especially the girls, that they don't just have to sit quietly and feel bad about what's going on. I've seen lots more students stand up and say, "Wait a minute. Something wrong is going on here." I like to think I've had something to do with that. You know, at the beginning, it was really hard and I was vilified by a lot of people. But now, people are more inclined to say, "Boy, she really sticks to her guns. She'll back up what she believes in. She's a really moxy lady." So, at least I have that to feel good about.

Case 10

Help, With Strings Attached

Emma Magleby[1]

In this case, a first-year teacher, Emma Magleby, describes the unanticipated struggles that resulted when a Chapter I aide was assigned to her classroom. The case revolves around a philosophical conflict regarding the teaching of mathematics. Whereas Emma focused her curriculum and instruction on collaborative mathematics problem solving and reasoning, the Chapter I program focused on remediation and skills.

My first teaching position was at Carlton Elementary School in the suburb of Newton City, where I was hired to teach fifth grade. Upon my first visit to the school, I felt that it had a positive atmosphere and a real feeling of collaboration among the educators. My room was adequate and my fellow fifth grade teachers were friendly and offered help whenever needed. I looked forward with great anticipation to having my own classroom and to getting paid for something that I had always wanted to do.

---

[1]Emma Magleby is a pseudonym.

At the beginning of the year I had 23 students, but by the end of the year my class had grown to 27. Most of the students were European American, one was African-American, one was Korean, and one was an American Indian. Four students were in the gifted and talented program, and one student received special education services in a pull-out program. I also had three students with behavior problems, whom I taught in my classroom using behavior modification techniques and contracts.

The school was situated on the edge of a business district and was partially surrounded by newly constructed homes. In general, the school was located in an area that was nice and well kept. However, within the school's boundaries were several run-down apartment complexes and a trailer court, areas not known as safe or nurturing environments. During the previous summer, one of my students had been raped by a trailer-court neighbor. I soon discovered that the trailer-court kids and students from the newly built homes did not mix much. One student from the trailer court never came to school with clean clothes and was sent home three times during the school year with lice. Very few of her fellow classmates talked or played with her despite my concerted efforts to encourage them to involve her in their informal school activities.

Many in the school viewed the trailer court and run-down apartments as "community eyesores" when contrasted with the upper middle-class homes that had recently been built in the area. Some of the teachers described their "problem students" as coming from these areas. One teacher was especially bothered by one family's lack of hygiene. Dirty clothes and the smell of urine were hard for her take. The parents from the trailer court were difficult to reach because they were seldom home or had no phones. It was apparent that many of these students were on their own to do their homework and get themselves fed. Unfortunately, some of the faculty members had little tolerance for the students' situations. Occasionally I heard comments about how much easier it would be if "we" did not have "them" within the school's boundaries.

Before the start of the school year, as I anxiously prepared my room and acquainted myself with the faculty, I was approached by Sandy Green who introduced herself as the Chapter I supervisor for the school. She was very kind, left me some math and reading test resources, and told me she had a teacher's aide who would be coming in each day to help my students in math.

I had heard of Chapter I before but, to be honest, I had never completely understood what it meant and what the function of the Chapter I program was in a school. After my first meeting with Sandy, I still did not know much about the program except that its focus was usually on math and reading and that an aide would be assigned to my classroom for math.

I immediately began to think about how I could use this aide most effectively. I brainstormed many ideas. He or she could model for the students how to solve problems as I presented the new concept for the day. The aide could work with small groups each day doing math journals. Perhaps the aide could assist in some of the direct teaching or create hands-on math tasks for the students to do. I was thrilled at the possibilities and looked forward to this collaborative teaching opportunity.

Two weeks after school began, I heard from Sandy again. She popped into my room and asked if I had a list of students to give her who needed help with math. Boy, did I have a list! I had not realized that my math lessons were going to be so novel. As a student at the university, I had developed some new ideas as to how I wanted to teach math. These ideas were very different from the structured math lessons I had endured as a student throughout elementary, junior high, and high school, in which the teacher went over the previous day's homework, explained the new concept, told us what formulas we needed to memorize, and gave independent seatwork assignments from the book. In contrast, I planned to engage students in math activities in which they could use divergent thinking skills and learn to write about math.

Though students liked the new approach, it required them to explore math in new ways. I felt that with this new approach, I was reaching students who had previously not excelled at math. However, I also found that those who had done well before were now having to expand their ideas about how math could be learned. I believed that having an aide would help me facilitate the kinds of activities I had planned during math time and give students another person to engage in mathematical dialogue. I listed for Sandy the seven or eight students whom I could see benefiting from extra help. She quickly wrote down their names and then asked me for a pretest to document their deficit in the unit we were covering.

"A pretest," I thought to myself. I had not given students a pretest. But I did know which students I was spending the most time with during math. Sandy quickly informed me that I had to have written work samples that demonstrated they had a deficit in the particular math skills we were working on. She suggested I just give all of the students one of the tests from the end of the chapter in the text to discover who needed help. I could not just give her my list because she had to have written evidence of the students' deficits.

I wondered how I could give her written documentation of the small group, hands-on math activities we had been doing for the past two weeks. Because I hadn't been following the formal structure of the math book, I struggled with the question of how I could test my students in a way that reflected what I wanted them to learn. How do you test divergent thinking or creative problem solving? Obviously, I wasn't going to be able to hand her a student's math journal entry and expect her to understand my mathematical goals and accept it as documentation. I felt frustrated. After unsuccessfully developing a written test that evaluated these things, I succumbed to using the first chapter pretest in the textbook, although I felt it was not an adequate measure of what I wanted students to learn.

After two days of pretesting my entire class and correcting the tests, I had a list of students for Sandy and copies of their tests. To my surprise, the eight students who received the lowest scores on the pretest in the book were different from those on my original list. Though many of the kids from the trailer court had been making progress with my new approach to math, they did not fare well on the written test. Although I found they were more creative in their problem solving and asked more questions that led them and other class members to greater discoveries, they appeared on the multiple-choice test as the ones needing the most help. But, at least now I would have a tutor for a half an hour each day to use as I pleased.

This was my first misunderstanding about how the Chapter I program was going to work in my classroom. Later that day, Sandy informed me that she would be sending an aide, Jennifer Land, to my classroom the following Monday. As I prepared meticulous lesson plans, I decided to have Jennifer spend the first couple of days observing the class. I felt this would be a good way for her to get to know the students and for me to get a feel for what she could do.

On Monday morning, Jennifer came in before school to introduce herself as the Chapter I aide assigned to my room. She told me a little bit about herself and asked where in the room she could work. I had set up a small table specifically for her and showed her where it was. She told me that she would be in at 10 A.M. that day and asked what page we were working on in the book. At the time, we were not working on a specific page. Instead, I was using the units in the table of contents as a guide to know what concepts I needed to teach, and students were doing activities in small groups to discover concepts about fractions with pattern blocks. So, I explained that I would like her to help students accomplish the task for that day and that in the future, I would have some specific tasks with which she could help. Jennifer was friendly and professional, and I felt very comfortable with her.

At 10 A.M., the students were working with pattern blocks in small groups trying to solve some fraction problems when Jennifer arrived. I was working with a group across the room and did not feel that I could easily break away. I watched from across the room as Jennifer sat down at her table. She observed for a moment and then one by one began calling the students on her list over to to her table.

When I was able to break away from the group I was helping, I went to speak with Jennifer. I suggested that instead of calling students over to her table, perhaps she could roam the room and observe the students. I hoped that by doing this she could get a feel for the activities we would be doing. She explained that her supervisor had told her to take five minutes with each child on the list to get to know them.

Though I preferred that she not pull the students away from the classroom activity they were engaged in, I felt it was important to allow her time to get to know the students personally, thus allowing her to do as her supervisor had asked. However, this created problems because I had assigned each person in the small groups a certain job, such as being the investigator or the scribe, so that everyone would feel part of the activity. As she pulled students over to the table, the groups had to compensate for the five minutes that their group member spent with the aide.

At the end of the math period, Jennifer walked up to me and said, "What a fun game! What math page will you be working on tomorrow?" I don't think she realized that the activity for that day was not a game but rather the math assignment and that we were not always going to be working out of the book.

As the weeks went on, I discovered a few more things about the Chapter I program in our school. First, only those students who had qualified on the unit pretest as needing help were to be served by the Chapter I aide. The aide needed to document each day how much time she had spent with each of the students on her list. This meant that she had little time to spend with the other students in the class who might be having some difficulty with a particular assignment.

Pulling the students over to the corner table to receive help created another problem: Many of them did not like being pulled aside. I tried to remedy the problem by suggesting that Jennifer roam the room and casually stop at the documented students' desks to help them. This approach did not work because other students (not on the official help list) would ask her questions and seek her help. These requests, she explained, took away from the time she could document having spent with those students on her list.

Throughout the year, the aide continued to pull students aside because that was the easiest way to facilitate personal help without distractions from other students. I frequently had to deal with children who refused to go to Jennifer's table to receive help. One day, after a major brawl during recess between several of my students, I discovered that the gap between the kids from the trailer court and those from the upper income areas was widening. One of the kids said he knew the trailer-court kids were dumb because they were always back at the table getting help during math.

A few weeks later, Sandy Green, the Chapter I supervisor, stopped by to say "hi." However, I think she had more on her mind than just a friendly hello. I had a feeling I was causing a few problems for her and her aide. I expressed to her some of my concerns, telling her about my small-group activities, and hands-on problem solving, and about the problems that resulted when students were pulled aside for help. She responded kindly, but suggested that perhaps I should use the text more—"After all," she said, "it was the skills in the text that the students were going to be tested on at the end of the year." She viewed my activities as games, and suggested that I do them at some other time of the day when the aide was not there. She also suggested rather strongly that I give instructions for the daily assignment before Jennifer came in to help; that way the students would be working independently when she came in and she would not interrupt "group games."

As the school year went on, my problems with Chapter I continued, and I found myself continually struggling with the same dilemmas. I wanted the assistance of an aide and believed that students could benefit from having help, but I struggled with the way that the help was offered. Furthermore, though the services of the aide were being given in the students' regular classroom environment so as to be inclusive, the act of pulling them aside caused many students to wonder about their own mathematical abilities. I frequently questioned whether this program was benefiting my students in a way that matched my own philosophical values as an educator. What could I do next year to both keep the benefits an aide could bring to the classroom and maintain the integrity of the program?

Case 11

In the Best Interests of the Child

as told by Heather and Bill Bonn

This case describes the tireless efforts of the Bonns to find an inclusive classroom for their son, Scott, who has Down syndrome. In their search, the Bonns encountered teachers, special educators, principals, and others who did not feel prepared to include him in the regular classroom in his neighborhood school. Part A describes Scott's early schooling, including an integrated Head Start program and special education classes, and the Bonns' struggle to place Scott in his neighborhood school. This part concludes with a disastrous meeting held to make a placement decision for Scott. Part B, which is in the Appendix of the teaching notes for this case (See Preparing Teachers For Inclusive Education), *describes what happened at the conclusion of the meeting, followed by Scott's experiences in regular classrooms at his neighborhood school and his parents' hopes for his future.*

PART A

By the time Scott was 10 years old, he had been in five different schools. Because he has Down syndrome, he began his schooling at 18 months, attending the only public special education school in the county once a week. At that time, all children with severe disabilities were bussed to this central location. Scott stayed at the special education school until he was $3\frac{1}{2}$. He could have stayed there until he was 21, but we wanted something different for him.

The district placement committee gave us very little choice about where we could place Scott. The options we were given were either a three-day-a-week cooperative preschool or a five-day-a-week preschool classroom that was housed in a high school. We felt that Scott would benefit much more by attending the longer program, so we placed him in the high school's program. Although we were frustrated by having so little choice in placements, we were pleased with the preschool program. It was Scott's first experience in an integrated setting. He was one of three students with disabilities in a classroom of 20 students. The teacher had an aide from the district's Special Education Office as well as a number of high school students who worked as assistants. Scott gained a lot from being with peers who did not have disabilities. And it helped the high school girls who were working with him to learn about people with disabilities. Having Scott in the classroom allowed them to see that he could learn; it just takes him a little bit longer than the other students.

However, it was here that we got our first insight into the ignorance and mistaken ideas people have about mental retardation and other disabilities. One day, the teacher showed us the reports on Down syndrome that the high school teaching assistants had written as an assignment. They included excerpts taken from library books written in the 1960s. One report inferred that children with Down syndrome were idiots, who couldn't be taught much. Yet, the teacher was very proud of the reports and had given many students As on them.

The teacher did little to adapt the curriculum for Scott. When things were too difficult for him to do in the classroom, he would be pulled out to work with the aide in the hallway on something else. In fact, we noticed that at times the other preschoolers were quicker to adapt to Scott's needs than were his teachers. Scott was mostly nonverbal at this time, able to make only "baa" sounds. The kids would ask Scott yes or no questions because that way they could get a clear answer from him. For example, rather than asking him, "Do you want the yellow crayon or the blue crayon?" they would ask him, "Do you want the yellow crayon, Scott?"

We did see an increase in his vocalizations while he was at this school. Scott also learned from his peers how to act like a student by watching what the other four-year-olds were doing. If they went to go sit at a certain table, then he would go and sit over there with them. He also learned how to take turns at that time.

After a year, the district required that Scott move again, this time to a Head Start program, which had a quota for students with disabilities that they needed to fill, and the district needed his spot in the high school-based preschool for younger children. This was Scott's third placement in as many years—a case of changing placements to fit the district's needs at the expense of the child's best interests. Scott has always had a problem adjusting to change, so leaving the high school and moving to Head Start was difficult. To him, it was a strange new place with a new teacher, new peers, and new assistants. At first he tested people all the time by refusing to do what he was told. But once he got used to the new routine he did much better. Adding to the difficulty of transition was the bus ride. Even though the school was only 2 miles away, each way took 50 minutes because Scott was the first of 15 students to be picked up and the last to be dropped off. After 50 minutes of bouncing around on the bus, he simply was not ready for school.

The Head Start program was a full-day, integrated program with 3 students with disabilities in a class of 30. An assistant worked with Scott on his Individualized Education Program (IEP) goals. Although he didn't have to leave the room to work on his goals, he did have to leave his group and sit with his assistant at a special table. He didn't like this at all; he wanted to stay with his peers, doing what they were doing. Throughout the year, he resisted having to be pulled out to work someplace else.

Even so, Head Start was a positive experience for Scott. It was there that he made some friends for the first time. He became much more self-confident and learned a lot of skills, including better table manners and personal hygiene skills such as washing his hands and brushing his teeth. He even learned some "life skills." Once he came home and started to cook a frozen waffle in the microwave for 66 minutes. Although he had learned some cooking concepts, we weren't ready to put him in charge of dinner! And, because his teachers took him to the rest room every hour and a half, he actually became toilet trained faster than his nondisabled cousin, who is the same age. Unfortunately, Scott regressed in a lot of ways after he left Head Start.

After a year at Head Start, Scott turned five and was eligible for kindergarten. We had two options: to send Scott to a special school for children with disabilities or to Hillview Elementary, the district's cluster school, which was five miles away. Although children with disabilities at Hillview were placed in a self-contained special education classroom for most of the day, they were also assigned to a regular classroom and were supposed to participate in activities with their age-group peers. Because we wanted Scott in an integrated setting as much as possible, we chose the cluster school.

At Hillview, Scott was placed in a self-contained special education class with children who ranged in age from 5 to 12, in grades kindergarten through six. Since only one other child was Scott's age, he spent most of the day with older children. During the morning session there was virtually no integration, even during recess. At lunch the students with disabilities all sat at the same table, with an assistant or teacher standing over them while they ate. On the few occasions when Scott was integrated with the kindergartners in the afternoon, there was always an assistant who stood close by. The regular kindergarten teacher made it clear to everyone that she did not want to have to deal with him if he acted up.

Scott was resistant to going into the regular classroom, where he was required to do regular, unadapted school work. In his special education class, the academic work was adapted to his level and he was engaged in more play and activities like cooking and art. Also, Scott didn't know any of the regular kids—all his friends were in the special education class. And sometimes he acted up. Scott did not always follow directions. He might not go stand in the line or he might refuse to participate. A couple of times he tried to wrestle with one of the other boys. Since Scott couldn't communicate verbally yet, it was his way of saying, "I want to play with you."

The only strategy they had for dealing with Scott when he acted up was to kick him out and send him back to the special education room—advice given to teachers by his special education teacher. This meant that if Scott refused to stand in line or to work on a new assignment, he had to leave. Sometimes a student would walk him back or the teacher would send a note to the special education teacher that said, "Send the assistant," and they would come and take Scott out.

Needless to say, we weren't pleased with this situation. We were frustrated that Scott wasn't being integrated enough, but we felt we had no say. We were told, "that's just the way it's done here." When we talked to the principal about our concerns, we were made to feel that it was a gift to us that Scott was being integrated at all. He said, "Be happy with what you are getting." We came to believe that the principal's and teachers' expectations of what kids with disabilities could do was very low. Later in the

year, when we again voiced our desire to the principal and special education teacher that Scott be integrated more, they decided to keep an anec-
dotal record of Scott's behavior during his integrated times. Over a
two-week period, they developed an eight-page record of negative events
without a single positive comment. It painted a picture of a child worse
that Satan! To us, this was an obvious case of prejudgment looking for
supportive data. However, the school did start to do some peer tutoring.
Some of the sixth grade students would come into the special education
classroom and work with Scott. He loved working with his tutors, and he
did very well for them. They worked on skills like counting objects, and
even taught an adaptive physical education program with the whole class.

Hillview had never been our ideal. We had always wanted Scott to
attend our neighborhood school, Coleridge Elementary. So even before
Scott first went to kindergarten, we had talked with the director of special
education about it. The director had told us, "I can't do it this year,
because we're having some trouble. We've got to get the neighborhood
schools that we already have set up and running smoothly. Then we'll add
more. Wait until next year."

So we waited. Then when Scott began kindergarten at Hillview, we
went back to the district office to say, "Remember last year you promised
us that Scott could go to his neighborhood school?" But the director we'd
spoken with had left the position. We were told by a staff member, "Oh,
you know, we've got a new director and we can't do that now."

But we kept asking. We told them that Scott needed to have playmates,
that he needed to socialize more with kids from his own neighborhood.
Much to our surprise the new director of special education contacted other
parents of children with special needs at Hillview and asked them if they
would be willing to move their children to Coleridge, making it the cluster
school instead of Hillview. The parents agreed and voted to change
schools. Then, some parents changed their minds and everything fell
apart. We were back to square one.

The year passed and it came time for Scott's IEP meeting to discuss his
placement for first grade. IEP meetings are always stressful for us because
usually it's only the two of us and six to eight professionals. Sometimes
what the professionals think is best for Scott is not what we, his parents,
think is best. We knew we wanted Scott to attend Coleridge Elementary,
and we felt there were several good reasons for this. It would mean that
Scott could go to school with his siblings and learn to interact socially and
build relationships with children in the neighborhood, whereas attending a
school outside the neighborhood would only prepare him for a segregated

setting after school. Attending the neighborhood school would also eliminate the isolation created by busing and, as a year-round school, would
avoid the regression Scott experienced over the long summer vacation.
Finally, Coleridge is a national award-winning school. We felt it offered a
better quality of education than Hillview.

Prior to the formal IEP meeting, we had had at least three preliminary
meetings in the spring in which we presented our perspectives on what
we thought would be the best program and placement for Scott. Each
time, the teacher, principal, or special education coordinator would
respond with a statement like, "I can't make that kind of a decision. I
need to talk to the district's director of special education." Then we
would wait weeks for a response. The formal IEP meeting wasn't scheduled until fall, at the start of the school year, and this extended IEP time
period raised our anxiety level and appeared to us to be a "wear-them-
out" strategy.

Before the IEP meeting in the fall, we approached a first grade teacher
at Coleridge Elementary and asked her if she would be willing to have
Scott in her class. She told us, "Oh sure, I'd be happy to have Scott in my
class." Right after that the principal from Coleridge came to see us. He
said that he did not like our going behind his back and talking to this
teacher because, he said, "Of course, she is going to say yes, but that may
only have been because she was afraid to say no to you." The principal felt
that we should have come to him first so that he could ask her in private
for "an honest answer."

So, this is where we stood when it came time for Scott's IEP meeting.
We knew what we wanted for Scott, but when we sat down we really felt
intimidated. The meeting was held in the conference room at a bank
because the district's conference room was too small to hold all the people
asked to attend. We sat facing the principal and special education teacher
from Hillview Elementary; the principal, the head kindergarten teacher,
and the head first-grade teacher from Coleridge Elementary; the school
district's attorney; and the district's new director of special education.
This time, we brought a person from the university as an advocate for
Scott and two people from the Legal Center for People with Disabilities,[1]
who were there to represent us in legal matters. The teacher we had first
approached at Coleridge, who had told us that she would be "happy" to
have Scott in her class, was not at the meeting.

We began the meeting by requesting that the district place Scott in a
special education classroom at Coleridge Elementary. The director said,

[1]Legal Center for People with Disabilities is a pseudonym.

"No way, the special education class is at Hillview. We tried to move it but it didn't work. This is where it's got to go."

"Okay," we said, "then we'd like to put Scott in a regular classroom at Coleridge. How much assistance would he need? Would he need a full-time aide?"

The head first-grade teacher from Coleridge was asked how she felt about having Scott in her classroom with an assistant. She said, "No, I wouldn't want that; I don't want an assistant in my classroom because that means I have to keep that person busy."

The director of special education then told us that it was not possible for Scott to attend the neighborhood school just now. But if we would just wait, he could promise "in good faith" to work on getting Scott to attend Coleridge by third grade. This was the second time we had heard a special education director promise to place Scott at Coleridge. We'd heard too much of, "Not this year, next year, next year." Still, we knew that we had to be willing to back off, even though we were so upset. We asked our representatives from the legal center to come out to the hall.

We said, "We give up. We can't take any more of this. If the director will put it in writing that Scott would be able to go to his neighborhood school next year, we'll wait. If they put it in writing, then it will have to happen." Our representatives agreed.

But when we went back into the room, we were told that the district's attorney had told the director that he could not offer anything in good faith. So they recanted: They would make no promises that Scott would ever attend his neighborhood school.

We argued that although Scott was now in a restrictive environment at Hillview, he had had many successes when he had been integrated in the preschool. But they said, "We can't do it, we don't have the support. We don't have the money or the space for a self-contained classroom."

With this refusal, we were at our wit's end. We said, "Well, forget it. We'll file for due process," and we got up and left.

Case 12

Building an Inclusive School: Vision, Leadership, and Community

as told by Bonnie Reynolds, Lisa Foster, and Sue McGhie

This case is based on an interview with Bonnie, a first grade teacher, Sue, the principal, and Lisa, the special education teacher at Spring Lake Elementary School, who narrate the story of how the staff, parents, and the community participated in building an inclusive school.

THE SETTING

Spring Lake Elementary School serves 650 children in a metropolitan area in the western part of the United States. The students are predominantly European American and of middle to lower socioeconomic status. Over the last several years, the community served by the school has been undergoing changes. The participation rate in the free and reduced-price lunch program has increased from 9% to 42%, and the transient rate has climbed from 10% to 39%. Today, the building has an open design without walls. There are no self-contained or special education classrooms. Before inclusion, however, 70 students participated in a resource pull-out program staffed by two special education teachers and a part-time aide.

BEFORE INCLUSIVE EDUCATION

"Although we didn't know it at the time," Sue, the principal, said, "we took our first steps toward becoming an inclusive school when we began to use cooperative learning in all of our classrooms. We wanted to help students become more involved in their learning, to start to own it more. We wanted to get them more excited about the things they were learning. That was six years ago."

The entire staff at Spring Lake had been using cooperative learning as a result of training they had received as part of the Accelerated Schools program (for background information, see Finnan, St. John, McCarthy, & Slovacek, 1996). Sue was very pleased with the changes that took place in teaching practices throughout the school, but she saw a problem, which she discussed with her staff during a building-wide meeting. "When I go into your classrooms," she said, "I see beautiful, well-prepared lessons with a lot of high-interest activities and kids who are very much involved, but about ten minutes into the lesson four or five kids get up and leave. A half hour to 45 minutes later they come back. The kids being pulled out for resource are not being included in some of the most important activities in our classrooms. They don't feel like they are part of what's going on. I'm very concerned because I'm not seeing peer relationships develop with these particular kids as they are with the rest of the class."

The faculty shared her concerns. Sue concluded, "Rather than generate solutions now, let's think about what we'd like to do and talk about it again later." As everyone was leaving the room, Lisa, a special education teacher, asked Sue, "Are we still meeting with Max's parents today? I'm sure that placing him in resource is the best thing to do."

"Yes, we're meeting this afternoon. Bring his complete file, will you? Max's parents are very worried about placing him in a special program."

At the meeting, Sue and Lisa explained to Max's parents that Max had fallen so far behind his peers that they believed it would be better for him to be in resource. Max's mother asked, "Will the other children look down on him because he goes to a different class?"

Max's father was more blunt, "Will they think he's stupid?"

"Many parents worry about that, but I don't see much negative labeling," Sue told them. "You know that Max isn't getting what he needs in a regular classroom," she explained. "In resource he'll get the extra help he needs so he can feel like he's having some success. Even if other children in his regular classroom have a problem, in resource we have all kinds of academic programs with tangible rewards that he can earn and feel good about. Resource," she said reassuringly, "is a safe haven where everyone is equal."

"Is this placement permanent?" Max's father asked.

"No," Lisa said, "we think of this placement as a way to help kids catch up."

"When will Max be able to go back into the classroom for everything?" he asked.

"When he's ready, we'll move him back to the regular classroom," Lisa reassured him.

"When will he be ready? How will you know?" he wondered.

"We'll have to see when he's ready. Right now, he qualifies for resource because he has tested well on aptitude tests, but he is three grade levels behind his age-mates. If he improves so that he is only two grade levels behind in reading, say, he'll go back in his regular classroom for reading again."

"Will he continue to get help if he's that far behind?" Max's mother asked.

"If he improves that much he won't qualify for resource anymore," Lisa said, "then his regular classroom teacher would work with him."

"How many kids ever get out of resource once they're placed there?" asked Max's father.

"Well," Lisa said, squirming a bit uncomfortably in her chair because she was having a hard time thinking of a student who had, "it's hard to say. Probably not many."

"A lot of our parents share your concerns, especially when they are first thinking about putting a child in resource," Sue said. "We want to reassure you that we do not think of these as permanent placements. We want all of our students to be in the classroom as much as possible."

A few weeks later, Bonnie, Lisa, and two other teachers sat at a table in the teachers' lounge talking before school. Sue sat in a lounge chair putting the finishing touches on her to-do list for the day. Other teachers drifted in and out of the room, pausing to chat for a few minutes. Lisa said, "I think being in a pull-out program makes my kids feel like they're different from the other kids. They tell me all the time that they wish they weren't in the 'stupid class.' The other kids pick up on it, too. Yesterday on the playground I heard a third grader say to one of my kids, 'You're stupid because you go to resource class.'"

A third grade teacher sitting at the table said, "Just as I was beginning a whole class activity the other day, one of my girls told one of Lisa's students, 'You can't do this kind of math. You go out to the other class.'"

"I work very hard," said a sixth grade teacher standing at the refrigerator, "to create an atmosphere of tolerance and respect in my classroom, but I was appalled to hear one of my best students say to a new boy in class, 'See that kid over there, he goes to that other class; he's stupid. They are in the stupid group and we are in the smart group.' I can't . . ."

"You know what I hate?" another teacher interrupted. "When a kid comes back from resource just when we've got a great cooperative lesson going. He's been left out, and there's no way to bring him into the lesson, so I say, 'Here's a coloring sheet', and sit him down to color for 30 minutes."

"I resent it," said a third grade teacher who had come into the lounge, "when kids come back from resource with toys or candy. I know, Lisa, that giving an immediate reward is important in what you do with these children, but my other kids don't think it's fair. A kid they consider dumb or one who isn't making it or is even a behavior problem comes back with these little rewards. I don't think it's fair, either. My other kids work hard every day, all day. They don't get toys and candy."

A fourth grade teacher related an incident that had occurred in her classroom. "Yesterday, Sarah came back from resource just as the class was beginning a math lesson. She told me, 'I don't need to do math today. I've already done it in resource.' I thought to myself, 'Well, that's right, I shouldn't have her do two math periods. Besides, I don't know whether she can do this assignment.' I told Sarah, 'Since Ms. Foster works with you on your math, why don't you find something to do in the creative corner?'"

"As classroom teachers," Bonnie added, "we don't feel total responsibility for a child in resource. We sometimes don't know what to do because we tell ourselves, 'She's resource's responsibility.' If she's not doing well in reading, math, or whatever, I can't really feel that it's my problem. I'm her homeroom supervisor, but it's resource's job to see that she learns these things."

"I'm not criticizing Lisa," the third grade teacher said to clarify her earlier comment. "I think our resource programs are excellent. They work better here than at the school where I used to teach. Lisa puts a lot of effort into working with us, and the kids are making real progress."

"Well," said Sue, "I'm sure that Lisa is doing a great job. The problem is that our resource program is a pull-out program. That by itself creates problems even when everyone is doing excellent work."

"What I would like," said a second grade teacher who had joined the group, "is to have some of my students *in* resource."

"Qualifying a child from your class for resource would be a problem," Lisa explained. "Just as an example, to be designated learning disabled (LD), a kid needs to be high ability but low achievement. He or she probably won't be far enough behind by the second grade to qualify."

"So we leave them in regular classrooms with no extra support until third grade. Then they are far enough behind to qualify for the program," another teacher chimed in.

"But I've got one boy who needs a lot of help, and I've got 25 kids!" the second grade teacher pleaded.

"I'm sorry," said Lisa. "There's nothing I can do."

Since it was nearing time for school to start, everyone left for their classrooms. Bonnie and Lisa walked down the hall together. "You didn't say much in there," Bonnie said. "What were you thinking?" she asked.

"You know, teachers ask me all the time what resource kids should be doing in their classrooms," Lisa responded. "I'm so overloaded. They just don't understand what I have to do. I want to tell them 'It's not my problem. It's *your* classroom!' Besides, when I suggest that we work out a contract for one of their kids, it's the last thing they want to do. *They* don't have time."

RETHINKING ASSUMPTIONS

After raising the idea that inclusion might be a way to solve the problems created by pull-out programs, Sue began speaking with teachers informally to get their reactions. The faculty had been thinking and talking about these issues for several weeks when Sue approached Bonnie on the playground. As they talked, Sue asked, "What would you think about the resource children being in the regular classroom instead of being pulled out?"

"Why would you do that!" Bonnie exclaimed in disbelief. "The reason they are being pulled out is that they aren't making it in the regular classroom. What makes you think that being in there they are suddenly going to start making it?" she asked, hoping Sue would give a reasonable explanation. Thinking of more reasons not to include resource kids in regular classrooms, Bonnie argued, "We don't have special education training, you know. We aren't going to be able to handle the needs of these children."

"Well, I'd like you to look at a school that's doing it," Sue said. "I've been talking to principals around the state and I've found a school that is already including resource kids in the regular classroom."

Bonnie turned her attention to an energetic discussion between some children. She was totally unconvinced by Sue's argument. She thought to herself, "This is not the way to go. I've been around children a long time. You can try and try a hundred different things and sometimes they still won't get it."

Seeing Lisa walking across the grounds, Bonnie waved to her. She was sure Lisa would agree that regular teachers would need special training to teach the resource kids effectively. Later that day, after telling Lisa what Sue had suggested, Bonnie said, "You know I'm not trained; I'm not qualified in special education. If children are identified as LD or as having Down syndrome, they need a different program, don't they?" Bonnie asked. "And aren't there special things that you do depending on how they've been identified? They need your expertise."

"Well, thank you," Lisa responded. "But it's a myth. People think we have these special magic wands. The kids come into our classroom, we wave our magic wand, then the kids go back to their classrooms."

"But," Bonnie persisted, "you do know more than a regular teacher about the different problems students have, and you have special techniques you use with them."

"I think special education teachers help create the myth," Lisa said. "It makes you feel good when a teacher expects you to solve impossible problems." She went on, "It's hard for us to get over the idea that we know something special, something wonderful about teaching these kids that nobody else knows. I have to learn to say, 'Sorry, no magic tricks and no magic wand. I'm just a teacher, like you are.'"

THE TRIP TO NEW CASTLE

Sue continued to talk to the faculty about her idea of fully including resource kids in regular classrooms. She decided to arrange for small groups of teachers to visit New Castle Elementary School, a Chapter I school in another city that had implemented inclusion successfully. At New Castle Elementary, Bonnie was so fascinated by a first grade classroom in which at-risk kids were fully included that she spent the entire day in that room. When she had a chance to talk to the teacher at lunch, Bonnie told her, "You have a marvelous program! The feeling in the classroom is so positive and all of the kids are excited about learning. Have any of your kids had serious problems?"

"Jimmy, who you saw working perfectly well with the other kids all morning, was in a center for behaviorally disturbed children a couple of years ago," the teacher told her. "He was completely out of control and unable to do his school work. Now, he's at grade level."

"Have you had any special training?" Bonnie asked.

"No, but I don't have to do everything by myself. I have two aides who work with me every day, and the special education teacher and other specialists in the school come into my class regularly to work with my kids. I'm really like a coordinator of all these people. Everyone in the school works together. When we run into a problem trying to include a child, we just figure something out."

"Are the kids who are at-risk as a whole catching up to the rest of the group?" Bonnie asked. "And how are the other kids doing?"

The teacher showed her the children's work and told her that the children who were considered at-risk were improving at a very fast rate and that the others were improving as expected. As Bonnie left the school, she thought to herself, "Maybe this actually can work!" When she returned to school, Bonnie and the other three first grade teachers talked about what they had seen at New Castle. At their regular team grade level meeting, held while Sue was in California to gather more information about inclusive programs, the four first grade teachers continued to work out their thoughts. During the meeting, Bonnie broached an idea that she had been thinking about: "If we could catch a lot of these kids early and really build some of their skills, plus give them a good feeling about school, I think they would go a long way."

"These kids are a problem, but whose problem are they?" asked one of the other first grade teachers.

"Who is going to help them catch up if we don't?" another teacher responded.

"We could have a first grade class with all of these kids in it with an aide and really give these kids the boost they need," Bonnie suggested. "But, one thing that would bother me about this idea," Bonnie continued, voicing a reservation about her own proposal, "is that the resource kids would still be separated from their classmates."

"I'm worried about that, too," said one of the other teachers. "Will Sue support it? She's so committed to inclusion that I can't see her going for something like this."

"At least we could try to teach them on a first grade level," Bonnie said, thinking aloud. "We wouldn't be dumbing down the curriculum. Even if it has some problems, wouldn't it be neat to have something like this in our school?"

As they talked, all four first grade teachers felt that their plan was beginning to gel. They decided to meet with Sue when she returned from

California. When they were able to get together, Bonnie summarized their plan, "One first grade class would take all of the kids we think are already beginning to fall behind. The teacher in that class would work hard to improve their skills and get them excited about learning. As much as possible, we'd use the regular first grade curriculum. We hope that by giving them a boost early they would be able to go into regular classrooms in the second grade. That way we would be able to achieve our goal of inclusion by second grade."

"And the rest of us will take larger classes, so the at-risk class can be smaller. That way the teacher in the at-risk class will be able to really focus on these kids," one of the other first grade teachers added.

Another teacher said, "We think this class will need an aide. An aide will be able to work with the kids so that each one will get one-on-one attention within the classroom."

Sue responded, "But we don't have any aides available for such a class."

The teacher continued, "We know, but we have an idea. As you told us last fall, whenever a building is funded, there is a small amount of money left over."

"That's true . . . ," Sue said.

"Yes," the teacher went on. "It's not enough to fund a full-time teacher, but there is enough for an aide. I know that we've always used that money to put an aide in the largest class to help the students. We're asking you to put that aide in the smaller, at-risk classroom."

"That would really change the way we do things," Sue said. Then she asked, "Who will teach this class? It won't be easy." For the first time the group fell completely silent. Since no decision had been reached after several minutes, Sue said, "It looks like we're not ready to decide this right now. We can think about it for a while and decide who's going to do it later."

"I'll volunteer to do it," Bonnie said apprehensively, "at least to get it started. I don't want this to lose momentum. As long as I know I have everyone's support and an aide, I think it can work."

After thinking for a few moments, Sue said, "We'll have to talk this over with the entire faculty." At the next faculty meeting, Sue told the teachers, "I'm ecstatic that a grade level team has taken the initiative to think through how to make our school more inclusive and serve the needs of our resource kids. You know that when the district tried to push an inclusion program a few years ago it didn't work. I think this will be different. I think it will be easier to support this proposal because it is coming from you. I'm very impressed that three of you are willing to carry a heavier load and one of you will work intensively with the at-risk students so they can get a shot in the arm." After a lengthy discussion of the idea, the faculty indicated its support, deciding that an at-risk first grade classroom would ultimately benefit the entire school.

THE FIRST YEARS OF IMPLEMENTATION

Reflecting on the first year of the plan, Bonnie described the class and her experience:

That first year, the at-risk class was composed of 18 students—16 who were starting first grade at a beginning kindergarten level and 2 (Shelby and Jay) who had already qualified for special education services. Shelby was labeled as intellectually handicapped and Jay had been diagnosed as having a communication disorder with autistic-like characteristics. Shelby and Jay could have absorbed every hour of my time because their needs were so great. My aide and I had to be careful to give everyone attention and to pull in additional resources to help Shelby and Jay.

I found that teaching was only part of my job. I became a coordinator of parent and high school volunteers as well as sixth grade peer tutors, all of whom helped to reinforce the skills I was teaching. I made it clear to parents at conferences that they were the most crucial part of the team to help their child succeed. I provided them with weekly homework packets with ideas to help. I also saw myself as part of a team composed of the special educator, the social worker, and the classroom aide. We all needed to be involved in sharing information and planning.

I tried to teach concepts in a variety of ways, hoping that the students would be able to connect with at least one of the approaches. Jay and Shelby ended up needing individualized reading programs, but the class allowed them to shine in other areas, like art and math for Jay and social interactions for Shelby. They weren't locked in to any one approach or program. I think that their abilities were stretched by the variety of opportunities in the classroom.

By the end of the year, the pre- and posttesting that Lisa conducted indicated that almost all of the students were on level in math and three quarters were on level in reading. I felt that the first year had been a successful one despite the myriad of problems that accompany

any new program. I knew that we had reached students who might have 'fallen through the cracks' had they not received the extra interventions we could provide in the at-risk classroom.

"It was rocky that first year, though" Sue said. "My expectations at the beginning weren't very high," she confessed. "I thought the kids were going to die, but they did the work."

Over the course of the first year, the faculty developed an overall plan to create an inclusive school. According to the plan, pull-out programs would be eliminated and special education services would be provided in classrooms; first grade would always have an at-risk classroom, but from second grade on, students would be fully included. Inclusion would be implemented in stages: one or two grade levels each year, beginning with grades 2 and 3. During the second year of implementation, when the students in Bonnie's classroom had been integrated into the second grade classrooms, Sue met with the teachers involved in inclusion weekly at lunchtime to talk about what was working well, what wasn't, and what changes could be made. At one of these early meetings, the teachers and Lisa voiced their concerns.

"We're not sure what to do," a teacher said. "How are we supposed to do everything?"

"This is an additional thing we've got to worry about. We didn't have to worry so much about these kids before," another said.

"Which ones in my class are Bonnie's kids?" one teacher wanted to know.

"Actually, the students who were in Bonnie's class are doing pretty well," Lisa said. "But I don't think we teachers are doing so well. Some days I feel like quitting! I have to divide my time between Bonnie's class, four second grades, and three third grade classes. I don't even know how to plan my schedule or where I should be to do the best job."

"You know," Sue said, "I don't really know what to do, either. We have to struggle through this together."

Later in the year, the faculty was more positive. "When things were rough early in the year, I was sure the kids who were having trouble were from Bonnie's at-risk group," a second grade teacher said. "Now, I find out that a kid I thought must have been one of hers wasn't, and a kid that was one of hers is doing just fine." Lisa described how the teachers and she had learned to work together effectively, "At first I tried to go to each class according to the activities that were planned. If someone was doing cooperative learning or something that I thought required extra help, I would go there, but the teachers wanted to know exactly when I was coming and have something on a regular basis. That was smart. It worked better."

"We're learning a number of ways to work with mixed ability groups," one teacher explained, "to trade students around in groups so that even though Lisa works with the kids who are struggling, she has different kids from the rest of the class at different times."

"It really helped me to know that Sue wasn't sure what to do either—that we all had to struggle together," another teacher said.

INVOLVING PARENTS
AND THE COMMUNITY

Reflecting on the early years of implementation, Sue said,

> Weekly meetings with the teachers in the integrated classrooms were essential to building an inclusive school. But working to involve the parents and the community was also important. We tried to get Spring Lake's parents involved very early in the effort to change the school. I asked some of the parents and members of the Community Council to arrange meetings in the community. They would invite five or six parents to their homes, and I'd come out to talk with them. I asked them what their dream school would be like. They described a school where all the children would be able to reach their potential, feel safe, and enjoy going. The parents wanted their children to have good memories of their school days as they grew older. They also wanted a school that would build their self-esteem, where no one would feel inferior or stupid.

Then, I asked them to come up with some priorities," Sue continued.

> It really took quite a while. The first year we started meeting, it took us six months to come up with priorities. But, once we started to talk about what it meant to promote the success of all children, I think the parents became more and more convinced that one of those priorities was to include all students in the regular classroom. Of course, not all the parents were sold on inclusion because they worried that it might dumb down the curriculum. And others were worried that their children would not get the attention and help they had gotten in resource.

Bonnie described one of the changes that the faculty felt was important in creating an inclusive school: eliminating letter grades and substituting a system of narrative reports. "We've moved the whole school to a non-graded system," Bonnie said. "the new report card is intended to give a lot more information about a child's progress. Instead of just a single grade for reading, it gives information about progress in different areas of reading. We hope that it's less stigmatizing than getting a D or an F. We try to communicate that the child needs to work on this or that, not that the child is a C child."

However, the nongraded system was a difficult adjustment for some parents," Sue said.

One mother complained that she didn't know how to reward her daughter anymore. She used to give her a certain amount of money for an A and a little bit less for a B. Some of the parents complained that they didn't know what good or satisfactory progress meant. They didn't know how to translate the new report cards into terms they were used to. As an administrator, I was pleased that parents were coming to us with their concerns. For inclusion to work, we had to change how we were teaching as well as evaluating students' progress. In order for us not to dumb down the curriculum, we needed to find ways to integrate the various subjects, so math lessons would be part of geography and so forth, and to think through how to provide assignments that are meaningful for students working at different levels. To do this required that teachers have more planning time. So, a group of parents and teachers began to brainstorm to find ways to provide planning time and training for the staff. The solution we came up with was to hire six specialists who are paid as part-time aides. They come in on Fridays and teach folk dancing, art, playground games, culture, cooking, and other things. Once a month, each grade level team is freed up all day on a Friday to plan and integrate the curriculum. We've also gotten several small grants to bring in consultants and specialists for staff development.

Lisa added, "This meets the community's need to have the kids in school. The kids love it, it meets the enrichment goal, and it gives teachers a large block of planning time each month. Our goal this year has been to develop one three- to six-week integrated unit across two disciplines, then teach it. Next year we hope to continue the process and develop new units."

LOOKING BACKWARD AND TO THE FUTURE

"After four years of implementation, we've learned a lot," Bonnie reflected. "One of the most important things is that there is a lot of powerful learning going on. When you keep your expectations high, the children will really surprise you. Another strength of inclusion is the positive environment. Students' self-esteem is better; they are not negatively identified with labels. The class feels more like a team. Also, you don't have to plan for the pull-out programs anymore."

"We think we've closed the gap between the resource kids and the others," Lisa said. "I think that they were actually being held back by being in resource."

"But, I have fears about funding in the future," Sue said. "First, I'm worried that special education will not continue to fund us if we don't keep the number of students up who are labeled; in other words, if our students don't fall so behind that they qualify for special education services, we may lose the funds that make their achievement possible."

"Although we no longer have pull-out programs and I work with all of the kids, even those who don't qualify for special services," Lisa said, "we still have to test and label children for resource in order to qualify for the money, and we still have to do all of the paperwork for a pull-out resource program."

"We met with district people to discuss this," Sue said.

They suggested using at-risk money, but that is only about $40,000 to split between 64 schools. We have to compete for this money. This year we were lucky, we got $5,000, which we used for aides and a reading club. Our second source of funds is also drying up." Sue continued, "We've been a centennial school, but this is our last year. We used the centennial money to pay for the aides who come in every Friday to provide enrichment programs. That money will soon be gone. So, what do we do next year? It's a continual battle to keep going forward. It doesn't take a lot of money to do things, but it's simply untrue that you can make real changes without money. We also need funding for all the additional staff development that inclusion requires: not just special education training but also training in decision making, thematic curriculum development, cooperative learning, portfolio assessment, and all the other innovations we're implementing.

"And it means teachers volunteering their time," Bonnie said, "spending an inordinate amount of time before and after school, working on their curriculum. But our philosophy is, if you identify a problem area, you brainstorm solutions. You do 'what ifs.' If you need additional money, you ask: 'How can we get it? What can we do?'"

"Another fear we have," Lisa said, "is that Sue will be reassigned to another school. When we started the training and other things to move toward inclusion, teachers asked, "Are we going to do this for a year, then have Sue take off?' Then it would have been just one more program that was never finished. Sue promised the faculty she would stay at least for the five-year implementation plan, and she has done that. Without that promise, most of the faculty wouldn't have done this."

"I've been in the building nine years," Sue said. "I don't know what will happen. I believe that a building needs a strong leader, but at some point changes have to become part of our ethic of how to teach children so that they will continue even without the administrator who was there when they started. I believe the changes we've made will continue."

"If Sue did leave," Lisa said, "I hope we could find someone with similar goals and values and philosophy. I hope we would be able to help interview so we could find a principal who fits. If we were to get a new principal who says, 'I'm sorry, we aren't doing accelerated schools or inclusion anymore,' I don't know what we'd do. But I don't think we could ever go back."

EPILOGUE

The year after this interview took place, Sue did leave to assume an administrative position at the district.

REFERENCE

Finnan, C., St. John, E. P., McCarthy, J., & Slovacek, S. P. (Eds.). (1996). Accelerated schools in action: Lessons from the field. Thousand Oaks, CA: Corwin Press.

Case 13

Inclusion for All? Dilemmas of a School's Move Toward Inclusion

as told by Lou Chestnut[1]

In this case, a kindergarten teacher with 25 years of teaching experience, including special education, talks about the first year of an inclusion program in an inner-city elementary school, which was introduced with the intention of reducing class sizes and correcting the inadequacies of traditional pull-out programs. In Part A, Lou describes how teachers in the school have adapted to inclusion differently. In Part B, he provides examples of students with behavior disorders and describes how they have influenced the learning environment in his inclusive classroom.

PART A

Until 10 years ago, Broadview was a prestigious suburban school. The mayor and many prominent businesspeople sent their children here. But

---

[1]Lou Chestnut is a pseudonym.

then people began moving out of the local neighborhoods and, eventually, what remained was subsidized housing. Now Broadview is known as an inner-city school. More than 90% of our students are on the free or reduced-price lunch program, and many come from one-parent homes. About 25% of our kids do not speak any English and many of the others are bilingual, with English as their second language. Many of our non-English speaking students and bilingual students are from migrant worker families. The school population is transient: New students enter the school as quickly as others leave, resulting in an 85% turnover. Yet, despite the high transiency rate, there is a nice sense of community among the migrant families. In the morning the parents walk with their children to school and come into the classroom to help their children put away their coats. They really create a family feeling.

This is the first year of an inclusion program at Broadview. It was not a sudden change, though. The entire faculty had been working on a strategic plan for moving toward inclusion for the past three years. It was really out of concern for the children—what the teachers could be doing that would be better for them—that motivated the teachers to make this change.

Prior to becoming an inclusion school, Broadview had a traditional dual system that separated the children in special education programs from the children in general education classes. Also, because of the makeup of the student population, there were a lot of separate pull-out programs in the school. Besides special education classes, we had Chapter I, a social skills program, speech classes, and language programs, including bilingual and ESL. All of these pull-out programs made the school day rather disjointed. Teachers found that the children were constantly being pulled out of the classroom; in some cases the kids were out of the classroom more than they were in it. The hallways were always full of kids going from one place to another. Teachers couldn't hold the kids accountable. It became impossible to know where anybody belonged at any given time. Even the students had trouble knowing where they were supposed to be. The teachers felt the situation was chaotic, but even more so, they felt that the pull-out programs weren't helping the kids learn. Students weren't connecting what they were learning in their pull-out classes to what was going on in their general education classes. Chapter I was doing its own thing; ESL was doing its own thing; all the programs were teaching different curricula. The faculty felt the kids were being pulled apart in little pieces.

A good example of this lack of consistency was between the Chapter I curriculum and our new literacy program, which we recently put in place.

Two years ago, we dropped our basal reading program and adopted a whole language approach. The new program attempts to give the kids all the strategies and skills in a rich text environment. This means not discounting things like phonics or skill work or spelling, but rather making sure that all learning is done in context, that skills aren't taught in an isolated fashion. However, Chapter I continued to use a phonics approach consisting of programmed readers that reinforced what had been taught through lots of repetition. The stories in the readers didn't make a lot of sense, and the sentences were short and stilted, not typical of the written language found in storybooks. In fact, very little reading went on, which was really detrimental to the kids in Chapter I, who missed their own reading class. Not surprisingly, the Chapter I and the general education classroom teachers rarely communicated with one another.

The new whole language curriculum was also at odds with traditional ways of structuring learning and classroom management. It takes a cooperative learning environment to achieve the goals of the whole language program. But creating this learning environment conflicted with the traditional ways of managing classroom behavior, in which the teacher talks and asks questions that students answer one at a time. Learning was not defined as a social activity, in fact, students helping each other solve problems or discuss issues was viewed as cheating. This conflict has been particularly apparent in the upper grades. It has been easier to use cooperative learning with younger kids, but older children were used to a disciplinary system that required them to work quietly on their own. So, they were not prepared to handle the new responsibilities that go along with cooperative learning. We have tried to introduce the older kids to cooperative situations slowly, with very specific ground rules. Even so, classroom management was made even more difficult for everybody because of the changes.

So, we became an inclusion school to create more consistency in the curriculum. Special education and all of the other separate programs are gone. Students are no longer pulled out for ESL, Chapter I, or resource, and only in rare cases are they even pulled out for counseling. Pull-out programs were just too disruptive, and the faculty felt we could not achieve the literacy goals outlined in the new program if what was going on in the pull-out classes was different from what was going on in the general education classrooms.

The new literacy program and inclusion brought about other major changes at Broadview as well, namely, smaller class sizes and teaming. We had long complained that our classes were too large for effective teaching—often there were 30 or more students per class. To implement the new curriculum changes effectively, we wanted class sizes of 15 students. We really grappled with how to achieve this. Knowing that classrooms of only 15 students wouldn't be feasible at every grade level, the faculty eventually adopted the idea of team-teaching. In some cases this meant bringing the pull-out teachers into the classrooms and having them team-teach along with the classroom teacher. In other cases, it meant dividing up the students among more teachers, which means smaller classes but teachers working alone during the day in separate classrooms. All faculty were given the option to transfer to another school if they were not receptive to this new plan. Most stayed, but a couple of the special education teachers told me at the beginning of this year that they felt they really had no other option but to stay. However, three special education teachers from other schools transferred to Broadview because they had heard of the inclusion program.

As a result, all grade levels have adopted a team concept. Now grade levels are known as teams: the sixth grade team, the fifth grade team, and so on. In addition to two general education teachers, each grade level team has, at least on paper, one full-time special educator or Chapter I teacher and an ESL/bilingual teacher. Grade level teams meet every week for 1 hour and 15 minutes to discuss their progress and to solve problems.

There are some excellent outcomes resulting from these teams working together. In the fourth grade team, for example, the ESL teacher and a general education teacher have the kids intermixed—the non-English speakers mixed in with the native speakers. From what I've seen, there is a lot of good language development going on in there, and even out in the playground there is good interaction among the kids. In the third grade, all the kids, including those with special needs as well as the non-English speakers, are completely dispersed among five teachers. These teachers really function as a team. They plan curriculum together and discuss the kids and shift them around all the time, depending on where their needs can best be met.

General education teachers have also teamed. In the fifth grade, two of them are doing some really interesting things in their classrooms. They have established all kinds of literacy-based centers where the kids are doing interactive learning, such as sharing their creative writings. Rarely do I see a kid off task in that room.

However, even though there are instances of successful teaming, it isn't working everywhere. Theoretically, each team is supposed to share teaching responsibilities equally; but what I've found is that responsibility is divided up according to areas of expertise. For instance, where teachers and specialists have tried to work together in the same classroom, the special education teacher will end up doing observations and one-on-one teaching, while the general education teacher will be up front presenting the lessons. This is because pull-out teachers (and I used to be one) haven't had a lot of experience managing a classroom from the beginning of the day to the end, but they are really good at doing one-on-one work. So there is something like a division of labor going on in some of these classrooms.

In the fifth grade, the teachers have not been able to do any cooperative learning with their students until this year. To get to this point they first had to solve some major problems with kids with behavior disorders who had been included in mainstream classes. Although the teachers have really worked at dispersing these students, the classroom in which the special education teacher is teaming has the two students with the most severe behavior disorders.

Inclusion and teaming has been least successful at the sixth grade level. The ESL teacher teaches the monolingual and bilingual kids in her own separate classroom; the special education teacher has also gone back to the old model, taking the kids with the most severe behavior disorders into a self-contained classroom; and the general education teachers get the rest of the kids. This means that the general education teachers have larger classes of students who are thought not to have problems, while the special education teacher has a smaller class with the most difficult kids. The general education teachers at the sixth grade level have returned to the traditional model of classroom instruction, in which the teacher assigns reading in texts, students complete questions at the end of the chapters, and some recitation and discussion of right and wrong answers occurs.

I think that as we moved toward inclusion, some teachers really didn't know enough about what to do, particularly those teaching in the upper grades. In other projects that I've been involved with over the years, I've seen that when teachers don't know what to do they will throw out the new ideas and go with what they know. Perhaps contributing to this situation in the sixth grade is that each team has one experienced teacher and one first-year teacher. In my experience, new teachers do not rock the boat. They do what they are told to do. So when someone with 20 years of experience tells a new teacher that cooperative learning groups don't work, the new teacher is not likely to try it and risk falling flat on her face.

Another problem that I've recognized is that it takes a lot of time for teams to really bond. Teams need time to talk together to figure out the best plan for individual students and to plan curriculum. But our only scheduled time to meet is on Thursdays for 1 hour and 15 minutes when the students leave early. This time often gets taken up by other things such as meeting with parents or administrative tasks. There is really too much to do in too little time. As a result, some of these teams have gone into survival mode: They just want to get through the day.

Right now there is a lot of hit or miss going on in the school. More reading is going on, with every classroom doing from 20 minutes to 1 hour every day, and class sizes are smaller than before. But at the same time, some of the teams are falling back into traditional models of instruction and aren't team-teaching. Most of the teachers are genuine about changing; they are not resisting. It's just very hard for them. The philosophy of the new literacy program and cooperative learning means that a teacher must become less of an assigner and teller, and more of a problem solver with kids. That's going to be hard for some teachers to learn. A couple of them are near retirement. The new teachers are willing and eager to try new things. I just hope that they will want to stay.

PART B

Although kids who have been diagnosed with severe behavior disorders have already been placed in a nearby cluster school, we still have some very disruptive kids. We are all grappling with how to deal with them. Inclusion and the new curriculum changes will only work as long as there is quick identification of the kids who are out of control along with support for teachers to either get them in control or remove them to the cluster school.

It takes only a few kids to ruin a classroom learning environment. I know that even the kindergarten teachers in this school have problem kids who disrupt their classrooms. In my classroom of 15 students, 3 have severe behavior problems. In the afternoon I have two aides who support me, but I still can't get done what I need to because these three kids are so disruptive. The other 12 kids really light up when I introduce new things. They want to learn, but my attention is constantly being drawn to these other kids.

For example, I can tell as soon as Sally comes through the classroom door what she is going to be like for the day. She sometimes has a look in her eye that I can only describe as distant and wild. When she has this look, I know she is going to run out of the classroom when we do something that she doesn't like to do. The simplest things provoke her, like if I ask her to sit down on the carpet with the class, or if I stand on the wrong side of her and she decides she doesn't like that. Before I got my aides I had to call the police three times to come and find her because I couldn't leave the other kids alone in the classroom to chase her. She is very disruptive in other ways, too. She throws crayons and will even eat them.

One of my aides is assigned to Sally full time in the afternoon. We have a very specific behavior program we use with her. She gets two warnings for disruptive behavior, and if she continues, she is sent to what we call the sitting seat. If she can't sit in the sitting seat, then we move her out into the hall to sit with the aide. This happens about twice a week. In order for Sally to return to her regular seat, she must tell me or the aide how she must behave. I actually get a lot done in the classroom when she is out in the hall.

Then there is Jake. He is a very bright little boy, but he has destroyed more things in the classroom than any student I have seen in 25 years of teaching. When he chooses to learn he picks things up very quickly, but most of the time he chooses to be destructive. If he is in a group circle, he will take somebody else's paper and destroy it, or he will pull somebody's hair, or kick somebody. He says profane words, which causes the whole class to react. We have tried many different strategies to involve him in a positive manner, such as giving him more power in group circles and letting him sit in the spotlight, but nothing has worked. The other aide I have works only with Jake. We have him on a behavior program similar to Sally's.

The third child with behavior problems is Bobby, who is visually handicapped and developmentally delayed. His behavior is not as severe as the other two. He usually only becomes disruptive when he can't participate because an activity is too challenging for him. When Bobby starts to get disruptive, we will go and sit by him and put our hand on him. He responds to this. We also give him something else to do. He is doing better now, although we still have to remind him how to sit.

We have lots of paperwork and observational data on these kids, so I have a good idea what is behind their behavior. The interventions we have tried with them are based on this information. I think that Sally's problem is cognitive. Sally's mother, who is 20, is limited in what she can do. So we think that Sally may be developmentally delayed. One thing we have found that works with Sally is to feed her before she comes into class. Her behavior is better when she eats. Because Sally has talked about her mom putting her in her room without letting her have dinner, we have speculated that Sally's mother uses food as a control. I think that Jake's problem is anger. Jake's father is in the penitentiary, so we think that this is a big source of his anger. But we really haven't found any behavioral strategy that works with him. Bobby is very frustrated because of his disabilities. We think he acts out the rage he feels when he can't participate equally with the other students in an activity. I'm not sure where we'll end up with Bobby. I have to spend so much time with the other two that I think he is missing out.

What is really frustrating about these situations is that I have no effective resources to deal with these kids, especially the two with the most severe problems. The resources that are available are not working. We have referred Sally and Jake for diagnosis, but this process takes a long time, and they both remain undiagnosed. Now that the special education teachers are classroom teachers, they are not as free to do observations in other classrooms. We have three counselors at the school and each counselor is given three grades. The counselor who has our grade is very ineffective. He really doesn't know how to work with kids, and I am not allowed to go to the other two. If we were a suburban school, these kids wouldn't be in my classroom because the parents wouldn't tolerate it. They would hear about Jake striking other students or Sally running out of the room, and they would call us and demand that something be done about them. I know that if we were a cluster school, both Sally and Jake would be in a room for students with behavior disorders.

It's rare when all the kids in my classroom are working together, and this makes me very sad. I think the potential is here to make enormous progress, but even with two aides we haven't been able to. This is very frustrating for me because things are not turning out like I expected. Instead, every day we take a deep breath and say, "Ok, let's see what we can get through today." We really are trying very hard to create a different sort of learning environment for the children. We have a great curriculum and we are always complimenting the children to encourage them. But I feel sad during those few moments of uninterrupted time when I can sit down with a book and read to my kids or do some writing with them, because then I see how much potential they have and how we could get so much further than we have.

Case 14

Conflicts in Collaboration[1]

Suzanne E. Wade

In this case, a reading specialist, Joan Baker, is attempting to work with content area teachers in a new role, that of consulting teacher. This role involves collaboration with teachers to provide instructional support to help students who are academically at risk or LD succeed in the regular classroom rather than be placed in remedial pull-out programs. However, in this case, Joan was not very successful. Analyzing the case helps us to understand the problems that specialists and regular education teachers may experience as they attempt to work together. More broadly, the case illustrates some of the problems any educator may face when attempting to change role expectations and collegial relationships in schools.

Joan Baker relaxed into her chair and sighed, "This is the first chance I've had to sit down all day." Enthusiastic shouts and running steps of the students could be heard through the window of her small office off the library. It was the end of school on a Friday afternoon, the first balmy day

---

[1]Reprinted by permission of the publisher from Shulman, J., *Case Methods in Teacher Education* (New York: Teachers College Press, © 1992 by Teachers College, Columbia University. All rights reserved.), pp. 97–106.

of April. Joan got up to pour herself a cup of coffee, then stood staring out the window. After several moments of reflection as she sipped her coffee, she turned and leaned against the window sill.

Well, you want to know what it's like trying to get content area teachers here to take some responsibility for teaching reading and learning strategies in their classes. It's been an exercise in futility. I think the teachers here are too lazy to really change much. Many have been teaching for 20 years; they're worn away, burned out. They have no incentive, except for a few individuals, and since no new teachers are coming in because of the freeze on hiring, there's no competition. Their focus isn't on how much the kid has learned anymore, it's on going through the motions of doing the job. They get no respect from the community, little pay, the kids are rude. Why should they change?

THE SETTING

Located in an affluent suburb of a large city in the Northeast, Wellington Junior High is a modern two-story building, serving approximately 500 pupils in grades 7, 8, and 9. Class size ranges from 22 to 26 pupils. The faculty are older and have had more years of teaching experience than teachers in the past did. Because of a decreasing student population and the district's consequent freeze on hiring, few new faculty members have been hired in recent years.

The policy of the school is to randomly assign students to classes without regard to ability, except in math. This policy of mainstreaming was designed to avoid stigmatizing students by exposing them to the regular curriculum wherever possible. However, this policy has resulted in frequent complaints from the faculty about the difficulty of dealing with the wide range in reading abilities that can be found in every classroom, from nonreaders to those who are able to read college material.

At the time, the school had one full-time reading specialist (Joan) and two part-time LD specialists. Joan's responsibilities included administering diagnostic tests to students with reading difficulties, teaching remedial reading to individuals and small groups of students, administering achievement tests to all classes on a yearly basis, conducting in-service workshops in reading, and acting as a consulting teacher to the regular classroom teachers in the school. The sole responsibility of the LD specialists was to work directly with the most disabled pupils several times a week, either individually or in small groups.

JOAN BAKER, READING SPECIALIST

Before coming to Wellington Junior High, Joan had been a reading specialist for several years in another state. She was now completing her third year at Wellington, which made her one of the youngest and newest members of the faculty. However, because of continuing budget problems in the district, she was not sure whether she would have a job there in the fall.

Joan enjoys working directly with individuals or small groups of students in her office. She feels that this gives her an opportunity to get to know the students well and to observe rather dramatic improvements in their reading skills. She also likes the freedom of choosing reading materials that match their reading levels and interest. But she realizes that tutoring and small group work is a luxury that the school can no longer afford. Providing direct services to only 30 or 40 students a week is doing little to alleviate reading problems in the school as a whole. As she says, "Many kids here are barely making it. Because their problems aren't severe and they're not disruptive, they're falling through the cracks." So becoming a consulting teacher to help general education teachers provide reading and learning strategy instruction in their classrooms is a role that she wants and needs to assume. However, despite her efforts and the encouragement of her well-respected principal, Joan feels that she has met with only limited success in this role. As she speaks, she presents a story of frustration—a "history of futility," as she put it:

> When I came here I found that lots of kids in this school didn't show growth and couldn't deal with school work. The first thing I did was pretest in order to get to know the teachers. We talked about test scores and the kids I was concerned about. That worked well. A lot of teachers were willing to talk about individual kids. But I don't think they followed any of my suggestions, like giving different assignments or having them read material they could handle.

> When I suggested to teachers that I work with small groups of remedial readers in the regular classroom, teachers wanted them removed. For example, Mary Calley, one of the history teachers, wanted to raise the class average on exams, and so was willing to let me work with her. But she viewed my role as remedial and separate from the classroom. She asked me to take out a small group of pupils who were having difficulty and work on organizational skills such as summarizing and finding the main idea.

She was insistent that I use regular classroom materials, which meant the textbook, and that was fine with me. Students in the small group were really cooperative, and we covered the chapter thoroughly in preparation for the upcoming exam. They not only developed outlines and diagrams for short essay questions, which Mary said would be the format of the exam, but also wrote questions they thought might be on the test. Unfortunately, not many of the students did very well on the exam. Not surprising! Without telling me, Mary dropped her original idea of having essay questions and used multiple-choice items exclusively.

Mary also wouldn't let students take the textbook home or even use it in study hall. Somehow she hoped it would get students to develop strategies other than committing the text to memory—to learn to quickly pick out the generalizations instead of getting bogged down in details. These are worthy goals, but she never taught the students these skills. This is where I could have helped, but she wouldn't consider my working with the class as a whole. And her tests emphasized factual-level material, which requires memorization of the text and lectures.

Joan feels that she has had some minor successes. One was a workshop on readability, which the principal required teachers to attend. The principal had told her to keep her lecture to 12 minutes, followed by hands-on activities for the remainder of the hour. As a result, Joan felt she gained some credibility and was then able to begin to work as a consulting teacher with a few content area teachers. But as Joan describes her work with the teachers, her frustration is evident:

I helped them develop unit and lesson plans, and made suggestions about how to deal with remedial readers in the regular classroom. I suggested things like preteaching vocabulary and using study guides and chapter summaries before reading an assignment. I had the most success with those least in need of change; they already had good teaching skills. I was able to do a few observations in classrooms, saying I wanted to watch particular kids. But mostly, I worked as a teacher's aide, and even a substitute teacher! I'll give you one example. Harold Whitmore, another one of the history teachers, agreed to collaborate with me on developing some innovative lesson plans and then trying them out in his classroom. I think he only agreed because the principal had personally suggested this to him to improve his teaching, which consisted mainly of lecture and questioning. The principal was right! Harold had a structured routine, distributing a weekly schedule of assignments and classroom activities. His style was not a reflection of his dedication to teaching but rather of doing the same thing every year.

The first problem I ran into was in scheduling planning meetings because of his many outside commitments. And, he'd often forget appointments when I *was* able to schedule them. But we did eventually get together and decide on the lessons that I would prepare. Although he wouldn't agree to my observing him teach, he said he would observe and evaluate demonstrations of lessons I'd teach in his classroom. I was pleased with that because I felt that I had my foot in the door. If he liked the lessons, he might be willing at some point to try them out himself. But, when I began to teach the first day, he left the room as soon as he had introduced me to the class and did not return until 10 minutes after the demonstration had ended, when he was supposed to take over! So, I found myself essentially being a substitute teacher, which would hardly bring about any change in his teaching. Well, I talked to him about how I needed his feedback on the lessons, and so he did stay in class after that. But he was never willing to teach any of the lessons himself, at least while I was there. I can't say that working with him had any effect on his teaching.

I had even less success working with another teacher that the principal had pressured into collaborating with me, mainly because this teacher was having a lot of classroom management problems. This was John Peterson, an eighth grade science teacher, who, surprisingly, seemed willing not only to let me observe his classes but to work together on lesson planning and teaching. Our discussions together concerned the need to find ways to teach a classroom of students who vary greatly in ability—to individualize instruction and deal with students who lack decoding skills.

Although I had no trouble scheduling meetings with him, trying to observe in his classroom was another matter. Once when I showed up for a previously scheduled observation, he said it was not a good day because he was going to go over a test and show a movie rather than introduce a new chapter in the textbook as planned. In fact, he told me that he often changed his plans like that. When I tried to schedule a time to observe a textbook-related lesson for the following week, he told me he doesn't plan far enough ahead to be able to say what would be a good day.

By sheer persistence, I managed to observe a couple of times and found that he really did have poor control of his classes. Although he has a fairly good rapport with students, his general passivity often resulted in wasted time with students, who just milled about the classroom. But the worst problem was the lack of textbooks. I couldn't have one to plan lessons with! I never did develop lesson plans or demonstrate them in his classroom. Instead, I just administered some informal diagnostic tests to some of the students. I doubt that the recommendations I made for these students were ever followed.

MARY CALLEY, HISTORY TEACHER

A 15-year veteran of the history department at Wellington, Mary teaches eighth grade American history. She had recently completed a doctorate in education, which focused on the role of women in history. Mary also has a strong interest in issues related to reading. She believes that the problem for most students is their inability to distinguish important from unimportant information and to draw generalizations from details: "There's a tremendous range in every class, from those who read at the third grade level to students who can read almost anything. But most aren't good at abstracting material—they're very literal minded. When they're working with the text, they can't organize the information into a framework; instead they wallow around in all the details and facts."

Mary wants to develop in her students a sense of history that expands their awareness and helps them become critical thinkers. She doesn't think this can be accomplished with her textbook, which she had no voice in selecting. To her, "the text is a piece of junk, filled with every American platitude. It has a fair amount of superpatriotism, which is dangerous. It also has a cardboard approach to historical personages and question–answer regurgitation. Most texts have been through so many different revisions that there's practically nothing left. Parents need texts more than pupils. My preference is to work with outlines."

Mary also wants to help students learn to organize information and abstract generalizations, but she is not sure of how to do it. Constant repetition by the teacher doing the generalizing, she guesses, is needed. Mary tries to individualize assignments and reading materials for the reading disabled in her classes to some extent, although she is worried about stigmatizing students in front of their peers. Most individualizing, she feels, has to be done outside of class, that is, handled privately. This is where she sees the reading specialist fitting in. Mary believes that the role of the specialist should be remedial and separate from the classroom:

A reading specialist can best work with content area teachers by taking groups of students out of the classroom, but still using the content materials, to teach organizational skills such as summarizing and finding the main idea. The reading teacher should try to keep tabs on who's getting what and what kinds of problems particular students are having. This is an almost impossible task for the classroom teacher.

Mary views the problem Joan faces in trying to work with content area teachers as one of resistance to change on the part of both the specialist and the teachers at the school. She readily acknowledges that most teachers in the school had been resistant to Joan's efforts to work with them in their classrooms. As she puts it, "Teachers prefer to be islands and are generally resistant to anything forced on them." At the same time, she sees Joan as having little interest in the resource role. She describes specialists in general as preferring the easier role of remediation, which isolates them from classrooms and teachers:

> Reading specialists want to stay isolated in their cubicles, working on a one-to-one basis instead of getting into classrooms. That's much easier than having to deal with 30 kids in every class. This is one reason they have trouble developing working relationships with content area teachers. I'm against the use of special or easier reading materials. This is one of the main reasons why there's a clash between content teachers and specialists. After the kid has been in a resource room for a while, the specialist will now say that he can handle regular classroom materials and assignments. But she's made this assessment based on the kid's handling of specially adapted materials, not the textbook. Then, when the kid is put back in the classroom, he still can't handle the work. So, he becomes discouraged and quickly withdraws.

HAROLD WHITMORE, HISTORY TEACHER

Harold is another eighth grade American history teacher, with about 20 years of teaching experience. He is actively involved in a number of extracurricular activities. Directing play rehearsals, for example, occupies a great deal of his time, not only after school but also during his planning periods. Although appearing to be perpetually busy, he does like to talk about his teaching, once he sits down and relaxes. Like Mary, he would like to help students develop critical thinking skills—"being able to think for themselves rather than parroting back information." He believes that to accomplish this, the teacher needs to be good: "It's the humanness and flexibility of the teacher rather than any one technique or philosophy of teaching that's responsible for learning." Given the fact that he has a part-time job as a car salesman, it is not surprising that he views teaching as selling: "A good teacher is a good salesman—good at establishing an intense, short-term relationship with the objective of getting a people to say, do, or feel something they wouldn't do on their own."

Despite his concern with developing critical thinking skills, which he shares with Mary, Harold's teaching style and use of the textbook is radically different. Whereas Mary covers a few topics in American history in great depth, with role-playing activities and primary source materials, Harold covers the entire textbook, relying primarily on lecture, having students write out answers to questions in the textbook, and quizzes. He describes the structure of his course in this way:

> I like to follow a basic routine each week. The activities and home-work are always outlined in detail on a handout that I give each week. On Monday, I'll introduce a chapter. I also have students read a column in the local newspaper for interpretive work with current events. On Tuesday, I test them on the newspaper column and have them complete the check-up questions in the first part of the text-book chapter. Wednesday, I finish lecturing on the chapter, which students have been assigned to read at home. Thursday, they work on all the end-of-the-chapter questions, and on Friday, I give a test on the chapter and check the questions they have completed.

Harold finds that his students have two problems in reading: a limited attention span and the inability to understand the main points of the text. To some extent, he believes that his teaching is affected by the wide range in reading ability in his classes: "It makes me more aware of their needs. I try to individualize by personal contact and by suggesting additional or alternative materials. But, because the textbook [the same one Mary uses and one he helped to select] is so superior, I don't find its use a problem."

Harold says that he welcomes the idea of collaboration, and he advocates an aggressive approach on the part of specialists. In contrast to Joan's negative attitude toward him and her belief that she has had little effect on his teaching, he describes Joan in positive terms and expresses the opinion that she has important things to offer content area teachers:

> The specialist should not wait for the teacher to generate ideas, but rather should approach the teacher with ideas and try them out. We

won't know if they work unless we try them. It's best handled by an aggressive attitude. As a classroom teacher, I used to have guilt feelings about not using resource people. But I didn't use them because they never approached me. Don't wait to be asked—come to me and ask if I've tried different things. Those who do wait around become a glorified teacher's aide to one or two teachers. You should assume that the content teacher is very busy and can't give up planning periods. We don't have time to set up elaborate reading programs. That's the responsibility of the reading person.

I see reading specialists now as being part of the woodwork. They need to come into the classrooms. The specialist should begin by finding a cluster of teachers to work with. When these teachers tell of what they are doing, others will be envious and start to fall in. My stereotype is a little old lady sitting in a room with one student. Another part of the stereotype is people who use elaborate obfuscating instruments in irrelevant ways, as razzle dazzle. No teacher likes to be overwhelmed by statistics.

But none of this is true of Joan. She's an exception to the stereotype—the model reading teacher. She's pleasantly aggressive and touches base with everyone at least once a month. Because she shows such an interest, the teacher is moved to put himself out. I like her approach to reading in the content areas. She has never attached reading to English. Instead, she sees reading as underlying all content areas. I also like her pre- and posttesting. She uses one simple test and doesn't try to impress us with jargon and numbers.

JOHN PETERSON, SCIENCE TEACHER

A relative newcomer, having been at Wellington for only three years, John is a young eighth grade earth science teacher. Like the other teachers, he would like his students to acquire both course-specific information and a way of thinking that they can apply to their everyday lives. As he said,

This is the only time they'll take an earth science class, so I'd like them to get some basic knowledge of the earth they live on. For a lofty aim, I'd like them to understand the scientific method—a way of problem solving—and apply it to everyday situations. Students learn best by doing. Especially as a science teacher, I agree with the saying: 'I hear and I forget; I do and I understand.' But because of

the realities of the classroom, I can only give them hands-on experience during lab periods. During the rest of the week, I have to rely
on the textbook, worksheets, and lectures. I also use films fairly frequently and occasionally show filmstrips and slides on such topics as
rock formations.

John identified several types of reading problems in his classes, including vocabulary and comprehension problems for a few students, and study
skills for most. And, he talked about what he sees as the best role for a
reading specialist. He reveals below several clues that help explain the
evasiveness that Joan found so frustrating:

> I'm not sure what a reading specialist could do working in my classes
> because you have to know the material. Joan was originally trained as
> a social studies teacher so I think she could help out in those areas.
> But to teach science, you have to be trained as a scientist. Another
> problem is that I don't like to plan more than a few days ahead.
> Scheduling lesson plans with someone else just won't work for me.
> What I would really like is to have the lowest ones—the learning dis-
> abled students, who are reading around the third grade level—out of
> my classes altogether because I don't have the time and attention to
> give them. That's how Joan could be the most useful.

JOAN BAKER'S FINAL THOUGHTS

You know, the teachers here really are resistant to change, extra work,
and evaluation. Even those who have been willing to work with me—
and they are few and far between—are vulnerable, defensive, and
unwilling to put much time into additional projects. There's a lot of
suspicion towards specialists in general, especially among older
teachers. The personality of the reading specialist is crucial. You have
to be friendly, bouncy, but not pushy. And you have to be careful to
deal with teachers with delicacy, tact, and flattery. Most important,
you have to be willing to accept a subservient role. The key is to gain
their trust and convince them that you are part of the group. You have
to view yourself as a service. That means you do it all.

AUTHOR INDEX

SUBJECT INDEX